CAMBRIDGE SOUTH ASIAN STUDIES

RELIGION UNDER BUREAUCRACY

A list of the books in the series will be found at the end of the volume

RELIGION UNDER BUREAUCRACY

Policy and administration for Hindu temples in south India

FRANKLIN A. PRESLER

Department of Political Science
Kalamazoo College

The right of the University of Cambridge to print and sell all manner of books was granted by Henry VIII in 1534. The University has printed and published continuously since 1584.

CAMBRIDGE UNIVERSITY PRESS

CAMBRIDGE
NEW YORK NEW ROCHELLE
MELBOURNE SYDNEY

CAMBRIDGE UNIVERSITY PRESS
Cambridge, New York, Melbourne, Madrid, Cape Town, Singapore, São Paulo

Cambridge University Press
The Edinburgh Building, Cambridge CB2 8RU, UK

Published in the United States of America by Cambridge University Press, New York

www.cambridge.org
Information on this title: www.cambridge.org/9780521321778

First published 1987
This digitally printed version 2008

A catalogue record for this publication is available from the British Library

Library of Congress Cataloguing in Publication data

Presler, Franklin A.
Religion under bureaucracy.
(Cambridge South Asian studies)
Bibliography.
Includes index.
1. Hinduism and state. 2. Temples, Hindu – India,
South. 3. Hinduism – India, South – Government.
I. Title. II. Series.
BL1153.7.S68P74 1987 294.5′35′068 86–17546

ISBN 978-0-521-32177-8 hardback
ISBN 978-0-521-05367-9 paperback

CONTENTS

To
Henry Hughes Presler
and
Marion Anders Presler

PREFACE

This book is an analysis of the relations of state, religion and politics in the south Indian state of Tamil Nadu. It represents research and reflection at various times over the period of a decade, and a growing conviction that religion–state relations need to be studied from a comparative and historical point of view.

The central focus is the important position Hindu temples occupy in modern Tamil Nadu politics, and the state's role in regulating and shaping them. Temples are significant in a multitude of ways in south Indian society and economy, and throughout the modern era have attracted the attention of governments and politicians.

From the perspective of religion–state relations, the study also explores aspects of change and development in twentieth-century Indian politics. The government's official policies toward religion provide a fruitful context from which to view, for example, the relation of political parties to sources of patronage and conflict, the effect of centralized "rational" administration on local practice and privilege, the consequences of bureaucratization for democratic politics, and the legacy of traditional theories of legitimacy in the "secular" state.

The present volume is a revised and much shortened version of my doctoral dissertation of the same title. The initial fieldwork in Tamil Nadu was carried out in 1973–74 and was supported by the Foreign Area Fellowship Program of the Social Science Research Council. I was helped by many individuals, among whom I would especially like to mention: Chaturvedi Badrinath, IAS, former Commissioner, Tamil Nadu Archives; Thiru A. Uttandaraman and Thiru Sarangapani Mudaliar, former Commissioners, HRCE; Thiru K.A. Govindarajan, HRCE; Thiru Kunrakudi Adigalar, Deviga Peravai; Thiru Swaminatha Gurukkal, South India Archaka Sangham; and Professor Chandra Mudaliar, Madras University. I was affiliated during that year with Madurai University.

I am deeply grateful to Lloyd I. Rudolph and Susanne Hoeber Rudolph for their support and interest over the years, beginning with my graduate study at the University of Chicago. The depth of their scholarship and the richness of their intellectual insight have shaped fundamentally my understanding of what political studies can be. It is a pleasure to acknowledge my debt to Arjun Appadurai and Carol A. Breckenridge, who were also doing dissertation research in 1973–74 and whose analyses inform this work significantly. For encouragement and insight offered at various stages I want also to thank Bernard S. Cohn, Leonard Binder, A.K. Ramanujan, Robert Frykenberg, David Washbrook, Edward Dimock, Maureen Patterson, Nicholas Dirks and Rakhahari Chattopadhyay.

A grant from Kalamazoo College enabled me to make a brief trip to Madras in 1981 in order to update some of the earlier research. The final revisions were undertaken during the summer of 1983 in the stimulating environment of a National Endowment for the Humanities Seminar, held at Columbia University under the direction of Ainslie Embree, on "Religion, Nationalism and Conflict: The South Asian Experience." My colleague David Barclay painstakingly read through the entire manuscript and offered many helpful suggestions. Portions of chapters 4 and 8 have appeared in articles entitled "The Structure and Consequences of Temple Policy in Tamil Nadu, 1967–81", in *Pacific Affairs* 56 (Summer 1983), and "The Legitimation of Religious Policy in Tamil Nadu", in Bardwell Smith, ed., *Religion and the Legitimation of Power in South Asia* (Leiden: E.J. Brill, 1978).

During the entire period I have been supported and helped in innumerable ways by Paula Presler. She has shared with me the joys and pains of doing research, and has gone over seemingly countless revisions of the manuscript. Although I am not sure she would agree, the book in many ways belongs as much to her as to me.

NOTES ON SOURCES, ABBREVIATIONS AND TRANSLITERATION

All government records cited are in the Tamil Nadu Archives, Madras. The following abbreviations are used in the citations:

BOR	Board of Revenue
Cons.	Consultations
E & PH	Education and Public Health
G.O.	Government Order
L & M	Local and Municipal
PH	Public Health
Proc.	Proceedings

Government Order citations include the following: number of Government Order; department; date. Consultations and Proceedings citations usually include the following: volume; date; page. In some of the mid-nineteenth-century documents, however, the citations are irregular; such cases are made clear in the text.

Tamil words and names are given in the form used in the government documents on which much of this research is based, although, in some cases, original spellings have been changed in the interests of overall consistency. The spelling of towns and districts is in accordance with contemporary usage. There are no diacritical marks.

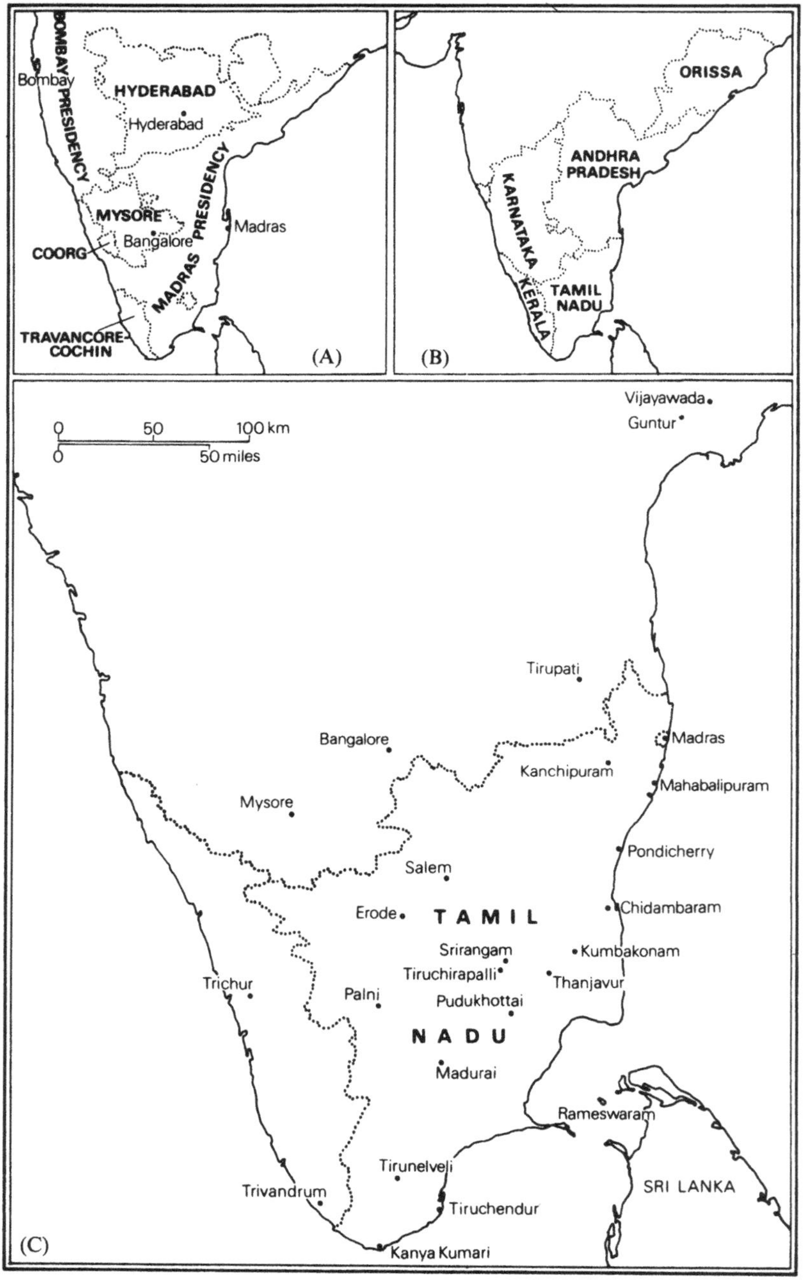

Map A Boundaries of Madras Presidency, 1947 (based on J.E. Schwartzberg, ed., *A Historical Atlas of South Asia*. Chicago and London, 1978)

Map B Southern India, 1975 (based on Schwartzberg, ed., *A Historical Atlas of South Asia*) The geographical jurisdiction of the department has shifted over the years. The original HRE Board had jurisdiction over the entire Madras Presidency, but this changed as state boundaries were redrawn along linguistic lines in the years following Independence. The HRCE today has jurisdiction only over temples in Tamil Nadu (known as Madras State until 1969). Separate although basically similar government departments exist in the other south Indian states.

Map C Southern India, 1975 (based on *The Times Atlas of the World*, 1975)

1

Introduction: studying religion–state relations

The past decade has seen a significant change in our perception of the relations of religion and politics. The once widespread belief that modern times would bring the inevitable decline of religion as a force in public life has been profoundly shaken. The interplay of religion and politics seems suddenly again a world-wide phenomenon, affecting both the "developing" world of Asia, Africa, the Middle East and Latin America, and the "developed" world of Europe and North America, and involving all the great religious traditions: Islam, Hinduism, Judaism, Christianity, Buddhism and their various sects. The prominence of religion in public life has reopened a whole set of issues which many people had regarded as closed, such as the role of religion in party politics, public education, family law, taxation, foreign relations and civic morality.[1]

The resurgence of religion poses many challenges to our understanding. As scholars search for explanations, clergy and politicians struggle with the more immediate problem of finding effective ways to address each new controversy as it emerges. Many urge as a basic principle that religion and politics be kept separate, that the health of both church and government can be ensured only when they are allowed considerable autonomy in their respective domains. This separation, it is said, is the only feasible arrangement given the increasing religious pluralism of most societies. But this prescription, however important, has not always been helpful in negotiating satisfactory relations between religion and the state. The problem remains universal, and is apparently intractable. We need to accept as a starting point the clear fact that religion and public life *do* penetrate each other, and reflect on how we might best interpret this fact. Greater specificity is needed regarding the different ways and contexts in which religion and politics intersect, the types of conflict which emerge, and the influence of economic, social, historical and cultural factors. Only then can we assess the meaning and consequences of what is clearly a world-wide phenomenon.

1 Ainslie T. Embree, "Religion, nationalism and conflict," in J.S. Bains and R.B. Jain, eds., *Contemporary political theory* (New Delhi: Radiant Publisher, 1980), p. 105.

This book is a study of religion and politics in the south Indian state of Tamil Nadu. It focuses on a central institution of south Indian religion, the Hindu temple, and explores its relation to the state. This institutional approach permits concentration on relatively stable features of the religion–politics relation, as distinguished from the more fleeting movements of political parties and public opinion, and identification of underlying, structural dimensions. It also provides an unusual position from which to view the activities of political parties, bureaucracy and interest groups, and to examine the effects on the political system of ideologies, patronage systems and legal structures related to religion.

The south Indian Hindu temple is a major institution. There are approximately fifty-two thousand temples in the state of Tamil Nadu, dotting the countryside, dominating the horizons of cities and shaping the life of both. Temples are also complex institutions, with complicated systems of internal organization and governance, economies based on endowments, offerings and highly detailed exchange relationships, and elaborate modes of worship rooted in history and tradition. Because of the wealth of the temple, primarily in the form of land endowments, because of the patronage which control of wealth brings, because of the significance of the temple in culture and society, and because of the deities residing in them, temples create economic and political power, and social and ritual status. Trustees in the larger temples are often prominent landlords, former rajahs and zamindars and other local notables. But countless south Indians of far lower social standing also care deeply about and vie for place in their local temples. Many aspects of life intersect in the temple.

Throughout the modern period, governments in south India have been deeply involved in temples. Their purpose has been to establish a presence in temple management, and thereby to regulate the use of the temple's material and symbolic resources. Inevitably, regulation has implied controlling the details of Hindu organization, economy and worship. This is true despite the fact that for at least a century the state has been committed to nonintervention in religion, and since 1947 has been constitutionally secular.

The key to this apparent contradiction lies partly in a structural conflict which has developed in the modern era between Hindu temples and the state. Modern state development in south India, as elsewhere, is in the direction of centralization of control, expansion of jurisdiction, autonomy, and rationality in administration.[2] These characteristics

[2] Charles Tilly, "Reflections on the history of European state-making," in Charles Tilly, ed., *The formation of national states in western Europe* (Princeton University Press, 1975), p. 70.

place the state in tension with other established institutions, and the resulting conflict is manifested in many political, institutional and cultural contexts, one of which is the temple. Indeed, Hindu temples more than any other institution seem to have represented a challenge to the modern south Indian state. The details of the challenge have varied at different times, but the challenge itself has been constant.

The twists and turns in the government's response over the past century and a half to the temple challenge have resulted in an extraordinarily complex temple–state relationship. The central purpose of this book is to analyze this relationship: the nature of the challenge, the response, and the structures and dynamics which have been the result. The analysis should also illuminate a number of more general issues crucial for understanding processes in postcolonial political systems, such as the effectiveness of legal–rational administration, the effect of bureaucracy on political representation, the importance of patronage for political parties, and the relationships between the centralized state and the localities.

I shall analyze the Tamil Nadu case through the state's central organizational vehicle for dealing with temples, the Hindu Religious and Charitable Endowments (Administration) Department (hereafter HRCE).[3] I shall focus especially on three HRCE initiatives: the effort to change the authority, functions and prerogatives of priests, trustees and other personnel; the effort to standardize temple landholdings and land use; and the effort to establish a central ecclesiastical organization directed by the state. These policies encompass central institutional dimensions of temples: *governance*, *economy*, and *religious life*. Taken together, they reveal a systematic attempt to penetrate the temple, to bring it within the orbit of state power and to ensure that it accommodates or furthers public purposes as defined by the state. HRCE administration in these areas is not uniformly effective. It has been stronger in religious life, weaker in governance and weakest in economy. This is somewhat ironic, since the state's authority over the religious dimension is far less clear than it is over the other two.

[3] The HRCE is the successor to the HRE Board, which was founded in 1926. The latter was an independent regulatory agency whereas the former, formed in 1952, is an executive department of the government. For most purposes, however, there is a single line of continuity between the two and, unless made necessary by the context, I shall refer to the state's administration of temples by the single designation "HRCE."

Interpreting religion–state relations

The Tamil Nadu case is a dramatic example of how entangled the institutional fortunes of religion and state can become, even in a society formally committed to "secularism." It is also an example, I think, which can shed light on characteristic features of religion–state interactions elsewhere. Rather than limit ourselves to country-by-country studies, or to the unique configurations associated with each of the great religious traditions, it seems useful to identify more general and characteristic patterns. What follows is an effort in this direction, one which focuses on the processes surrounding the emergence of the modern state, and the modern state's almost universal tendency to propagate its vision of rationality.

The emergence of the modern state involves processes basic to political development in all countries and extraordinarily significant for religion. The characteristic direction everywhere in the world is towards the expansive "rational" state – autonomous, differentiated, centralized and internally coordinated.[4] Almost without exception, modern governments see religion – its beliefs and practices, its leaders and institutions – as a potential or actual threat to this expansion. The reverse is equally true. Religious leaders, worried about modernization and about what the changing political order portends for religion, develop strategies to defend their domains from state encroachment. Each side is concerned to defend its authority and legitimacy. Religion–state relations are not static. The conflict is sometimes subdued and at other times explicit, but both sides are continually alert to one another and to change in the larger environment of the society. The result is continuing structural tension. To analyze this tension, it is useful to view it in terms of three central dimensions: a *political* conflict between governmental and religious elites; an *institutional* conflict over the use of economic and cultural resources; and a *cultural* conflict over legitimacy, authority and the definition of the ideal society.

The political conflict between governmental officials and religious elites tends to be the first manifestation of underlying tensions. Centralizing states typically begin with attacks on ecclesiastical properties and benefices and on the status and influence of the religious elite. As they find their positions jeopardized, religious leaders (bishops, abbots, priests, monks) search for ways to save their positions, sometimes through resisting the state's incursions, other times through forging an alliance with it. These strategies have made for high drama: Henry VIII

[4] Tilly, "Reflections," p. 70.

and Thomas More, the French Revolution and the "nonjuring" Catholic clergy, Ataturk's abolition of the Caliphate. In Tamil Nadu, as we shall see, the state has moved to undercut many prerogatives enjoyed by temple elites, such as control over temple land and income, religious authority, and local prestige and status; the elites, in turn, have not lacked means of resisting, at least temporarily, the state's threat.

Lying behind the political struggle is a set of tensions between institutions of religion and the state as the latter press to exert influence over an ever-widening range of social activities, including economy, property, welfare, law and education. State expansion is accompanied by "demands that these vital areas be brought directly under state control," that the state be "sovereign."[5] In Tamil Nadu, the state has claimed sovereignty in a wide variety of areas: land and tenancy reforms, supervision of education, changes in inheritance, property and charity laws, and efforts to channel religious wealth in socially "progressive" ways. The state's claim in these areas has posed direct, major challenges for Hindu temples.

In a sense, the cultural conflict between the modern state and more traditional religion lies behind and is logically prior to the previous two. At issue are the basic values, understandings and symbols in terms of which shared social purpose and unity are possible. Especially important is the issue of legitimacy. The growth of the modern state is accompanied by major shifts in the structure, procedure and goals of public power, often in directions not entirely compatible with those of the past. Legitimacy in the premodern era was often tied institutionally and ideologically to religion. Modernizing states usually stake out independent claims, resting their rule on written constitutions, statutory laws, formal procedure, and actual performance in such areas as physical health, economic prosperity and national security.[6] Even states which maintain a religious connection, such as extreme cases of theocracy, attempt to enhance their own autonomy.[7]

The conflict over legitimacy is not necessarily expressed fully or formally. It can be mediated through very narrow and specific disputes and, indeed, this is the common pattern. After all, the modern state does not spring into being all at once; it forms slowly, incrementally. Conflicts over legitimacy thus occur case by case, as when the state moves into an area, such as education or priest selection, which heretofore had been

[5] Donald Eugene Smith, *Religion and political development* (Boston: Little, Brown and Co., 1970), p. 97.

[6] Smith, *Religion*, p. 116; Raymond Grew, ed., *Crises of political development in Europe and the United States* (Princeton University Press, 1978), pp. 19–20.

[7] Embree, "Religion."

more or less autonomous. Here state officials must justify the state's right to take charge, and their justification often represents a quite different interpretation of the state's relation to and purpose in society. New categories and definitions may be introduced, different goals and meanings may be appealed to. The new interpretation is thus essentially a cultural act. The state is successful to the extent that its cultural interpretation becomes dominant, edging out the other, previously established, religiously based views.

In Tamil Nadu religion–state relations are marked by cultural conflict of a complex kind. The Indian state is constitutionally secular. For ordinary purposes, this is understood as meaning that religion and state coexist, but in separate realms, with "noninterference" and the "wall of separation" being the standard for their interaction. To be legitimate, therefore, the Tamil Nadu government must redefine its relation to temples as something other than control. Thus, control is called "supervision," "protection," or "oversight"; religion is labelled a "cultural heritage"; and temples are defined as "public trusts" or "monuments." Conflict also surrounds the relationships among state agencies. For example, the HRCE has a view of the Hindu temple which is vigorously resisted by other state agencies, especially the courts and the Revenue Department, as well as by temple spokesmen in the localities. Unravelling the strands of these conflicts will be a major task throughout this study.

Religious policy and political development

The combined force of the political, institutional and cultural challenges explains why religion–state relations are a central issue in modern state formation. Yet the direction of the state's response is not automatic; history gives evidence of many different patterns. In general, though, we can say that the strategy that a particular state follows is conditioned by the underlying strength of the regime, by the support and opposition it receives from political elites, and by procedures, jurisdictions and managerial styles in the state's administrative agencies. These can be elaborated briefly.

Policy must always take into account underlying *regime strength*. It is not always true that the state will be made more secure and that its control will be augmented by an expansive, domineering approach to religion. Officials must evaluate the nature of religious leadership, and the extent of popular loyalty to religion in order to avoid precipitating general resistance to the state's claim to sovereignty and legitimacy.[8]

[8] Tilly, "Reflections," p. 35.

State officials in modern south India have repeatedly had to make these sorts of calculations. For example, British colonial administrators in the nineteenth century perceived religion in India to be an especially sensitive and often dangerous force, which needed to be handled with great tact and sensitivity. Muslims and Hindus were believed to be highly volatile when their religious privileges, beliefs and institutions were threatened. The 1857 Mutiny especially, but many other smaller incidents as well, reinforced this belief. Threats to colonial power could of course come from many quarters, but the British believed that the threat from religion was perhaps the most significant. They were by no means always as confident of the Empire's basic security as their public statements would suggest.

British policy thus vacillated between two basic strategies. One implied expansion: assert the state's sovereignty and spread the administrative net over all religious institutions. Local officials could keep tabs on trouble spots, and state financial and political interests could be protected. The second strategy implied separation and noninterference: religion was too explosive. State interests were best ensured by severing all connections and by refusing to pass laws which could in any way offend religious sensibilities.

Each strategy had supporters. Noninterference found its main supporters at the higher levels of government, in Calcutta and London, and expansion tended to be favored by lower provincial and local officials. Cutting across this general pattern, however, is the fact that different departments at the same organizational level tended to emphasize those strategies which conformed best to their particular organizational interests. Everyone, of course, at whatever level or in whatever department, defended his views as being the most consistent with the cultural and political traditions of both British and traditional Indian governments. Not surprisingly, actual state policy tended to combine features of state expansionism and nonintervention.

Political support and opposition also weigh heavily in formulating religious policy. Religion affects a variety of social, economic and cultural interests; a policy which benefits and draws support from one group may damage and be opposed by another. As state activities widen in scope and detail, new segments of the population are mobilized and for the first time enter the political arena, sometimes to oppose and at other times to support the state.[9] Religious policy may now become part of the government's overall strategy of building support for itself in society. A particular policy may strengthen existing alliances between

[9] Ibid. p. 32.

the regime and its supporters, forge new ones, and diffuse opposition. The interactions between religious policy and politics enter a new, quite different and, for the state, immensely important phase.

In south India in the nineteenth and twentieth centuries, newly mobilized groups began to claim and achieve representation in state agencies.[10] Indians became especially influential in the courts, municipal councils, provincial assemblies and other advisory boards. Many were new entrants to politics, English-educated and living in urban centers; others were older elites from the countryside. All had much to gain from political activity, and especially from issues relating to temple finance and administration. The colonial state, in turn, increasingly needed the support of the emerging Indian political and administrative classes. As the twentieth century opened, Indians were taking over more and more pivotal positions, so much so, indeed, that older established state agencies, and the British officers who primarily staffed them, found their jurisdictions threatened. The clearest evidence of this is the HRCE itself. Its formation heralded a dramatic expansion of the state's initiatives in religion, but was brought about only under the auspices of the elected Indian government set up under the Montagu–Chelmsford Reforms. The British had long resisted changing the pattern of religious policy; for the emerging political classes, however, the reformed temple administration was an important vehicle for political growth and gain.

The *interaction among state agencies* is a third factor shaping religion–state relations. New policies often upset the existing balance among government agencies, and affect long-standing jurisdictional boundaries, prerogatives and responsibilities, introducing periods of uncertainty, rivalry and imbalance. Administrators are frequently quite parochial and conservative. A policy designed to benefit the state in overall terms may well be subverted as administrators jockey to protect their positions, resources and power. Smooth administration may eventually be reestablished, based either on compromise or on dominance by one side. However, well-entrenched agencies may in the end successfully resist the new policy. A standoff results, with no resolution of conflict, and concerted state action may simply not be possible. The formal attributes of legal–rational authority, in other words, do not immunize government agencies from struggles for power or from the inefficiencies to which such struggles lead.[11]

[10] Ibid. p. 35.

[11] Lloyd I. and Susanne Hoeber Rudolph, "Authority and power in bureaucratic and patrimonial administration: a revisionist interpretation of Weber on bureaucracy," *World Politics* 31 (January 1979): 195–227.

In south India, interagency conflicts have been and remain a crucial variable in temple administration. Especially important are conflicts among three agencies: the HRCE, the judiciary and the Board of Revenue. These are agencies with vested jurisdictional interests, and strong but fundamentally different administrative traditions and interpretations of the Hindu temple. The structure of temple–state relations is shaped in pivotal ways by these conflicts.

Levels of stateness, administrative ineffectiveness and the concept of secularism

This perspective on religion–state relations can be clarified by some further comments in three areas. The first relates to the dynamic quality of religion–state relations, the second to the problem of government ineffectiveness, and the third to the concept of secularism.

It is important to emphasize that the structure and intensity of religion–state interactions can vary considerably over time. Constitutions and legal systems, it is true, make for relatively stable patterns, but there is still room for change. Recently several authors have found it useful to think in terms of J.P. Nettl's notion that there can be levels or degrees of "stateness," and that the level in any given country can rise and decline over both the long term and the short term. High stateness means that the state assumes, and society in turn expects it to assume, basic responsibility for law and order, for setting public purposes and for attaining them.[12] At such times, the state is firmly differentiated from other organizations: it is autonomous, centralized and formally coordinated.[13] In turn, persons associated with the state – bureaucrats, military officers, prime ministers, judges – enjoy enormous prestige and authority. Their definitions of the public interest are, for the time being at least, compelling and legitimate. The state in these circumstances may be described as enjoying constitutive powers; it is strategically placed to shape society in a wide range of areas. It selects public values, certifies some groups as having public standing and rejects other groups as illegitimate, and defines the overarching principles which guide the use

[12] J.P. Nettl, "The state as a conceptual variable," *World Politics* 20 (July 1968): 559–92. For an application of the concept of stateness in the all-India context, see Lloyd I. and Susanne Hoeber Rudolph, *In pursuit of Lakshmi: the political economy of the Indian state* (University of Chicago Press, forthcoming).

[13] Charles Tilly, ed., *The formation of national states in western Europe* (Princeton University Press, 1975), p. 638. For a recent analysis of the subsequent use of Nettl's concept of "stateness," see Gabriel Ben-Dor, *State and conflict in the Middle East: the emergence of the postcolonial state* (New York: Praeger, 1983), esp. chs. 1–2.

of public coercion. High stateness, in other words, gives government remarkable power. Low stateness, on the other hand, is marked by the relative absence of the features outlined above. Nettl notes that the strength of the state, its level of stateness, is the product both of long-range historical and cultural traditions and of more proximate political, economic and social factors.

The Tamil Nadu state enjoys relatively high stateness in matters of religion for three especially important reasons. First, south Indian kings historically had important connections with religion and temples. The cultural expression of this connection is the concept of the state as "protector" of religion generally and of temples specifically. Some would argue that the HRCE is simply performing the contemporary version of this traditional role. Second, the modern Indian state is regarded, especially since Independence, as a positive countervailing force to traditional society. Insofar as temples can be said to embody old and traditional patterns, the state enjoys considerable public support in its effort to bring temples under control. Third, there is the ever present struggle for "place" – for economic, social and political position – in the face of scarcity. Much of Indian public life involves constant jockeying for status, privilege and opportunity. The state, more than any other single agency, is in a position to affect the outcome of these struggles. Through its own employment, and through laws which regulate how others give employment, the state has become the great gatekeeper of place. This is as true in temple matters as it is in other areas.

High stateness inevitably affects the profile of political representation in temple matters. The state's preeminence places critics and opposition groups at a disadvantage; the burden of proof rests heavily on them, and it is difficult to influence policy through "normal" channels. The state, for its part, is able to claim legitimacy for its policies by appealing to its historic role as protector. Governments also can shape the broader environment in which policy is made. On a number of occasions, as we shall see, governments have designated, in a quasi-corporatist fashion, particular organizations as *the* legitimate representatives of society's interests, in return for which the organizations have observed certain restraints on their demands and activities.[14]

Other groups, in contrast, are dismissed as bothersome interferences,

[14] On the corporatist concept, see Philippe C. Schmitter, "Interest intermediation and modes of societal change in western Europe," *Comparative Political Studies* 10 (April 1977): 7–35; "Still the century of corporatism?" *Review of Politics* 36 (January 1974): 85–131.

as "politically" motivated "special" interests. Yet no government or political party has been able to resist incorporating the temple into its broader political strategy; whenever possible, temple resources, symbolic and material, have been used to build, stabilize or extend networks of power and influence.

High stateness does not, however, guarantee governmental effectiveness. Administration includes cultural dimensions which may seriously undercut policy. Government officers have distinct images of the world they administer and distinct languages to describe and control that world. The categories used for analysis, the way problems are defined, and the procedures applied to address those problems come together in clusters of ideas and sentiments, or "theories." A particular agency's theory is not necessarily or even usually stated explicitly; it is embodied in regulations, and draws on the agency's history and organizational style, and on the professional culture of its officers. When different agencies have different theories, the rivalries and conflicts which result are far more than just petty squabbles; involved are identities and public purposes to which administrators may be genuinely and deeply committed. The result can be paralysis.

Colonial and postcolonial administrations face problems of a rather special sort. Because the culture of the colonial society is very different from that of the west, colonial rule requires from the outset an act of interpretation. Without forsaking the most compelling precedents of the home government, administrators try to fashion a set of categories and procedures which will be appropriate to both. And this interpretive act is precisely what colonial administrators sharply disagree over: which facet of western experience is the relevant analogue? To what extent can that analogue be applied in the colony? To what extent is the indigenous reality distinct? How should its distinctiveness be treated? The disagreements among strong-minded officials with deep professional commitments inevitably hamper the government's overall effectiveness.

As it happens, down to the present day the south Indian temple has served as a rich and unending source for this sort of intellectual argumentation among administrators, temple officials, lawyers and scholars. The three issues examined in this study – governance, economy, religious life – lend themselves to diverse and conflicting interpretations. We shall focus especially on the theories of the HRCE, the Board of Revenue, and the judiciary, and the relation of each of them to the south Indian temple. Each claims to have captured the "real" nature of the temple, and their disagreements have profoundly affected the dynamics of the temple–state relationship.

Finally, because this book departs from most others on Indian religion–state relations in that it does not adopt the concept of secularism as a basic orientation to the subject, a word of explanation may perhaps be in order. Without question, secularism is a central component of India's national identity and public philosophy.[15] As a legal concept, secularism's meaning is in principle clear: it means "non-establishment" (no established state religion) and "religious freedom" (freedom to practice religion, subject to minimal constraints in the interests of public order and morality). Secularism has also been described as "noninterference" and as a "wall of separation."

But these descriptions do not capture the dynamics and details of actual religion–state interactions. A complete and impenetrable "wall" is unlikely in any country.[16] Religion is a dimension of individual and social activity and, as such, is mixed inextricably with other areas, including economy, health, education and culture. Since modern states take more and more initiative in these areas, the "wall" is easily breached. The HRCE is a major instance of this breach. The constitutionality of the HRCE has been upheld by the Indian Supreme Court on the grounds that temples are public trusts for which the state has a direct responsibility.[17] In actual fact, of course, "temple as public trust" is difficult to distinguish from "temple as religion." "Noninterference" is also a nice slogan, but a poor guide to practice.

Religious policy, in other words, cannot be studied primarily through reference to the formal principle of secularism. The state's policy at any given time is an outcome of many factors: the law and Constitution, to be sure; but also party competition, individual, group and organizational interests; ideology; material advantage; and long-term regime interests. Religion–state relations change over time, and religious policy is subject to the same sorts of political pressures as policy in any other area.

One implication of adopting a primarily political rather than legal approach to religion–state relations is that we no longer expect religious policy to be "rational" in a formal sense. Politics involves compromise and adjustment; substantive policies are based not only on merit and reason but also on influence and competing interests. What is formally

[15] The leading discussion, still excellent in its wealth of detail, is Donald E. Smith, *India as a secular state* (Princeton University Press, 1963). However, Smith's analysis is seriously limited by the preoccupation with what he assumes is American practice. For an excellent critique, see Marc Gallanter, "Secularism: East and West," *Comparative Studies in Society and History* 7 (January 1965): 113–72.

[16] For an important analysis for the United States, see Mark Dewolfe Howe, *The garden and the wilderness* (University of Chicago Press, 1965).

[17] The major case is *Commissioner of Hindu Religious Endowments, Madras v. Lakshmindra Thirta Swamiar of Sri Srirur Mutt* (1954) S.C.R. 1005.

rational is not always politically rational.[18] This political understanding keeps in view the basic fact that Hindu temples possess material and symbolic resources of great importance to individuals, groups and the state. Religious policy affects the way these resources are distributed – denied to some and secured for others – which is why policy so often embroils local notables, political parties and state agencies in conflict.

The structure of the book

Any one of several historical periods could be chosen as a starting point for an examination of the contemporary temple–state relationship in Tamil Nadu. The year 1842 is often cited as an important juncture because of the British policy of withdrawal; the year 1863 marks the beginning of a major broadening of participation in temple affairs under the aegis of British local self-government legislation; and 1887 brings the judiciary in a major way into temple administration. Each of these dates is important and, as we shall see in the next chapter, provides an essential component of the nineteenth-century legacy.

For several reasons, however, it seems most appropriate that this study's primary focus be the period which begins in 1926. I am concerned especially with the implications for religion of the modern bureaucratic state, and the year 1926 marks the founding of the Hindu Religious Endowments Board, from which has developed the state's central administrative apparatus, the HRCE. Also, the nineteenth century has been well explored in recent years by scholars who have focused on particular temples, issues or regions.[19] This scholarship has already made it clear that Hindu temples had a significant impact on policies of the nineteenth-century colonial state. What is of interest for this study are the continuities between the nineteenth-century pattern and the contemporary Tamil Nadu state, and also the specific role the religion–state link has played in the contemporary political system: in parties, patronage, and representation, in centralization, bureaucracy and law.

The research for this study was conducted in India and England during 1973–74, with a shorter trip to India in 1981. One of the most fruitful aspects of the research experience was the effort to combine the

[18] For a useful discussion of this distinction, see Aaron Wildavsky, *The politics of the budgetary process* (Boston: Little, Brown and Company, 1974), pp. 189–94.

[19] See especially the works cited in the bibliography by Arjun Appadurai, Christopher Baker, Carol Appadurai Breckenridge, Nicholas Dirks, C.J. Fuller, Burton Stein.

political scientist's techniques of field interviews and the historian's use of archival materials. My hope was to interpret, in a disciplined manner, current temple–state issues in light of modern south Indian history and culture. My research was in part a study of contemporary Indian political culture and, at the most general level, I was especially interested to explore citizen views regarding the scope of legitimate state activity and the prerogatives enjoyed by those in positions of governmental authority. The field of religion and state proved to be an extremely fruitful field for these explorations.

This small note on research method helps explain the manner in which the material is presented in the chapters which follow. The kind of information available on temple governance, economy and religion – the three major areas of temple administration discussed in this book – varies significantly. For example, statistical information on contemporary temple economies is sketchy, and thus subject to misinterpretation. Further, the material is not always in the public domain. Consequently, although the discussion of economy in chapters 5 and 6 draws on some contemporary materials, the weight of evidence is drawn mainly from the historical archives available to me at the time of research. Temple governance, however, is an area that lends itself to field inquiry. It is a highly publicized subject of constant public and private speculation; thus, the argument regarding governance in chapters 3 and 4 is informed significantly by contemporary information available through interviews, field observation and the press. The availability of information on temple religion, discussed in chapters 7 and 8, is more equally balanced, and I have been able to use both historical and contemporary evidence.

2
The temple connection in the nineteenth century

A little-recognized aspect of modern south Indian history is that the British colonial state penetrated Hindu religious institutions, both temples and *maths* (monasteries), deeply and systematically. This penetration was something that was neither unknown at the time nor unintentional. The state's relationship to the temple was formalized early in the nineteenth century and was a constant feature of the next century and a half of imperial rule. In form and intensity the state's activity varied over the years, but the Madras government consistently maintained that a measure of control was essential both for the state's security and income, and for society's welfare.

This fact is insufficiently noted in the historiography of British colonial rule in India. The general impression is that by the mid nineteenth century the British government had abandoned most policies which involved it directly with Hindu institutions, primarily as a result of pressure from Christian Evangelicals in England, reinforced later by the experience of the Indian Mutiny. This understanding of what happened has been advanced so many times in so many different contexts that it has become the standard interpretation of British colonial rule in India. In 1943, for example, a government committee took it as an established fact that "By 5th September 1843 the government parted with all control over religious institutions."[1]

[1] "Report of the nonofficial committee constituted to examine the workings of the Hindu Religious Endowments Act" (G.O. 5634 PH 12 May 1943), pp. 2–3. For a study of the nineteenth century based in part on this impression, see David Washbrook, *The emergence of provincial politics: the Madras Presidency 1870–1920* (Cambridge University Press, 1976). Washbrook writes:

> British attitudes towards religion and social life led to a further reduction of state influence. Formally by 1863, but in practice as early as 1840, the British had severed the relationship of their government to the institutions of religion and so had relinquished control of the vast economic and emotional resources of the temples. (p. 331)

A study which provides detailed background for the policy of "withdrawal" is E. Daniel Potts, "Missionaries and the beginnings of the secular state in India," in Donovan Williams and E. Daniel Potts, eds., *Indian history in honour of Cuthbert Collin Davies* (New York: Asia Publishing House, 1973), pp. 113–36.

It is true that the pressure in the nineteenth century to withdraw was enormous. A powerful coalition in England exerted unrelenting pressure on Parliament and the East India Company, and "withdrawal" became an ideology of great force. In time this pressure affected Madras, but the response of the local government was unenthusiastic, a mixture of resistance, reluctant accommodation and deception. In some cases, the details and intensity of control were modified; in others control was simply shifted to other agencies or buried in hidden institutional arrangements.

The cumulative effects of these pressures, however, did change the overall profile of state intervention. Subjected continuously to conflicting currents, temple policy slowly lost coherence and direction. Consensus over the basic goals and boundaries of state policy was lost, and government agencies developed vested interests in particular ways of doing things. Various corporate groups and individuals sensed opportunity in this uncertainty. By the end of the nineteenth century, temple politics had entered a new phase. Conflicting analyses of the temple and of the nature of the temple problem competed with one another. But at a general level, the ideology of withdrawal was countered by a concept of protection drawn from south Indian traditions.

The legacy of these years is crucial for understanding the evolution of the temple–state relation in this century.[2] The purpose of this chapter is to highlight briefly the institutional, political and ideological issues involved, and the way in which they converged in the Hindu Religious Endowments Board in the 1920s. As will quickly become clear, the stakes involved were high, especially for the state.

The state's interest

Before the commotion over "withdrawal" in the second half of the nineteenth century, the state's interest was understood in fairly straightforward terms. Regulation VII of 1817 was the first legislation on religious institutions in Madras and according to its Preamble:

> Considerable endowments have been granted in money, or by assignments of land, or of the produce or portions of the produce of land by the former Governments of this country, as well as by the British Government, and by individuals for the support of mosques, Hindu temples, colleges and choultries, and for other pious and beneficial purposes; and ... *endowments* [*are*] *in many instances appropriated, contrary to the intentions of the donors, to the personal use*

[2] The history of the controversy up to 1841 is reviewed thoroughly in a memorandum by Henry Chamier, Chief Secretary of the Revenue Department, in *Revenue* Cons., 12 April 1841, 519: 3183ff.

of the individuals in immediate charge and possession of such endowments; and . . . *it is the duty of the Government to provide that such endowments be applied according to the real intent and will of the grantor.*[3]

To fulfill this duty, Regulation VII vested with the Board of Revenue and its district officers "the general superintendence of all endowments in land or money."

This was a very broad mandate indeed, governed by an equally broad concept of the "duty of government." Soon, in fact, the Board of Revenue and its officers were drawn intimately into temple administration. What concretely did this mean? In terms of governance, it meant that government officials effectively became supervisors of temple trustees. The Board recognized two categories of temple trustees: those who acquired their office through some form of inheritance, i.e., direct descent, election by a hereditary electorate, selection by the heir of the founder; and those selected by an officer of the state. District collectors determined which category applied in each temple, and then either supervised or themselves appointed the temple trustees.

The collector's control was equally sweeping with regard to temple finances. If he discovered that temple land was uncared for or was misused – usually because appropriated by a trustee – the collector was empowered to "take over" the temple's management himself. His office then oversaw cultivation, collected rents, spent what was necessary for maintaining irrigation or other facilities and remitted the balance to the temple for worship and other activities.

All this was done for a fee; the government did not provide the services of its administrators *gratis*. When all the temple payments or fees were added together they resulted in a fairly sizeable income for the government over and above expenses. Thus, in 1837, it was reported that the government would lose Rs. 81,636–0–11 if temple supervision was terminated.[4] Also, the temple's own funds were kept in the government treasuries.

In time, more and more temples were found to be mismanaged and were "taken over." The Board of Revenue defended this policy as an "absolute necessity" in 1838:

Instances are constantly brought under their [i.e., Collectors'] consideration in which villages entrusted to the administration of the Pagoda Functionaries are

[3] *The Madras Endowments and Escheats Regulation, 1817* (Regulation VII of 1817), emphasis added. This and other laws and regulations may be found in *The Madras code*, 4 vols. (Madras: Government Press, 1940).

[4] *Revenue* Cons., 29 May 1837, 436: 3035.

entirely neglected, the sources of irrigation permitted to decline, the fair dues of Government thereby rendered insecure, and the revenues of the Pagodas decline... From these causes it has been found absolutely necessary to interfere summarily and eject the managers... and to entrust the Native Revenue Officers with the direct administration of the lands.[5]

Actually, the financial nexus between state and temples was more complicated than the simple profit from supervision. The state was also making annual allowances to many temples. In schematic form the situation was as follows:

In the past, zamindars, petty chieftains and local rulers had made donations to temples, which was the origin of much of the land temples now owned. In part to establish continuity with local laws and customs, the British in the early years had also paid duties and made donations. Donations of land were not always permanent, however. They could be and often were taken back, perhaps by the original donor, more likely by one of his successors. The British called this recovery "resuming the land" or "resumption." Although it was not absolutely necessary to do so, the British often gave compensation in the form of money allowances to temples which lost land through resumption, so that the temples would not be left without income. From the point of view of the temple, however, money allowances were inferior to control over land itself. There was no guarantee that the government would not change its policy and discontinue payments in future years, and payments were in any case seldom adjusted for inflation.[6]

Now, insofar as the Madras authorities in 1837 were able to compare a temple's allowance with the lot parcel on which it was based, the system of resuming certain lands and converting them into allowances had worked to the advantage of the government. That is, in the ten years prior to 1837, the government paid allowances annually averaging Rs. 565,923 for resumed lands from which the actual tax income was Rs. 749,613, amounting to a "profit" of Rs. 183,690. But even this was not the complete picture. Other allowances existed which the government recognized as obligatory but which, because the records had been lost, were no longer traceable to specific parcels of resumed lands. When these "gratuitous" allowances, as the British called them, were added to the allowances already mentioned, the total paid by government

[5] BOR Proc., 1 October 1838, 1628: 12845–58.

[6] This system is described in detail in ch. 5 below. The dynamic of grantee and grantor relationships has similarities to that of "prebendal feudalism" as described by Max Weber. See *Economy and society*, eds. Guenther Roth and Claus Wittich, 3 vols. (New York: Bedminister Press, 1968), vol. 1, pp. 259ff.

in 1837 as allowances to temples and *maths* was Rs. 901,529.[7]

The effect of allowances was to give the government added political leverage. Allowances were paid only if the Board of Revenue was satisfied that the temple was being kept in good condition and that the allowance was being used for "appropriate" purposes. Significantly, Rs. 216,250 went to institutions under "private" management, which effectively expanded the government's influence beyond those temples directly under its control.[8]

The Board of Revenue, in fact, was inclined to a sweeping view of the state's responsibilities. It argued that temple income from land was, in the final analysis, an appropriation of state revenues.[9] On this reading, temples were creatures of the state, supported by an ever-increasing share of alienated state funds. Some officials argued, in fact, that almost four-fifths of the total accounted income of Hindu religious institutions, Rs. 2,082,857 out of Rs. 2,682,555, originated in this way.[10]

The "withdrawal" policy

In the early decades of the nineteenth century, the temple–state relationship outlined above came under increasingly vocal attack by groups in England on the grounds that it amounted to support by a Christian government of non-Christian and sometimes offensive religious practices.[11]

[7] Calculated from "Abstract statement of the money allowances paid from the public treasury for the support of Hindoo and Mahommedan religious establishments both under the management of an average of ten years from fusly 1233 to 1242 both inclusive in the provinces under the Madras Presidency," BOR Proc., serial no. 1559: general no. 115765ff.

[8] Ibid.

[9] In 1835, for example, the Secretary of the Board of Revenue wrote: "The total amount of Revenue annually appropriated for religious and charitable purposes is estimated at Rs. 4,056, 287–12–2 1/2 of which Rs. 3,361,107–13–4 3/4 is the amount of the revenue from lands etc. and the allowances paid from the public treasury *which may be considered generally as appropriations of the revenue of the state*"; emphasis added (BOR Proc., 17 August 1835, serial no. 1462: nos. 10–11).

[10] Calculated from "Abstract statement showing average revenue."

[11] The norm here was often expressed as that of "noninterference." But noninterference had another implication not quite as amenable to the wishes of the Christian Evangelicals. Noninterference could be taken to mean that the British government ought not to interfere with or forbid acts which had the sanction of religious custom and yet clearly violated deeply held British (and allegedly universal) standards of morality. In 1828, for example, the Governor-General, Lord Bentinck, finally outlawed the practice of *suttee* or widow-burning. For many years, the problem had been discussed without resolution, partly because of the fear that this would interfere with Hindu religion. Among the many sources on this controversy and English Evangelicals generally, see Potts, "Missionaries and the beginnings"; Francis G. Hutchins, *The illusion of permanence: British imperialism in India* (Princeton University Press, 1967), especially ch. 1; Vincent A. Smith, *The Oxford history of India* (Oxford University Press, 1923), pp. 663 ff.

In 1833, word reached Madras that the home government had decided that there must be some change in policy. There followed a period of controversy and negotiation which, with varying degrees of intensity, continued over the rest of the century.

Public attention in England tended to focus on the government's "support" and "patronage" of the Hindu religion as evidenced by the presence of government officers at Hindu festivals and by donations and allowances to temples. Yet, far more was at stake. Large sums, intimately affecting the state's own finances, were involved. Also, in Madras, temple lands included some of the best agricultural land in the Presidency, in the continued upkeep and productivity of which the state had a major interest. There were also political implications. Trustee appointments and money allowances enabled local officers to monitor local politics and influence local notables. In short, completely terminating the connection with Hindu temples could not but affect the existing structure of control in the Presidency.

It is not surprising, therefore, that Madras resisted the new policy of withdrawal. "Withdrawal" quickly became separated into several sub-issues. The government proved willing, after some discussion, to withdraw insofar as explicitly "religious" matters were concerned. These were the well-publicized "ceremonial practices," especially obnoxious to critics in England, where the state made donations for traditional rituals, participated in festivals, and enforced temple cart pulling. The government also, though much more reluctantly, recognized "independent" trustees, i.e., trustees whose appointment would not be regulated by the state. Depending on circumstances, temples were handed over to local rajahs or influential zamindars, or were placed in the charge of village panchayats or newly constituted committees, or of temple priests and other functionaries.[12] But the government so circumscribed the new trustees' formal powers that their authority did not extend much beyond supervising rituals, collecting offerings and trying to keep peace among other temple functionaries. "It might be practicable," the Board of Revenue had cautiously written, to relieve "the European functionary" from direct interference in temples' "internal concerns," and to leave this duty to competent and carefully selected *dharmakurtas* (permanent managers). But Madras officials doggedly and vehemently resisted granting any authority that could

[12] The "different modes which were adopted according to local circumstances and feelings" are described in *Revenue* Cons., 8 April 1946, no. 1.

affect the financial, political and administrative structure of state–temple relations.[13]

The Madras Board of Revenue's arguments against placing temple lands under the new trustees summarize many aspects of the government's overall objection to the "withdrawal" policy. The only persons who will gain through handing over lands, the BOR argued, will be the trustees. The government, the cultivators and the temples themselves will lose. Freed from state control, most trustees will exploit the land for short-term personal gain. They will lease it out to relatives or political allies and take much of the income for themselves. Lacking steady financial support, temple rituals and functions will be cut back, and the physical premises will be neglected. In time, the temples will fall irreversibly into disrepair and, because of fraudulent leasing, ultimately lose the titles to their land.

The BOR also felt that withdrawal would jeopardize government revenue and political stability. The land itself was in danger. Productivity usually depended on irrigation, especially in the paddy-growing regions of Thanjavur district. Corrupt and ambitious trustees, it was feared, would not make the expenditures necessary to keep these irrigation facilities in good repair. In a very short time, irrigation could break down, rendering large tracts unfit for cultivation and upsetting the economy of whole villages. The result would be a precipitous decline in government revenue, with an added and distinct possibility of widespread civil unrest.

Under the existing system, the Board went on, cultivators know what is owed to the government and to the temple, and plan their crops accordingly. Supervision by the Revenue Department ensures that each party with an interest in the land – temple, cultivator and government – gets its fair share. If the government withdrew, the ordinary cultivator's security and fortune would decline rapidly. Deprived of the state's protection, cultivators would be exposed, as one writer put it, to "rapaciousness of men [i.e., trustees] having only a temporary interest in the lands."[14] Dissatisfaction with the government itself could not but grow rapidly.

The picture of the temple which emerges from the Board of Revenue's description is that of an institution with few if any defenses against those

[13] Letter of 1 October 1838, quoted in *Revenue* Cons., 12 April 1841, 519: 3183 ff. For a discussion of what should and what should not be left to these managers, see BOR Proc., 1 October 1838, 1628: 12845ff.

[14] This was the phrase used by the Government of India to describe what it considered to be the melodramatic view of Madras officials. Letter no. 951, 20 September, 1845, in *Revenue*, Cons., 8 April 1846.

who would exploit it, especially against the trustees. The basic reason was that temples depended, in the final analysis, on land in the continued upkeep of which there was no authority, other than the state, with a clear and lasting stake. As Governor Elphinstone put it in 1840:

It appears to me that this right [of interference] could not be given up without injustice to the people and without the risk of great loss to the revenues of Government. Some check of this nature appears to me to be indispensably requisite as a precaution and remedy against the tendency to neglect and decay which I believe is everywhere observable in lands in which the actual managers have only a life interest ... and which in a country like this where everything depends upon the efficient maintenance of the means of irrigation, would not only entail ruin upon the property itself but which might involve that of a whole district.[15]

Elphinstone's general conclusion was that a continued involvement was at once the government's duty and right:

It cannot be doubted that if the right of summary interference was abandoned, the property of the Pagodas would be speedily embezzled and alienated. The Government it is true would be no losers by this, but the people would look upon such a state of things with deep dissatisfaction, and would justly consider that they were denied that protection which Government is assuredly bound to afford.[16]

Elphinstone became Governor of Madras in 1837. Over the next several years, he sent a number of memoranda to the Government of India in Calcutta in which he tried to unravel what was at issue in the argument over "interference" and "withdrawal." A reasonable ground of complaint against existing policy, he wrote, is that the government is making a financial profit from its connection with temples. He therefore agreed that the annual surplus of Rs. 81,363 should be given up, particularly because it was being used by "ignorant persons" in England as a pretext to agitate about complex issues they did not understand. But "interference" is basically a vague category, Elphinstone noted. The government can interfere in several ways: "to support, to protect, to destroy ... to impede or to molest."[17] Interference to protect, he argued, is surely the government's duty. That is, the government must necessarily attempt to ensure that land or money endowed for specified purposes be protected from misuse and embezzlement, and this included endowments for religious purposes.

Implicitly, Elphinstone argued, the London Court of Directors'

[15] *Revenue*, Cons., 9 June 1840, 497: 2674 ff.
[16] Ibid.
[17] Letter of 12 February 1841, in G.O. 210 Public 2 March 1841.

policy already recognized this duty since it provided that when executive action was terminated the jurisdiction over mismanagement and misappropriation would be taken up by the judicial system:

The Court of Directors manifestly intend that ample protection shall be given to Native Religious institutions ... for they declare that *such protection is to be given through the medium of the Courts of Justice* at the same time that they desire that Pagoda Funds shall not be managed or appropriated by Government officers.[18]

The notion that anything fundamental is changed by handing over this jurisdiction to the courts is simply muddled thinking, Elphinstone believed: "The interference is the same upon whichever party the duty of protection devolves."[19]

To summarize, the policy of withdrawal did not in fact lead to a "parting of all control over religious institutions." In the areas most critical to the government – lands, allowances and temple accounts in treasuries – the connection and control remained substantially the same. And in the areas where changes were made – trustee appointments and religious practices – the long-term result ironically was to set in motion forces which eventually increased rather than decreased the state's intervention.

The role of local committees and courts

The 1843 policy of handing over responsibility for the religious side of the temple to independent managers may have been of lesser significance to the government, but was very important to those in the localities most immediately affected by the change. Indeed the policy was severely criticized later in the century as irresponsible and shortsighted. The argument was that withdrawal created a "new class of managers" who then went on to claim hereditary status. Not only were these claims fraudulent and not based on local custom and usage, they made trustees out of persons without any particular interest in or dedication to their temples. New managers used their relative independence from government control to advance their personal fortunes, excessively spending and misappropriating temple funds.[20] Arguments soon began to be heard for closer government control. Withdrawal, in other words,

[18] Ibid.
[19] Ibid.
[20] These arguments are reviewed in "Report of the nonofficial committee," pp. 8–15. See also, Ernest J. Trevelyan, *Hindu law as administered in British India* (Calcutta: Thacker, Spink and Co., 1912), p. 551.

ironically created new demands for intervention. It brought new groups to power and excluded others, with both sides looking to the government's policy as the major influence on their positions.

Growing pressure to resolve these and other difficulties led to a new piece of legislation, the Religious Endowment Act of 1863 (Act XX of 1863), which superseded the remaining portions of the old 1817 Regulation. The most important departure, at least in intent, was the elimination of the Board of Revenue's primary jurisdiction. This was accomplished through a twofold approach: some of the BOR's historical jurisdiction was handed over to local governments, and some to the judiciary. The centerpiece was a system of local "area committees," the members of which held office for life and were normally chosen by election. The committees were responsible for what came to be called the "non-hereditary temples" in their particular districts: i.e., temples whose trustees had "traditionally" been nominated or chosen by the government. Area committees had many of the responsibilities formerly exercised by revenue officers, such as appointing trustees, ensuring order among temple personnel and taking care that temple funds were not mismanaged or misappropriated. Area committees did not have jurisdiction, however, over "hereditary temples": i.e., temples whose managers had not previously been selected by government officers. These temples were relatively free from any direct outside control, although their trustees could be sued in the courts for alleged mismanagement.[21]

The local area committees prefigured Lord Ripon's more extensive local self-government measures a decade later and, like them, resulted in new groups mobilizing and entering the political arena. Internal temple alignments and relations between temples and society were again thrown into uncertainty, temple–state relations became more complex, and new pressures converged on those exercising the state's authority.[22]

The second tier set up by Act XX was the jurisdiction of the courts. In part, the courts' authority was focused on problems expected to occur in the "hereditary temples." In cases of disputed hereditary succession, for example, the court could, on appeal, appoint an interim manager until the disputants had settled their rights in a regular civil suit. But the court's actual jurisdiction was broader and included non-hereditary

[21] For a general discussion of the background and provisions of Act XX of 1863, see Chandra Y. Mudaliar, *The secular state and religious institutions in India: a study of the administration of Hindu public trusts in Madras* (Wiesbaden: Franz Steiner, 1974), pp. 16 ff.

[22] For a comparable pattern elsewhere, see Charles Tilly, "Reflections on the history of European state-making," in Charles Tilly, ed., *The formation of national states in western Europe* (Princeton University Press, 1975), pp. 31–8.

temples also. For example, the court could demand that specific duties be performed by the trustee or priest of any temple, or even by a member of an area committee. Directly or indirectly, then, the court was in a position to exercise some control over all types of temples.[23]

It should be emphasized that the court's jurisdiction was not entirely new. The earlier policy of withdrawal, as Governor Elphinstone had argued, had been limited to the "executive" side of government; the "judicial" side always retained its jurisdiction. The significance of Act XX lies in the fact that, in formalizing this role, it laid the foundation for a rapid expansion in the scope and detail of the court's jurisdiction. By the beginning of the twentieth century, the court was preeminent. Initially it was an awkward jurisdiction and difficult to use effectively. Suits had to be initiated by outside allegations of malfeasance, breach of trust or neglect of duty before the court could intervene, and these suits were rarely completely successful since the defendant usually controlled the financial accounts and land records which were the subject of the dispute.[24]

In 1887 a new section was added to the Civil Procedure Code which effectively transformed the courts into the state's central agency in temple matters. Under new section 539, the Attorney-General, acting on his *own* initiative, was empowered to bring suit to prevent temple mismanagement in both hereditary and non-hereditary temples. This was tantamount to acknowledging once again, as Regulation VII of 1817 had acknowledged, the state's direct interest in and responsibility for temple administration.

The most significant feature of section 539 dealt with what were called temple "schemes." A court was empowered to settle a "scheme of administration" on a temple if the court deemed that no other short-range remedy was possible.[25]

This step had far-reaching implications. A "scheme" typically prescribed in detail the way in which a temple was to be administered. It could specify the respective duties and privileges of different temple functionaries, the uses to which temple funds were to be put, and even the kinds of rituals to be conducted. The court was effectively in a

[23] Trevelyan, *Hindu law*, pp. 552–63.

[24] T.L. Venkatarama Aiyer, *Mulla on the Code of Civil Procedure Act V of 1908*, 13th edn (Bombay: N.M. Tripathi, 1965–67), pp. 407–8.

[25] There is some disagreement over whether provisions in a "scheme" were merely declaratory, or were executable as well. Apparently, the determination of this question depended on the exact wording of a court's ruling in each case. This and other questions regarding the court's scheme-making powers under both the original Section 539 and the revised Sections 92–3 in Act V of 1908 are discussed in Trevelyan, *Hindu law*, p. 517, 545–8; and in Venkatarama Aiyer, *Mulla*, pp. 387–98.

position to chart a temple's future development, economically, administratively and religiously.

As a footnote, it is of interest that Section 539 was borrowed in part from an English law known as Romilly's Act. Sir John Romilly was a Benthamite member of the Second Law Commission (1856) whose report incorporated many Utilitarian ideas. Among these was a disregard for the Whig doctrine of separating "judicial" and "executive" powers.[26] It is no surprise, then, that Section 539 constituted a marked expansion of the judiciary's jurisdiction.

Two decades later, in 1908, Section 539 was revised into Sections 92 and 93 of the Civil Procedure Code. Judicial intervention was made still easier. Persons without specific personal interest were permitted to initiate suits. Previously, the plaintiff had legal standing only through some financial or religious relation to the temple. Also, it was not necessary that the suit be based on *prima facie* evidence. It was enough that "the direction of the court is deemed necessary" in some way.[27] Clearly, there were few, if any limits, to judicial intervention.

This does not mean that there was a sudden or dramatic decline in temple mismanagement. But it did mean that, after 1908, the Government of India firmly resisted any further expansion of the state's powers. The Government of India pointed over and over again to the very real power and discretion the courts now exercised. As it wrote in 1912:

> The successful termination of the Tirupati temple case proves the possibilities inherent in the existing powers of the civil courts. It has always, the Government of India believes, been the weak point in the case of the Madras reformers that they have been inclined to ignore these great potentialities.[28]

The Government of India also had a ready explanation of why, despite the broad powers of the court, effective oversight of the temples had not been achieved. It was not because of inadequate legislation, but because of a "lack of public spiritedness" on the part of native Indians. As it wrote in 1899, in a typical dispatch:

> The Government of India [is] not satisfied that there [is] anything to show that, given the public spirit necessary to put the machinery in motion, the law could not be effectively enforced against peccant trustees of temples ... [In] these circumstances, the Government of India do not consider that the need for legislation has been established.[29]

[26] Eric Stokes, *The English Utilitarians and India* (Oxford University Press, 1959), p. 63; Venkatarama Aiyer, *Mulla*, p. 387.

[27] Trevelyan, *Hindu law*, p. 561; Venkatarama Aiyer, *Mulla*, pp. 400–6.

[28] G.O. 627 Public 28 May 1912.

[29] G.O. 223 Public 2 March 1900.

Those who were pressing for a tightening up of temple administration, the government went on, assumed that temples were somehow analogous to churches in the West, an assumption with which the government disagreed:

A laxity in the management of religious endowments which might appear to be scandalous to Englishmen or to natives of India imbued with our ideas, would almost certainly be regarded in an entirely different light by the great body of Hindu worshippers, who look upon an offering to a priest of Brahman as a religious act. [30]

Whether because they were "imbued with" English ideas or for other reasons, an increasingly vocal group of Indians in public life continued to press for an even more active, direct and once again genuinely "executive" presence in temple affairs. Their efforts achieved success in the form of the Hindu Religious Endowment Board, established by the HRE Act of 1925.

The HRE Board

The end of World War I brought a reversal in basic British policy towards the Indian Empire. The British declaration that the war was fought for the principle of "national self-determination," and the increasing strength of the Indian political movement led to a new momentum towards self-government for India. The Government of India Act, 1919 (generally known as the Montagu–Chelmsford Reforms) provided for elected provincial councils, with jurisdiction over specified areas. Among the powers "transferred" to elected Indian representatives was authority over religious endowments.[31] This was a

[30] Ibid. This general view is reflected more recently by J. Duncan M. Derrett in his "The reform of Hindu religious endowments," in Donald E. Smith, ed., *South Asian politics and religion* (Princeton University Press, 1966), pp. 311–36. In a memorial in 1911, however, several Madras residents sought to disabuse the Government of India of this conception of the Madras Hindu community. The GOI's view, they argued, was based on facts which might be true of north India, but not of the south: "Every attempt hitherto made had the cordial support and concurrence of the Government of Madras, but we were not fortunate enough to receive the support of the Government of India, as their views have been largely coloured by the prejudices of the people of Bengal where in most of the institutions the superintendent or the Mahont as he is called is taken as possessing vested personal interests inexplicably involved in the affairs of the religious institutions. The state of things in this Presidency is absolutely different" (G.O. 627 Public 28 May 1912).

[31] The best constitutional discussion of the background, structure and operation of the Montagu–Chelmsford system of dyarchy is still Reginald Coupland, *The Indian problem: report on the constitutional problem in India* (Oxford University Press, 1944), chs. 5–6. For a study of the workings of dyarchy in Madras Presidency specifically, see Christopher J. Baker, *The politics of south India 1920–1937* (Cambridge University Press, 1976), especially chs. 1–2.

momentous event for the structure of temple–state relations in Tamil Nadu. It led in 1926 to the formation of the Hindu Religious Endowments Board (HRE Board) and after Independence to its successor, the Hindu Religious and Charitable Endowments (Administration) Department (HRCE).

The HRE Act (Madras Act II of 1927) passed in 1926 by the Madras Legislative Council was a comprehensive effort to address long-standing problems in Hindu temples, but the reception to it was not entirely cordial.[32] The break with "withdrawal" led to a lasting debate over the nature of "noninterference" and secularism, and the emphasis on independent "executive" action led to repeated conflicts with older agencies such as the Board of Revenue and the courts. Temple officials were not enthusiastic. Thus, the new HRE Board began its work in an atmosphere of animosity and mutual suspicion. Moreover, the broader political, social and intellectual tenor of the ruling party was an issue. The 1920 elections had seen the defeat of the Swarajists, a breakaway Congress group, by the Justice Party. The Justice Party had been founded in 1916 by a group of upper-caste non-Brahmins who emphasized non-Brahmin culture and literature and demanded a greater role for non-Brahmins in education, politics and administration. To the extent that the nationalist Congress was perceived as dominated by Brahmins, Justice Party members were antagonistic to it.[33]

This context significantly shaped the reception of the new legislation. The HRE Act was initiated by a government controlled by the Justice Party, a party with an aggressive ideology whose relation to Hindu

[32] The legislative history is complicated. Soon after the Madras Act I of 1925 was passed there were questions about its technical legality. To remove these, and to introduce some further modifications, a second comprehensive statute was enacted late in 1926, called the Hindu Religious Endowments Act of 1927 or Madras Act II of 1927. In most of the secondary literature, 1927 is taken to be the beginning date. In fact, though, the HRE Board began its work soon after the passage of Act I of 1925. The next major revision came with the Hindu Religious and Charitable Endowments Act (XIX) of 1951, which replaced the HRE Board by the Hindu Religious and Charitable Endowments (Administration) Department (HRCE). This was followed by the HRCE Act (XXII) of 1959. For an analysis in detail, see Mudaliar, *Secular state*; also, V. Rajasikhamani, *The Tamil Nadu Hindu Religious and Charitable Endowments Act XXII of 1959* (Madras: B. Sundaralingam, 1971?).

[33] Of the several works on the early history of the Justice Party, see Eugene F. Irschick, *Politics and social conflict in south India: the non-Brahman movement and Tamil separatism 1916–1929* (Berkeley: University of California Press, 1969); Marguerite Ross Barnett, *The politics of cultural nationalism in south India* (Princeton University Press, 1976), chs. 1–3; P. Spratt, *D.M.K. in power* (Bombay: Nachiketa Publications, 1970), chs. 1–2. Charles A. Ryerson cites much of the extensive literature on the non-Brahmin movement, especially regarding its origins and development in the nineteenth century, in his "'Meaning and modernization' in Tamil India: primordial sentiments and sanskritization" (Unpublished Ph.D. dissertation, Columbia University, 1979), especially ch. 3. For a somewhat different perspective on the ideology of the movement, see Baker's *Politics of south India*.

orthodoxy was problematic. Many who previously had supported an expanded state role suddenly found reason to back off, fearful that the actual effect of the act would be to further the Justice Party's particular vision of south Indian culture and, in so doing, radically undercut traditional Hindu practices and orthodoxy. Opinion about the bill, in other words, did not necessarily fall neatly along party lines.

The HRE Act would clearly tighten the relation between state and temple. Its central feature was a Board of Commissioners, located in Madras city, appointed by the government, and vested with the "general superintendence of all religious endowments."

Dispersed jurisdictions, resulting from the confusions of the nineteenth century, were to be gathered together and consolidated. Authority would shift away from the courts, and the "executive" rather than the "judiciary" would become the state's paramount agency. The powers of area committees, especially, were to be eroded. Local, elected self-government would be subordinated to centralized, nominated administration.

These political and administrative implications were clearly understood from the outset, in broad outline if not in every detail. The act was thus one of the most controversial and important pieces of legislation in Madras Presidency under the Montagu–Chelmsford Reforms. The formal legislative debate over the act extended over three years and in printed form runs to more than a thousand pages. It is impossible to do justice here to the wealth of information and detail which can be found in these debates. At an ideological level, discussion revolved around the merits of two contrasting principles for temple–state relation: noninterference and protection. Fastening on a key nineteenth-century term, the bill's opponents attacked the HRE bill as a deep and flagrant intervention in the religious affairs of Hindus, and thus contrary to the long-standing British guarantee of *noninterference*. The bill's supporters, in contrast, sought support from south Indian culture, particularly from the principle that *protection* of Hindu temples by the state is an ancient Indian tradition, a tradition moreover which is expected by the Indian public and which is essential to the welfare of the institutions themselves. The debates gave a lasting imprint to this distinction, which has continued to shape nearly all subsequent argument about temple–state relations in Tamil Nadu.

The government's major defense for the new HRE Board was that it re-established state "protection," an ancient south Indian tradition. Under Hindu rule, the argument went, kings and rajahs had always protected Hindu religious institutions. Local rulers built temples, endowed them with lands, took an interest in how they were managed, and made certain that their successors would do the same. Temples in fact symbolized the legitimacy and authority of kings; building and restoring temples was a royal prerogative, at once an obligation and an opportunity. Even in the twentieth century, Hindu rulers in such princely states as Mysore, Travancore and Cochin maintained this tradition. Protection is a principle accepted by the Hindu public, and is essential for the welfare of temples themselves, asserted the government's supporters.[34]

Much of this argument was made by P. Venkataramana Rao Nayudu, the government's expert witness. Recent history, he argued, proves that temples are harmed when the state is no longer active. Deterioration began immediately after 1842, when the British ended active supervision. Since then the "government has not been doing its duty to its subjects," and this is the "standing grievance of the Hindu community."[35] "Withdrawal," in fact, was a policy forced by the "missionary lobby" in Madras and London in the hope that Hinduism would suffer. And that is precisely what had happened:

> They [the missionaries] asked the government to hand them [the temples] over to Indian management and said that their objects would be realised only if those institutions were handed over to Indian management. They were thus handed over and subsequent events have clearly proved that what they said was quite true. From the time they were handed over to the Indian management until now, it is plain that many of the temples have ceased to exist and many poor fellows became rich at the expense of such temples.[36]

Those who opposed the HRE Act appealed to the British precedent of "noninterference." As a minority in the legislature, the opposition's only real hope lay with the Madras governor, who, under the Montagu–Chelmsford Reforms, could veto provincial legislation. The debates are therefore filled with strategic quotations from nineteenth-century "guarantees." In the course of one speech, an opponent first quoted Queen Victoria's proclamation of 1858:[37]

> Firmly relying ourselves on the truth of Christianity, acknowledging with gratitude the solace of religion, we disclaim alike the right and desire to impose our convictions on any of our subjects. We declare it to be our royal will and pleasure that none be in any wise favoured, none molested or disquieted, by reason of their religious faith or observances, but that all shall alike enjoy the equal and impartial protection of the law; and we do strictly charge and enjoin all those who may be in authority under us *that they abstain from all interference*

[34] For an earlier and succinct statement of the "essential functions of government" in regard to temple supervision, and how these were maintained in the native states as distinct from British India, see Muttuswami Aiyer report in G.O. 72–74 Legislative 26 May 1894.

[35] *Proceedings*, 17 September 1926.

[36] *Proceedings*, March–April 1923.

[37] *Proceedings*, 25–31 August 1926.

with the religious belief or worship of any of our subjects on pain of our highest displeasure.

He then went on to quote the Montagu–Chelmsford Report, which also warned against interference "in questions of religious nature or bound up with religious beliefs, which it is the duty of Government to respect and leave alone." He concluded by citing a speech by the Viceroy, Lord Reading:

There is the fundamental principle of the British Government in India which the British Parliament has taken care should be preserved: *the freedom of religion from interference.* You will remember – these are my final words – that the provisions of our constitution make it imperative, as it seems to me, upon the Governor-General to consider not only whether the Bill affects religion but how far it affects it and what its consequences may involve.

The HRE Board contradicted these "guarantees" in every detail, the opponents declared. S. Satyamurti, the leading spokesman for the opposition, particularly criticized two details. One was the "extraordinary" provision regarding *dhittams* (temple budgets). *Dhittams*, he noted, determine

how many coconuts should be broken, how many seers [a unit of measurement] of oil are to be used for *abhishekam* purposes [i.e., bathing the idol] and how many *panchamruthams* have to be made.[38]

Is it proper, he asked, that decisions regarding these matters should be vested with "secular" authority? The Board and the committees had the power to approve or disapprove temple budgets. What if the Board or a committee refused to sanction expenditures for religiously required rituals?

This is the crux of my objection to this section. According to modern notions, to the committees and to the Board it will seem a wastage for instance to have a thousand plantains on the head of the deity or two thousand coconuts . . . But we believe that by offering these rich and varied offerings to the deities in the temples we are doing something meritorious.

In a clear reference to the Justice Party he asked, "Are you going to vest in all these committees and the Board, without any test [of their orthodoxy] whatever, the right to determine the *dhittam*?"[39]

[38] *Proceedings*, 25–31 August 1926.

[39] Satyamurti added, correctly, that the right to appeal to higher judicial authority was scarcely a remedy. The appeal had to be paid for by the plaintiff and, until the final order was received, the Committee's decision was legally binding. Moreover, the appeals process was simply a matter of "appealing from one secular body to another secular body." The provision, he warned, vests "arbitrary power in the Committees and the Board . . . and is likely to work great mischief and harm and insult the religious feelings of the people" (*Proceedings*, 13 September 1926).

Satyamurti also attacked the power which the bill gave the HRE Board over the legal principle of *cy pres*. Under the *cy pres* principle, temples were regarded legally as trusts, and a court could direct a temple's surplus income to some other purpose, possibly but not necessarily related to the temple from which the surplus derived. Under the bill, the HRE Board, rather than the courts, would have this jurisdiction. Satyamurti argued that the Board might well manipulate temple budgets to create *artificial* surpluses, and that these would then be spent on projects furthering the political interests of the ruling party. The first part of this fear was not altogether without foundation. The major sponsors of the HRE bill, including the Chief Minister, the Raja of Panagal, had often stated their opposition to "extravagant expenditures," and, more ominously, expenditures in what they called "wrong directions."[40]

Satyamurti's fears were real enough and his objections not without force. But the references to nineteenth-century "withdrawal" could not carry much weight; everyone realized that withdrawal had never been a complete description of nineteenth-century British policy, especially in south India. On closer examination, indeed, it becomes clear that the real objection was not to interference as such, but to the projected departure from *existing* forms of interference. Behind the opposition was the perception of a change in the political and administrative structure of the Presidency. The shift from the courts to the Board was a major symbol of this change. Those who opposed the HRE Act perceived correctly that the HRE Board foreshadowed important changes in temple–state relations: the growth of central power and the decline of local authorities, the ascendency of administration based on bureaucratic rules and region-wide directives, the decline of contextually oriented courts. The long hours spent debating the HRE bill reflected a deep uncertainty over what these changes would mean.

Clearly threatened were local autonomy and identity. Diversity – in temple organization, traditions and practices – was being rejected in favor of centralization and uniformity. The immense differences among temples were to be subsumed under a few classifications and categories, and all were now to be administered according to a common set of rules. At stake were long-standing local patterns, rooted in particular communities, histories and cultures.[41]

[40] *Proceedings*, 11 September 1926.

[41] On the distinction and interaction between local custom and orthodox Hinduism, see the anthropological literature on "great" and "little" traditions, e.g., McKim Marriott, "Little communities in an indigenous civilization," in McKim Marriott, ed., *Village India* (University of Chicago Press, 1955); Milton Singer, *When a great tradition modernizes* (New York: Praeger, 1972).

Some, indeed, argued that the concept of the "Hindu temple" was itself an innovation. A representative from South Kanara district argued that the temples of his area were not "Hindu" at all, but belonged to separate and independent "communities." A representative from Malabar, in a long and impassioned speech, pointed out the unique features of the temples in his area:

Sir, the very idea of communal ownership is foreign to people in Malabar except in some parts of Palghat. Each *tarawad* is a self-contained unit. It has got its own tanks, its own burial grounds, its own temples, and everything that is absolutely necessary for the ordinary wants of the members of the *tarawad.* As is seen in other parts of the Presidency, we have not got a common burial ground or a temple or a threshing ground or anything like that. People live separately from one another and you don't find the custom of living in streets. Practically in the whole of Malabar there are no streets except as I said in Palghat. Each *tarawad* lives quite detached and separate from others. Therefore it is necessary for each *tarawad* to have its own temple.[42]

In the eyes of the opponents, essentially political calculations lay at the heart of the HRE legislation. The HRE Board would enhance the power of the center and would benefit the political party controlling the center. In the short run, this would mean that local temple resources would be used to strengthen the Justice Party. Moreover, compared with the courts, the HRE Board was distant, unfamiliar and, it was feared, likely to be contemptuous of local customs. Is this, one opponent asked, the ultimate meaning of the Montagu–Chelmsford Reforms, for which all present had worked so hard?

The constitution of the Board, investing it with enormous and extensive powers, clothing it with an amount of finality, taking away the jurisdiction of the civil courts . . . constitute [sic] . . . the storm centers of this Bill . . . Hitherto we have been trying for the transference of power from the old bureaucracy. Now, after getting the power transferred from the old bureaucracy, there is a tendency on the part of some of us not only to retain that power and use it but also to trench on the domains of others.[43]

Another Councillor put the meaning of the new arrangements succinctly:

Of course, this creates a new field of pasture for some people influential with the ministry to get billets; but how far the Board or the Boards are going to serve the purpose for which they are constituted is in the laps of the Gods.[44]

[42] *Proceedings*, 3 August 1926; 26 August 1926.
[43] *Proceedings*, 3 April 1923.
[44] Ibid.

Beyond these short-term political consequences, the HRE bill also implied a more significant structural change in the temple–state relationship. At one level, the argument that the HRE Board simply continued the principle of protection in a new modern form was quite plausible. But the continuity was more than offset by a major discontinuity. Sriman Mayasaya, one of the bill's most forceful opponents, made a telling distinction. He was quite aware that a close connection used to exist between the state and temples. But the nature of the state in earlier times was profoundly different:

It has been said that the kings in the past interfered with the religious endowments and why then do you now object to the interference of the State as now constituted? The very constitution of the State will show the difference. Our kings in the old days, the Hindu kings, endowed properties for the temples and maths. They appointed trustees or constituted themselves as trustees. That is how they exercised the kingly duty of interfering with the temple properties. But what is the case now? The Government ... has nothing to do with the endowments of the properties of the Hindus, yet wants to interfere with the religious institutions.[45]

Sriman Mayasaya was pointing out that in the twentieth century the state's link with temples had changed profoundly. In pre-British days the state and temples had been mutually supportive. The state supported the temple with land, while the temple supported the state's legitimacy with various symbolic resources. Protection had real substantive meaning in the context of this exchange. The modern state, however, is separate from, and quite self-consciously does not base its legitimacy on, temples. For the opponents of the HRE Board, this separateness was fundamental. It made the appeal to protection spurious, robbed the HRE Board of its legitimacy, and became a warning of changes to come.

Conclusion

In the broader historical sense, the inauguration of the HRE Board did settle at least one thing. It ended the long argument, which had begun in the 1830s, between Madras officialdom and the proponents of withdrawal in favor of the former. "Protection" replaced "noninterference" as the central ideological underpinning of actual practice. But beneath this victory lay tensions over the concrete direction protection should take. Part of the success of "protection" as a legitimating principle, indeed, lies precisely in its capacity to convey multiple meanings and

[45] *Proceedings*, 26 August 1926.

values. The uneven record of subsequent temple administration is rooted in these tensions. Both the HRE Board and its successor, the HRCE, have been enmeshed in intractable disputes with agencies whose jurisdictions they were intended to supersede: the localities, courts and Board of Revenue. These conflicts – over governance, economy and religious life – will be explored in subsequent chapters.

3

Governance: the necessity for order

In the HRCE, and among educated south Indians more generally, there is an image of temples as poorly organized, badly governed and corrupt. Temples are regarded as a "problem," a continuing scandal. The atmosphere in many temples does not help this image. To their critics, temples seem noisy, chaotic and full of extraneous activity which disrupts quiet worship. According to the standard view, the reason for this state of affairs is not hard to find. The immense resources of temples are constantly exploited for personal gain – by temple functionaries and trustees, by contractors, merchants, politicians and others pursuing status, honor and profit. According to this view, the solution to the problem is also clear. Corruption and mismanagement need to be brought under control, the perpetrators ousted and prosecuted, and the temples reorganized for the benefit of devout Hindu worshippers.

This image is not especially new. It was in fact substantially the same in the nineteenth century, and led directly to state intervention. Without vigilant state protection, it was argued, temples inevitably decline, preyed upon by those who manage to get a hold over them. This was the central argument used in the 1920s to justify setting up the HRE Board, an argument affirmed many times since. The state must gain control and reorganize the temples, so that temples can fulfill their religious mission.

Governance was thus uppermost when the HRE Board began its work. However, after over a half century of administration by the HRE Board and its successor, the HRCE, the problems remain substantially the same. Disputes abound among worshippers, priests, trustees and government officers (executive officers); succession from trustee to trustee is irregular and often bitter; temple wealth is misused; temple lands are often occupied by squatters and other unauthorized persons, and rents are often not collected.

The seeming intractability of the "temple problem" is puzzling. The general thesis explored here is that the HRCE's failure stems from an absence of agreement in south Indian society about the fundamental theory of the temple. My use of "theory" here follows that of Samuel H. Beer in his classic effort to understand the complexities of political representation in British society. Beer found several forms of representation:

Each of the principal forms has been associated with a cluster of ideas and sentiments toward government and society in general and toward representation in particular. Such a cluster we may call a theory providing we understand by "theory" not necessarily the product of a political philosopher, but rather an operative ideal of people in politics.[1]

Similarly, in the world of temple administration there are not one but several "clusters of ideas and sentiments." Each defines differently what temples are and what they should be. I shall call these clusters theories, with the understanding that a "theory" is rarely stated explicitly, and is rather, as Beer puts it, "an operative ideal of people" about temples. Theory conflict is the rule rather than the exception; the HRCE is constantly embroiled in disagreements over fundamentals. It is an oversimplification, in other words, to identify HRCE failures as the result simply of corruption or inefficiency. The theory conflicts are deep and enduring, and their effects on administration are systematic. The main theories or images of the temple are associated with four political and institutional arenas: the HRCE, the court, the political party and the locality. Each theory is logically tied to a particular form of temple organization; to particular rules and procedures for governance; to a particular economy and form of financial management; and even to a particular concept of religion. Most important here, each theory implies a particular kind of state presence.

My general thesis, then, is that theory conflict over the basic nature of the temple lies at the root of HRCE administrative failures. The fact that there is no basic agreement shapes the behavior of all individuals, groups and institutions active in temple affairs. As might be expected, the situation is in part a legacy of colonial experience. With British rule came a set of western categories, assumptions and organizational forms which sat uneasily with those of south Indian culture and history. But colonialism is not the whole story. The problem stems also from the fact that temples engage an unusually diverse set of groups and individuals, with structurally very different interests, and culturally very different assumptions. Some sense of this diversity is suggested by the fact that those who are typically interested in temple matters include lawyers,

[1] Samuel H. Beer, "The representation of interests in British government: historical background," *American Political Science Review* 51 (September 1957): 613–14. Other authors use other terms to get at the same issue. Examples include "paradigm" (Thomas S. Kuhn), "conceptual models" (Graham Allison), "models" (Morton Halperin), "images" (Michael Polanyi).

priests, landowners, tenants, bureaucrats, urban educated elites, caste groups, legislators, district judges, government development workers, grain wholesalers, *panchayat* boards, newspaper journalists and ordinary worshippers.

To disentangle the threads of this situation is no easy task. The different operative ideals or theories are for the most part unstated and implicit, and each is complicated by interactions with others, so that none falls into a water-tight compartment. Any formal outline is necessarily to this extent arbitrary, yet some abstraction is necessary. For governance issues, the HRCE's own theory is clearly of utmost importance. But its significance will be apparent only if preceded first by a description of the world of the south Indian temple in its own terms, artificially isolated from the HRCE. The contrast between this world and the HRCE's assumptions will soon emerge clearly.

The south Indian temple

As was noted in the Introduction, we are dealing with an institution of great complexity. Space does not permit a review of the recent and extensive literature on south Indian temples; this would take us far afield of our central focus on HRCE administration. I shall only suggest in schematic outline central features of the temple as an institution, relying at crucial points on Arjun Appadurai's important study *Worship and conflict under colonial rule.*[2] To make an otherwise abstract discussion as concrete as possible, I shall include examples as the discussion proceeds. I shall begin, as Appadurai does, with a brief account of temple honors, or *mariyathe*.

Late one evening in April of 1974, having concluded a long interview with the manager of the Sri Ranganathaswami temple in Srirangam, one of the most important Vaisnava temples, I happened upon the ritual of *raja mariyathe*, or kingly honors. To the beat of drums and music of the *nagaswaram*, the deity was being carried in procession through one of the temple's interior streets. The procession stopped near me, and each of seven men was honored. I was told that the men included a *konar*, a watchman, and five or six friends of one of the temple trustees. The officiating *stanikar* wrapped each recipient's head with a cloth and then placed on it briefly the *sadagopam*, or golden crown, imprinted with the feet of the lord Vishnu. It was a small group that was present, and not much notice was taken by those who walked by. But there was

[2] Arjun Appadurai, *Worship and conflict under colonial rule: a south Indian case* (Cambridge University Press, 1981).

nonetheless an extraordinary sense about the ceremony. There seemed a closeness and familiarity with the deity on the part of those receiving *mariyathe*, markedly contrasting with the distance from the deity, even withdrawal, on the part of the rest of us.

According to the HRCE assistant commissioner (AC) at Tiruchirapalli, *mariyathe* rituals are an unending source of administrative difficulty. Temple government is formally headed by trustees, and the competition for these posts is often intense. Much of the assistant commissioner's time is taken up with the effort to handle trustee conflicts. Trusteeship is desirable, among other reasons, because of *mariyathe*; trustees enjoy precedence. Moreover, since trustees often represent their communities, competition for trustee posts, and competition among trustees for precedence, translate easily into larger caste conflicts over status, wealth and power. One of the HRCE's strategies, the assistant commissioner reported, is to appoint trustees from each dominant community in the hopes of minimizing conflict.

Even this approach does not guarantee harmony. The AC described the case of a neighboring temple's annual ten-day festival, each day of which is financed by a separate donor (*kattalaidar*).[3] A dispute arose over whether the first honors on a given day should go to the *kattalaidar* or to a member of the local *panchayat*. The conflict was really between an isolated but wealthy donor, on the one hand, and the "local people," on the other. At least this is how the AC interpreted it. If serious, these conflicts over rituals must eventually be decided by the HRCE deputy commissioner (DC), whose judgment can be appealed to the civil courts. These authorities, the AC noted, decide "who is the lawful person to receive first honors."

Mariyathe is traditionally granted also to prominent dignitaries. The practice has become quite controversial in recent years, particularly when it involves politicians and government ministers who are well known atheists or at least deeply skeptical. Commenting on the general practice in 1973, the Estimates Committee of the Tamil Nadu Legislative Assembly wrote:

> In conclusion, the committee desires to refer to the prevalent practice of temple honours and *parivattam* being accorded to VIPs on their visits to the temple. The committee is not able to ascertain the origin of this practice; nor is there any evidence to establish any sanction there for in the *agamas* or rituals ... Above all the practice is contradictory to the concept of equality before God and equal treatment in the presence of God. The high and the low, the mighty and the

[3] On the nature of *kattalais*, see Carol Appadurai Breckenridge, "'Dry-nurse of Siva': withdrawal and temple endowments, 1833–1863" (mimeo, 1976).

meek, the rich and the poor are alike, and the children of God and must be treated as such in the presence of God. Humility is an essential attribute of a devotee. Such being the case nothing that accentuated distinction of rank, position or power can not [*sic*] be said to be in accordance with the divinity. Moreover, presentation of *parivattam* involves expenditure and there seems to be no legitimate sanction for the same. The committee is also constrained to observe that in recent times, the practice has been extended to many people in the category of VIPs without any restraint or restriction.[4]

The committee concluded by strongly recommending that the ritual of temple honors be discontinued.

Mariyathe is a good illustration of the way in which a temple's broader political and social context affects its internal rituals and processes. In his book, Appadurai clarifies the reasons why individuals and corporate groups have such an investment in *mariyathe* and in temple affairs generally.[5] Temples are pivotal institutions in local society, Appadurai argues, in part because temple deities preside over a "redistributive" process which at once defines the community socially and sustains it materially. Quoting Marshall Sahlins on redistribution, Appadurai includes the south Indian temple as an institution which "generates the spirit of unity, codifies ... and stipulates ... social order and social action."[6]

To understand these functions, the temple must be viewed not as a single, unbroken entity, but as an aggregate of parts. For example, each component of a temple's complex ritual cycle is subsidized by a "great diversity of donors," whose donations initiate the redistributive process.[7] A central resource is honors, which may take the form of the deity's silk vestments, priority in drinking the water sanctified by contact with the deity, a garland, or – as with the ceremony I witnessed in Srirangam – placing a gold crown on the head. All those in any way involved in honors rituals – donor, temple staff, worshippers – benefit in a general sense. Yet, the particular character of each honors ceremony and the order in which honors are distributed both *denote* and *constitute* "culturally privileged roles in relationship to the deity" and thus impose a ranking within the community. This is a crucial point, and it would be well to quote Appadurai at some length.

[4] Tamil Nadu Legislative Assembly, Committee on Estimates, 1972–73, *Hindu Religious and Charitable Endowments (Administration) Department*, p. 16.

[5] Appadurai's analysis of *mariyathe* elaborates an earlier, more general account. See Arjun Appadurai and Carol Appadurai Breckenridge, "The south Indian temple: authority, honor and redistribution," *Contributions to Indian Sociology* (NS) 10 (1976): 187–211.

[6] Appadurai, *Worship and conflict*, p. 34.

[7] Ibid. p. 29.

That is, the receipt of specific honors, in any given context, *renders authoritative* the individual's share (*panku*) in the temple conceived as a redistributive process. Such a share would be composed of the right to offer service (*kainkaryam*) to the deity, either through endowment (*upayam*) or through prescribed ritual function; the right to move the resources allocated for the specific ritual event; the right to command the relevant persons involved in the actualization of the given ritual; the right to perform some single part of a complex ritual event; and, finally, the right to worship the deity by simply witnessing the ritual. Depending on whether one was a donor, a temple servant, or a worshipper, and depending on the particular ritual event in question, one's share in the ritual process would have a different concrete content. The sum total of one's rights, over time, would constitute one's share in the ritual and redistributive process of the temple.[8]

Appadurai goes on to argue that each redistributive process is relatively autonomous. That is, particular groups and individuals view themselves as having independent relationships to the deity, not "subject to the control of their fellow worshippers":

The most important fact about these various forms of service is that they are all relatively autonomous forms of participation in the overall ritual and redistributive process of the temple. Each person or group involved in service of any kind thus possesses an inalienable and privileged relationship to the sovereign deity concretized in some sort of "share" (*panku*), and embodied and rendered authoritative by some sort of honor.[9]

The presence of numerous shares, each claiming autonomy, means that any order among the shares is something of an achievement, representing what Appadurai calls a "delicate consensus," easily threatened by changes in the social and political environment.[10] Indeed, control over a particular share is never entirely secure; there are always others in the wings, waiting to marshal whatever influence they can to oust the present shareholders from their positions.

The general concept of "shares" moves the analysis beyond the confines of the formal *mariyathe* ritual. A breakdown of consensus over shares is always serious. The government records include a fairly detailed account of one such breakdown, which occurred in the 1930s in a little village of South Arcot district.[11] Its basic features are repeated, in general outline if not in precise detail, throughout the south Indian countryside many times each year. The trouble in the Karamani Kuppam village related to the conduct of the annual *Masi Makhan* festival in February. The festival included a procession by Adi-Dravidas

[8] Ibid. p. 36.
[9] Ibid. p. 46.
[10] Ibid. p. 47.
[11] G.O. 463 Public 17 March 1938.

(as the records referred to the untouchable community), carrying their tutelary goddess Mariyaman to the seaside. The customary route of the procession took the Adi-Dravidas through fields before they were able to reach the road leading to the ocean. The Adi-Dravidas had been trying since at least 1918 to have this route changed to one which would proceed along the village's main street. The clear intention, and herein lay the difficulty, was to have a route which would take the Adi-Dravidas past the village's main Siva temple, worshipped in by higher caste villagers.

In 1937, the Adi-Dravida leaders petitioned the deputy superintendent of police to permit them to change the route, and also asked that he issue a restraining order against any attempt by caste Hindus to prevent the change. The deputy superintendent refused, on the grounds that the Adi-Dravidas were "trying to set up a new right"; the Adi-Dravidas reluctantly followed his ruling. The same request was made and refused again in 1938, but this time the Adi-Dravidas took matters into their own hands. On the night of the festival they gathered on a plain near the railway tracks and threw stones at the caste Hindus and a few police officers assembled nearby. The police called for reinforcements, at which point the Adi-Dravidas fled.

As this illustrates, access to the temple, even to the temple's physical proximity, is important in local society. To have access is in a sense to have a share, and with shares go privilege, precedence and control. How temple shares are controlled affects politics in the villages and districts, at the levels of both individual and political party competition. The modern western reader may be inclined to dismiss temple honors as "merely" symbolic and derivative from the "real" politics of wealth, status and power. But the symbolic temple interactions are deeply consequential.[12] Temples in all their dimensions are arenas where people pursue strategies designed to protect, enhance or stabilize social position and rank. The temple has a competitive, political character.

If the temple is from one point of view a competitive political arena, it is from another point of view the victor's spoils. That is, the temple is itself a resource or, rather, an aggregation of resources. Some resources we have already mentioned: rights in worship, such as proximity, *mariyathe*, precedence in the receipt of divine leavings (*prasadam*); offices, such as trustee, priest, *kattalaidar*. Others are resources which can be controlled as a consequence of controlling worship and offices: tenancy on the temple's land; commercial contracts to renovate a temple

[12] On this point, see Appadurai and Breckenridge, "The south Indian temple."

tower or sell a temple's paddy harvest. The losses and gains in temple competition involve the control of resources such as these.

Structure and conflict in the temple are especially articulated at important rituals and occasions. Illustrating this is another government report, also drawn from the HRE Board's early years.[13]

Late in April 1937, the Madras government received a telegram from Nidamangalam town in Thanjavur district. The cable was from a local politician, protesting against the arrest of several persons belonging to the Justice Party. The cable pleaded, "Pray immediate enquiry and prevention forever of politics in public religious festivals."

A report filed later by the sub-divisional magistrate made clear that the issue involved a temple cart. This was nothing unusual; cart-pulling festivals were often prime occasions for trouble. Very old and often three stories high, south Indian temple carts are mammoth wooden structures, to which are secured very thick ropes. Pulling the cart requires teams of hundreds and even thousands of men. The carts are used at least once each year to take the temple deities out in procession around the city's main streets.

The cart festival of the Sanathanarayanaswami temple occurred on 25 April. The celebrations were about to reach their peak at 9:30 in the morning, with thousands of onlookers lining the streets. Suddenly the flag of the Indian National Congress party was hoisted and displayed from within the cart. In the context of local Nidamangalam politics there was no doubt about what the flag signified or what was being claimed. Relations between the Congress and Justice parties had been "strained" for at least a year, centering particularly around elections to the panchayat board. The Congress group was led by two brothers, members of a wealthy and powerful landowning (*mirasdar*) family referred to in the records as the Odayar family. The brothers were influential in the temple, and had in fact supplied the two thousand or so laborers pulling the temple cart that day.

When the Congress flag appeared, one Armugam Chettiar, presumably from the Justice Party, went immediately to the sub-inspector of police to object. The sub-inspector replied that the complaint needed to be put in writing. Either because he lacked pen and paper, or because he perceived this as a delaying tactic, Armugam Chettiar went to the temple trustee, who in turn referred him to the Odayar brothers. The latter shrugged away any responsibility; after all, they said, the only persons in the cart along with the idols are temple servants, such as priests,

[13] Details of this incident are contained in G.O. 3274 LA 26 August 1937; G.O. 1177 Public 12 July 1937. See also, G.O. 1693 Public 10 October 1938.

drummers and musicians. With this, Armugam Chettiar took matters into his own hands and laid himself down in front of the cart wheels, declaring that he would not permit the procession to proceed as long as the Congress flag was flying.

The sub-magistrate was called. He asked the trustee to remove the flag, but the trustee said he was helpless. The magistrate then asked Armugam Chettiar to move. Chettiar, now joined by four others, declared his intention to perform *satyagraha*, whereupon the sub-magistrate declared them an unlawful assembly and arrested them. The five were released later in the day after the cart-pulling was over. Closing his report to the Madras government, the sub-magistrate reported his conviction that it had not been practical to order the flag's removal. Two thousand men hired by the Odayars were pulling the cart, whereas the police force at his command had been very small. A serious breach of the peace could have resulted.

Change is a constant feature of temple life. The perpetual struggle for "shares" – "shares" in the sense of precedence, entry, donation, honors, *prasadam* – is affected by assertions of rights to shares hitherto denied, by new donations, and by the wider social and political environment. Because any change, however small, affects the overall distribution of privilege in the whole, new claims to place are always a problem.[14] Claims by lower caste groups of rights to temple entry are vigorously contested; Brahmin priests deny that others have the right to serve; caste Hindus fight to prevent Adi-Dravidas from taking their procession before the village temple. Some groups and individuals may choose to gain a share through financially endowing a ritual or portion of a festival; others forge social and political alliances to achieve influence. There are many plausible strategies, depending on local circumstance and opportunity. In general, we can assume that when the social, economic and political environment is stable, the structure of temple control is relatively stable; when broader social structures are fragile, the structure of governance is likely also to be fragile and unstable.

Clearly, the south Indian temple is not completely self-contained. Its boundaries with broader society are open and fluid. In one sense, the temple is especially pivotal in the larger social environment: its primary resource, proximity to the deity and the status this gives, cannot be found elsewhere, and often brings highly valued material resources as

[14] Carol Appadurai Breckenridge, "Betel-nut and honor: exchange-relationships and temple-entry in a south Indian temple" (paper read at the annual meeting of the Association for Asian Studies, March 1975), p. 2 and *passim*. Breckenridge argues that changes in the pattern of access to "external" festivals are less disruptive than changes in "internal" ritual.

well. But, by the same token, resources are present in society which can affect the temple profoundly: chief among these are the state's legal and cultural authority, and the influence of political office, economic wealth and social status. The temple and the broader social system interact constantly.

To summarize, the south Indian temple is an arena in which are distributed and redistributed highly valued material and symbolic resources. The temple's structure at any given time is equivalent to control of these resources, confirmed periodically in temple rituals such as *puja*, *mariyathe*, processions and festivals. Thus, relations among temple actors, e.g., priest, trustee, tenant, caste, landlord and government, have a dynamic quality. Privileged access is in a daily contest with relative deprivation.

The HRCE's theory of temples

When we turn to the HRCE, we find an image very different from that just presented. What from the vantage of those in the temples appears as normal and appropriate is viewed by the HRCE as disorganization at best and chaos and corruption at worst. The HRCE sees its central task to be that of reorganizing the temple to make it governable in an orderly way. The HRCE's theory can be stated fairly simply. It is that temples should be religious, public, and non-political. They should be governed by rules consistently applied by persons chosen for their positions by objective qualifications. Stated thus simply, the theory seems harmless enough, but in fact it pits the HRCE continuously against trustees, priests and most others active in temple affairs.

The first element in the HRCE's image is that temples must be regarded as *religious* – not economic, social or political – institutions. Religion gives the temple its central identity and its paramount purpose. The spiritual dimension sets the temple apart, at least in principle, from all other institutions, and requires that boundaries be placed between its roles and processes and those of the larger society. The religious core is the ritual of *puja*, in which the priest stands as an intermediary between the deity and the worshipping devotee.

This view implicitly contrasts the "religious" to the "secular." This was originally a western distinction but it has been adapted and is today of crucial importance. HRCE officers routinely speak of the temple as having two "sides": a religious side and a secular side. The essential side, the side which defines the temple as such, is the religious. The secular side involves all that supports the religious side: land, finances, administration. The religious side cannot be altered without changing the temple's very nature; protecting it is therefore critical. The secular side is only a matter of convenience; its form can be changed at any time without interfering with the temple's nature.

The religious–secular distinction is used repeatedly to defend the HRCE against the charge that it violates the principle of secularism. HRCE policies, it is said, affect only the "secular" matters, such as governance, organization and economy. But the distinction loses its precision in concrete circumstances. "Secular" innovations can have "religious" implications, and protecting the "religious" side has without question affected the content of the religion itself. This issue will be discussed in detail in later chapters, but it will be useful to have some introduction to the range of issues involved. This can be done by noting briefly the HRCE's policy on priests.

Priests are, in the departmental view, a temple's preeminent religious functionaries. Priests stand as intermediaries between the deity and the worshipper especially when they conduct the *puja*. As such, the office of priest is limited to performing these rituals. Especially, it is not inherently connected with land. This is a clear implication of the distinction between the religious and the secular. Priests have long argued that with their office goes a traditional right to land, either of ownership or use. For the HRCE, however, landownership is a matter of economy, not religion. How priests are supported – whether through land, salaries or fees – is only a matter of detail. For years the HRCE has challenged the claims priests make to temple lands.

The HRCE's position that it must protect the religious function means that it gives considerable attention to whether or not the ritual is being performed correctly. If the rituals are to be efficacious, the sacred words and rubrics must be followed precisely. Priests need to be well versed in the *agamas*, the sacred texts which prescribe temple rituals. But priests are scandalously ignorant, in the HRCE view. Certainly they have no formal training, as modern educators would understand education; a priest becomes a priest because members of his family have always been priests and because his *jati* makes him eligible to be one.

The HRCE's response has been to move gradually toward a policy of providing religious education for priests. In 1970, for example, the HRCE commissioner sent a letter to the secretary of the South India Archaka Association in which he wrote:

> It is proposed to start Agama Patasalas. I am to request you to send a scheme for the same ... Training schools should be started for the training of priests. An examination has to be prescribed and a certificate has to be issued.[15]

[15] I am grateful to the Secretary, South India Archaka Sangham, for much of this and subsequent information on the SIAS.

The letter went on into the details connected with starting such a school. How many pupils should it have? What would be the expenses for furniture, books, boarding and rooming facilities? What would be the salaries for the school principal, instructors and office staff? All this is designed to guarantee that the *agamas* are accurately followed and therefore that the temple's religious side is preserved. The logic of the HRCE view is to make education *the* central qualification for the priesthood, with birth an incidental and perhaps unnecessary criterion.

The second element in the HRCE's image is that temples are *public* institutions. That is, temples are part of the cultural heritage of the whole Tamil (or Indian) community, not simply a local resource.[16] Temples belong to, and must benefit, the entire society; they are not the special preserve of any individual or group, and they should not be vehicles through which individuals and groups pursue their special concerns.

Reinforcing this view is the fact that the HRCE is bureaucratic in form and inspiration, and modern bureaucracies tend to favor frameworks which universalize their administration as much as possible.[17] In temple administration, this has pitted the HRCE against local particularities, whatever their source. In a way, the issue comes down to technicalities of classification. Every government needs frameworks to classify the items under jurisdiction. In the nineteenth century, local revenue officers were relatively more respectful of local differences. Even the Board of Revenue's more general distinctions – notably between "public" and "private," "denominational" and "non-denominational," "hereditary" and "non-hereditary" – were designed to capture presumed differences among religious institutions. Yet, from the vantage of local villagers, whose temple had a distinct name, history and identity, even these distinctions must already have seemed artificial. But the HRCE is far more radical.

The effective HRCE posture is that all temples should be under state control. As the HRE Board wrote in its first annual report, temples are in "chaotic condition" and the efforts of "public spirited worshippers" have little effect "in the absence of a public body working continuously

[16] This was also the view stated by the Government of India's Hindu Religious Endowments Commission, 1960–62. See its *Report* (Government of India: Ministry of Law, 1962) ch. 4, especially, pp. 41–2. See also J. Duncan M. Derrett's discussion of the Commission's views, in *Religion, law and the state in India* (New York: Free Press, 1968), ch. 14.

[17] As Weber pointed out, universalization is part of what bureaucracies mean by rationality. Rationality in temple administration has had important implications both for how temples are classified and for how many are incorporated under department control.

to take vigilant steps."[18] Religious institutions are in bad shape whatever their formal and legal status.

For the HRCE the category of "hereditary" (temple, priest, trustee) is especially troublesome. Well entrenched in law and precedent, "hereditary" temples were "excepted" from crucial provisions of the original HRE Act. The department was never happy with this, and attacked the "excepted" temple category as simply a strategy by powerful zamindars, prominent trustees and other "vested interests" to avoid having the law apply to themselves.[19] The "excepted" temple category was finally abolished in 1959, over thirty years later. The categories of "hereditary priest" and "hereditary trustee" remain, although the department has successfully reduced the actual number and powers of those who still enjoy these classifications.

How does the HRCE prefer to classify temples? On the basis of wealth. For the HRCE, there are only two types of temple: "listed" temples, with incomes of Rs. 20,000 or more, and "non-listed" temples with incomes of less than Rs. 20,000. The logic of this classification follows from the premise that all temples are equally the heritage of the general Tamil public, and that the HRCE's supervision is formally limited to the "secular" side. Once differences of sect, denomination, locality and history are set aside, the problem of classification can be settled pragmatically on the basis of what particular problem needs to be addressed. And, viewed in narrow "secular" terms, the most general problem temples face involves finances. Temples are places where money changes hands, frequently in questionable ways. The department's job, then, is to see that the money is managed properly. Because they are wealthy, "listed" temples are more important than "unlisted" ones, so listed temples are administered by deputy commissioners, who are just below the commissioner in rank and authority. Non-listed temples are overseen by assistant commissioners.

If all temples are "public," there can be no theoretical grounds for any of them remaining outside the HRCE's supervision. Expanding its coverage was therefore a major concern in the HRCE's early years.

[18] G.O. 1337 L&M 9 April 1927.

[19] In 1943, a committee appointed by the government on the HRE Board's work wrote (G.O. 5634 PH 12 May 1943, p. 14):

> It seems to us that the virtual immunity from control of certain body [sic] of trustees is not conductive to the proper administration of religious institutions which are public and it is not possible to understand why a person who assumes the office of trustee of a public temple should not be subject to a liability... We have given our anxious consideration and we think that all hereditary trustees should be placed on the same footing and that the Board should be given the power of removal of hereditary trustees in the first instance.

Departmental effectiveness was measured in part by how many temples were annually brought under control. The number of temples covered increased dramatically in the first three decades until it stabilized after World War II. In 1973, 11,015 temples and *maths* were under HRCE administration. Collectively they owned 441,004 acres of land, some of it the best paddy-growing land in the state. Six hundred seventy-two were "listed", having annual incomes exceeding Rs. 20,000, and several had incomes above Rs. 100,000.[20] The wealthiest temple, the hill temple of Dhandayuthapani Swami of Palani, had an income of over Rs. 55 lakhs (Rs. 5,500,000), most of it derived from land and offerings.

For years the HRCE did not actually know how many temples there were. An investigation undertaken in the early 1970s revealed that an additional 41,306 institutions had, as HRCE officials put it, "escaped" departmental control. Though generally small, the newly identified temples were all endowed and together owned 201,343 acres.[21] Many had "escaped" because their trustees in the past had been regarded as "hereditary" or their temples as "private." The HRCE knows that its claims to jurisdiction over these temples will be challenged in the courts, usually by temple trustees. In an interesting sidelight on the HRCE's approach to these claims, one officer explained to me:

> When we take over a new temple, we make an arrangement willingly to appoint as trustee the man already acting in that capacity. In so doing, we avoid two problems. First, court action is avoided on the abstract issue of the temple's status at that time. Second, having accepted the HRCE appointment once, the trustee cannot later claim that his post is hereditary or, at least, such a claim is weakened should it be made three years later when we want to appoint a new trustee.[22]

The HRCE rarely views claims to exemption from the standard rules of the department with sympathy. Its bias is reinforced by the standard procedure followed in hearing such cases. The cases are not heard by the assistant commissioner, who is likely to know the most about a given temple's circumstances, but by the deputy commissioner who, unhampered by special knowledge and involvement, is naturally more likely to render a final decision consistent with abstract principles.

The corollary of the principles that temples are religious and public is

[20] Tamil Nadu Legislative Assembly, Committee on Estimates 1972–73, *Hindu Religious and Charitable Endowments* (*Administration*) *Department*, p. 6.

[21] "Report on the investigation of lands by special staff up to 30.6.1974" (Madras: HRCE mimeo, n.d.). Despite the investigation, statistics on temple numbers, land and income are sketchy and often inconsistent. Moreover, figures do not always distinguish between temples and maths, and temples under the HRCE and those that are not.

[22] Personal interview, 27 April 1974.

the third element of the HRCE's theory: temples are *not* political or, rather, ought not to be. For the HRCE, politics is a disturbing force which comes from the outside and is the central threat facing south Indian temples. Politics threatens temple governance, economy and religion. Politics benefits groups and individuals at the expense of the temple itself. The only long term solution is to isolate temples from politics of any kind, to de-politicize them. This is synonymous, in the HRCE's view, with reorganizing temples into units to which universal rules and regulations can be applied. Temples must become, in short, arenas for efficient management, not politics.[23]

The HRCE sees itself as the central instrument to effect this change. For this reason, we must probe more deeply into the department's own character. Every large organization develops its own routines and traditions. Decisions and choices made in the early years, in response to specific contexts and pressures, become the central assumptions, values and procedures of later years. Managerial styles develop, along with standardized rules and regulations. Together, these amount to an organizational culture which is absolutely crucial to the way the organization operates.

There are several aspects to the HRCE's organizational culture. One is the pronounced thrust towards centralization. HRCE rules and procedures are formulated at the central administrative offices in Madras. They are shaped primarily by the state government, in conjunction with expert advice offered by the HRCE, and reflect the considerations of abstract policy, state-level politics, and overall HRCE organizational needs.

The HRCE itself is highly centralized. The central decision-making authority lies in Madras city, from which radiates out a vast administrative network encompassing districts, towns, villages and the countryside. Consisting of commissioners, executive officers (EOs), inspectors, auditors and clerks, this network is charged with implementing the policies of the center, to which it is accountable.

In the past three decades everything has been done to make the HRCE into a career civil service organized along the same principles as regular

[23] This is an assumption which has obvious parallels in other contexts. Politics is viewed as dysfunctional by administrators in a wide variety of professional, quasi-professional and governmental areas, e.g., hospitals, universities, legal firms, bureaucracies. For a similar set of issues in the Indian context, see Susanne Hoeber Rudolph and Lloyd I. Rudolph, *Education and politics in India: studies in organization, society and policy* (Cambridge, Mass.: Harvard University Press, 1972), ch. 1. For an analysis of the preference for "normative" apolitical sorts of control exerted in professional and quasi-professional organizations, see Amitai Etzioni, *A comparative analysis of complex organizations* (New York: Free Press, 1961).

government bureaucracies. Officials are paid as in any government bureaucracy, in accordance with fixed salary scales and promotion and seniority rules.[24] Recruitment is based on criteria basically similar to those for any government bureaucracy, except that a certain amount of legal training is needed at the higher grades. There is no special religious requirement, other than to be a "Hindu" which in practice embraces a wide variety of belief and practice. No special knowledge of temple ritual, history or sacred scriptures is required. In their religious views, HRCE personnel range from the very devout and orthodox, to the openly skeptical and contemptuous. It must be added, however, that whatever their starting point, HRCE officials often become fascinated with their work, and accumulate vast knowledge and understanding over the years.

As civil servants, HRCE officers are oriented not to the particular temple to which they may be attached for the time being, but to the HRCE and its more general goals. Careers depend on performance, after all, which leads officers, often despite themselves, to administer their temples along the pattern desired by the center.

This centralized administration has penetrated temples deeply. Illustrating this most clearly is the post of Executive Officer and the HRCE's control of temple budgets. Executive Officers (EOs) have become central in most temples since the 1950s. The origin of the EO post is revealing. In the original 1927 act, HRE Board policies had to be implemented, if they were to be implemented at all, by temple trustees and managers. But since these trustees and managers resented the Board's incursions into what they considered their areas of personal authority, its policies were often ignored or thwarted.

This situation began to change in 1935, when an amendment act (Act XII of 1935) enabled the HRE Board, under certain conditions, to suspend trustees or managers and replace them with its own agents. "Notification," as it was called, occurred when the Board was satisfied that it was "in the interests of the proper administration of the endowments of a temple." It often, and eventually nearly always, meant

[24] Section 12(1) of the HRCE Act, 1959, reads in part:

> The commissioner, deputy commissioners, assistant commissioners and other officers and servants including executive officers of religious institutions employed for the purposes of this Act shall be servants of the government and their salaries, allowances, pension and other remuneration shall be paid in the first instance out of the Consolidated Fund of the State.

The HRCE reimburses these funds out of its "Tamil Nadu Hindu Religious and Charitable Endowments Administration Fund," derived from temple "contributions." See below, p. 55.

that a salaried EO replaced the incumbent trustees or manager. The EO had almost unchecked authority to address what the HRE Board had identified as the temple's crisis. He was to "exercise such powers and perform such duties" as were vested in him by the Board. Significantly, notification could occur in all temples, including those under "hereditary" trustees and those under court "schemes."

The 1935 amendment was of great significance. Even though still constrained by quasi-judicial procedures, the state nonetheless now had a vehicle by which to bring temples directly under central administrative control. By 1940, five years after the act was passed, 217 EOs had been appointed.[25] A further step was taken in the 1959 act, which eliminated both the need for a judicial hearing, and the implication that an EO would be appointed only if it were necessary to dismiss the existing trustee. EOs were quickly appointed in many new temples. By the 1970s, EOs were a common feature of temples – now, however, co-existing and sharing responsibility with trustees. Large, "listed" temples usually have an EO working full time within the temple premises; smaller temples are often grouped together, with two or three sharing a single EO.

In the early years, each notification was based on a unique set of circumstances, so that the specific role of EOs differed widely from temple to temple. Also, they were paid directly by their respective temples; salaries ranged, in 1940, all the way from Rs. 2 1/2 to Rs. 400 per month, and there were no rules for recruitment or qualification.[26] By the 1970s, in contrast, the duties and careers of EOs had become formalized and rule-governed. In 1959 EOs became members of a separate civil service cadre, employed and paid directly by the state. The service now consists of five grades, with specified educational qualifications and rules for promotion. EOs in grade five must have passed the eighth standard in secondary school; grade three officers must have a BA; and grade one officers must have the equivalent of a law degree.

The EO is the center of temple government for most routine matters. He is responsible for keeping order, and for reshaping a temple so that it

[25] G.O. 1878 E&PH 5 May 1941.

[26] In 1941, the following description of EOs was given (G.O. 1878 E&PH 5 May 1941):

> No qualification is insisted on either as regards education, health or age. Some of the EOs have had no English education of any kind. They range from the ages of 19 to 69 and are not governed by any rules. The salary conditions of service of each EO are governed by the particular order of the Board appointed him, and no general rules exist regarding the qualifications required for these EOs, their method of recruitment, their conditions of service ... Much of the odium which is attached to the administration of the Board is due to the manner in which these EOs have been appointed. It is necessary, for the purpose of satisfying public opinion, that there should be some rules ...

can conform better to the HRCE's image of temples as religious, public and non-political. At the heart of this responsibility is the temple budget (*dhittam*), a central vehicle influencing the temple's future course.

A temple's *dhittam* for the coming year must be submitted to the HRCE for approval. The *dhittam* covers the entire range of temple expenditure: salaries, building and maintenance costs, and daily, periodic and annual rituals and festivals. Budgets should, according to the HRCE Act, take account of "established usages" and traditions, and worshippers should be given an opportunity to register their suggestions and complaints. To this extent preparing the budget is, as a leading commentator put it, "a matter of the temple's internal administration," as distinguished from the state's jurisdiction.[27] But the final authority over all budgets is still the HRCE commissioner, who can include, reject or modify each proposed expenditure, including those for rituals and festivals. As the HRCE Act puts it, the commissioner will pass such "orders as he may think fit on such proposals."[28]

The HRCE's basic contention is that budgets should enhance the religious and downplay the political. The fact that it is not always possible to arrive at a clear definition of "religious" and "political," even in the abstract, seems to matter not at all; the HRCE moves confidently where others fear to tread.

An example is budgeting for large annual temple festivals, famous throughout India and abroad. The HRCE traditionally views these very critically. According to HRCE officers, festivals are less religious and more political occasions. Temple trustees like to spend extravagant sums of money in order to reflect their prestige and enhance their local power. From an early HRCE administration report:

> The policy of "spiritualization" begun in the last two years has continued and the Board has the pleasure in informing the Government that as a result every important temple has *spent less on what may be called merely the showy side on occasions of festivals and more on the truly religious aspect* and religious instruction. More attention has been paid to the organization of lectures ... in a religious atmosphere.[29]

HRCE officials still find that temple festival expenditures are too high. They scrutinize the temple budget each year in a seemingly endless effort to keep down expenditures.

[27] V. Rajasikhamani, *The Tamil Nadu Hindu Religious and Charitable Endowments Act XII of 1959* (Madras: B. Sundaralingam, 1971?)
[28] HRCE Act of 1959, sect. 58(3).
[29] G.O. 55 Public Health 9 January 1943, p. 22, emphasis added.

From custodial to managerial administration

The historical significance of both the HRCE's image of the temple and its bureaucratic style is highlighted when we return again to the temple in its locality. From the perspective of those directly affected – the priest, trustee, or worshipper – the changes brought on by the HRCE are striking. The locus, content and scope of the state's administration look very different today, when its agent is the HRCE, from what it was in the early nineteenth century, when its agent was the local collector. The contrast is one between custodial and managerial administration.[30]

In the early nineteenth century, when the collector was the agent of the state, administration was custodial, local and limited. Regulation VII of 1817 placed with the Board of Revenue and its agents a general responsibility to ensure the orderly conduct of temple affairs. Procedurally, protection was conducted on a relatively *ad hoc* basis. Problems were taken up as they came along, consideration was given to the different customs of different localities, and the exigencies of local politics were an important element in decision making. A collector, in any case, had a great deal else to do; temples were a minor, and frequently resented, part of his job. We can assume that state authority ordinarily weighed relatively lightly on temple trustees and priests, becoming direct and concrete only when difficulties arose: when there was a trustee succession, or a dispute, or an allegation of mismanagement.

In contrast, HRCE administration today is centralized, continuous and managerial. *Ad hoc* decisions and the multiplicity of local customs, precedents and relationships to which the nineteenth-century collector gave consideration have been replaced by a few bureaucratic rules and categories. No longer a part-time, secondary responsibility, temple administration involves an extensive bureaucracy with its own "theory" of the temples. Finally, today's HRCE does not operate primarily in times of crisis, but on a daily and routine basis, applying its energies to the most ordinary affairs of the temple.

What particularly bothers those in the localities is that under the new, managerial state the temple seems to gain so little. In the more traditional state there was an exchange of mutual benefit: rulers and kings made donations (of land, of money, of jewelry), in return for which they acquired material and symbolic rewards in the forms of status, honor, power. Under the HRCE, this organic exchange relationship is broken, or at least made less tangible. The temples receive the dubious assurance that temple administration is now conducted for their own

[30] I am grateful to Burton Stein for first drawing my attention to this way of identifying the change in the nineteenth-century British colonial state.

"good" and in the "public interest." But more immediately perceived is the state's thinly disguised challenge to all existing temple roles and relationships, along with its use of temple resources in ways that seem more to benefit the government and its political purposes. It is scarcely surprising that temple personnel are less than enthusiastic about the new bargain that has been struck.

Moreover, the temple have to *pay* for this new arrangement, in the form of "contributions" to support the HRCE bureaucracy. In other words, in the new temple–state relationship, the state does not donate money or land to support the temple; it *extracts* money from it. Temples are assessed a percentage of their annual incomes to support the HRCE's administration, the amount ranging from two percent for temples earning less than Rs. 1,000 a year, to seven percent for those earning over Rs. 200,000.

Not unnaturally, many temple personnel are reluctant to keep their side of this bargain, particularly when money paid out to the HRCE is money taken away from the support of existing temple salaries, services and rituals. It is notoriously difficult to get the temples to pay their contributions, and even more so when the local trustee wields influence in political circle in Madras. The following figures give some idea of the dimensions of the contribution problem. In 1965–66, the HRCE budget was Rs. 1,790,000 with an additional Rs. 510,759 in audit costs. The contributions and audit fees collected that year nearly equalled, but still fell short of, the budget. More than one-half the fees actually collected were technically arrears from previous years. In other words, for the year 1965–66, the HRCE was able to collect *less than one-half* the actual amount required to support itself.[31] In 1973, the government officially estimated that the total amount of contribution arrears due from temples was no less than Rs. 6,000,000.[32]

Conclusion

Non-payment of contributions is the local expression of the several tensions and conflicts we have identified in this chapter. There is a

[31] Calculated from data provided in Madras legislative Assembly, Committee on Estimates, 1965–66, *Hindu Religious and Charitable Endowments (Administration) Department.*

[32] Personal communication. The reason that this vast debt to the HRCE does not immediately terminate administration is that the HRCE's expenditures are in the first instance paid from the state's "Consolidated Fund." The HRCE is supposed to reimburse the state from temple "contributions." The problem of non-contribution by temples has been a leading characteristic of HRCE administration from the beginning.

conflict between the ways the HRCE, on the one hand, and temple personnel and others in the localities, on the other, perceive the temple and the purposes of state administration. Effectively, this conflict over the underlying nature of the temple erodes the efficacy of protection as a justification for HRCE control of temples. The struggle for contributions, on which the department depends for its very existence, partly results from the lack of consensus between the administrators and those who are administered.

In searching for contributions, the HRCE thinks it is making a reasonable request which is in the temples' own interest as permanent public institutions. From the vantage point of the localities, contributions siphon off valuable temple income for the support of a far-off and alien bureaucracy which is as threatening as it is benevolent.

Officers in the HRCE hope that their own professional identity and purposes are not confused with those of the politicians who frequently interfere with HRCE administration. Many people in the localities, however, perceive the HRCE, the party government and central politicians *collectively* as a force threatening local autonomy and the traditional processes by which temple resources were distributed.

I have described these changes in administration – from custodianship to management, from locality to center – as abstract changes in the character and scope of the state's authority. But for those in the localities, the changes are anything but abstract. HRCE administration has a profound effect on temple organization and governance. Access, privilege and power, and the processes by which these are distributed, are directly threatened by the reformist, managerial HRCE, functioning in terms of its own theory and definition of what needs to be done. Trustees, priests and others have found their positions challenged by the new agents of the state. New strategies, therefore, have been required of those intent on pursuing power, status and profit in their local temple.

4
Governance: trustees and the courts

An analysis of HRCE governance requires a closer look at the temple's top legal authority, the Board of Trustees. Boards usually have three to five members, and appointments are usually highly coveted. Trustees receive special consideration in temple rituals, in the receipt of honors and in other dignities; they can shape the consideration others receive. Trustees also influence the way the temple's material resources are used. Trustees may be able to help a friend obtain a lease to temple land, rent a space within the temple to sell ritual necessities, or obtain lucrative building and renovation (*tiruppani*) contracts. Even modestly endowed institutions possess land and income that, when used carefully, can be extremely influential.

For the HRCE, trustees are the wild card upsetting the smooth flow of temple management. Gaining control over trustees, itself no easy task, is a precondition to controlling the temple. HRCE officers report that trustees are seldom truly dedicated to their temples. They use their offices to elevate their own prestige, to further their political careers, or to increase their personal income. It is a theme which has been sounded many times over the years: the typical trustee is ambitious, unscrupulous, corrupt, the root cause of temple disorder and decline.

If the temple were reconstructed according to the HRCE's ideal image, there probably would be no trustees at all. But in that case the conclusion would be almost inescapable that temples are state institutions. Since the HRCE is nominally committed to secular principles, it has limited itself to trying to control who gets trusteeships and how trustees conduct themselves in office.

At the temple's very center, then, there is a built-in conflict over institutional control. On the one side is the Board of Trustees, the corporate body legally in charge. On the other side is the HRCE. At first sight, the contest appears very uneven, almost entirely in the HRCE's favor. The HRCE can draw on the statutory powers given in the HRCE Act, on its large organizational resources, on the day-to-day efforts of the local EO, and on more informal political pressures. Also, one legacy of the repeated accusations made against trustees over the past century is that the moral burden of proof rests more on the trustees than on the

HRCE. Though it is unfair to many dedicated individuals, trustees tend in the public mind to be viewed suspiciously as the cause of the "temple problem." The HRCE, in contrast, insists that its purpose is disinterested, merely to protect part of the Tamil cultural heritage.

Yet trustees are not helpless. Time and again, they have shown themselves able to manipulate law and politics to advantage. They have been able to counter the HRCE's efforts by using two powerful instruments: the political system, to which as a government department the HRCE is accountable, and the court system, with which it shares jurisdiction. Pressure from the political system has transformed trusteeship into a form of patronage, reintroducing politics back into the temple, though it is a new kind of politics and comes from a different level. The effect of the court is a bit more complicated, involving yet another theory and image of the temple. We shall deal first with the court, and then with politics.

The courts: deadlock between "judicial" and "executive" procedures

The HRCE's difficulty with the court is really a legacy of the many changes in temple administration over the past century and a half. These changes have so fragmented the state's authority that the HRCE is highly dependent on other government agencies to accomplish its work. The initial jurisdiction over temples in the nineteenth century lay with the Board of Revenue. Over the next century the BOR's authority was progressively eroded, first by the policy of "withdrawal," then by area committees, and then by the judiciary. Each time it was hoped that the change would end the "temple problem." By the 1880s jurisdiction was so dissipated that the courts, drawing on their inherent prestige, found that they had little difficulty in taking on a major role.

By the twentieth century, however, it was evident that the court's jurisdiction had not been entirely successful either. Some believed that the courts had in fact failed miserably. Courts were slow, inefficient and inflexible; protracted litigation drained away temple wealth. "Ousting the jurisdiction of the courts" became the rallying cry for reform in the 1920s and led directly to the 1927 HRE Act and the HRE Board. An "executive" department unhampered by the older policies of "withdrawal," it was hoped, could bring the timely intervention and quick remedy which had been desperately needed for so long.

But for those who defended the courts, and there were and still are many who do, much more than efficiency was at stake. Jurisdiction is tied to policy. An "executive" administration might be faster, but it also would have different content. When the HRE Act was being debated in the late 1920s, the actual consequences of "executive" administration lay in the future and could not be described in detail. But enough was known about the proposed Board to know that its inauguration would mark a sharp break with judicial precedents. This was why ousting the courts was, as the opposition leader, S. Satyamurti, put it, "one of the main objections ... to this bill becoming law."[1] Then and now, the court's jurisdiction implies a particular definition of and operative ideal for temple administration.

Rights, custom and usage, property

By the early twentieth century the court had developed a powerful and influential interpretation of what was at issue in temples. Its approach had developed gradually in the nineteenth century, from elements of both the Indian and English experience. It was bolstered by an impressive body of case law and precedent. The analysis was systematic, forcefully articulated and intellectually persuasive. It remains influential today. Three concepts are of special importance in the judicial view: "rights," "property" and "custom and usage" (*mamool*).

In the court's understanding, temples can be analyzed as consisting of "rights," which are of several types: rights to offices, such as trustee and priest; rights to precedence, such as in receiving honors and *prasadam* (leavings of offerings, consecrated food); rights to "shares," such as in the temple's income or in its management. There are even rights involving who is and who is not allowed to enter the temple. All these rights are in some sense rights to "property."[2] To be sure, property here is used in an extended, elastic sense. But the Civil Procedure Code itself opened the door for the court's flexible interpretation when it declared that "religious offices" based on custom or belief have a property "aspect." This principle has been applied liberally.

Temples, then, consist of complexes of individual and group rights to property or property-like offices and status. But how are the rights in specific temples to be determined? In the early nineteenth century, British judges had hoped to find general answers to this question in classical religious texts, but this solution turned out to be less helpful than it had at first seemed.[3] In 1868, in a decision of great importance,

[1] Madras Legislative Council, *Proceedings*, 14 September 1926, p. 703.

[2] Ernest John Trevelyan, *Hindu law as administered in British India* (Calcutta: Thacker, Spink and Co., 1912), pp. 4–5.

[3] For a discussion of this, see Lloyd I. Rudolph and Susanne Hoeber Rudolph, *The modernity of tradition: political development in India* (University of Chicago Press, 1969), pt 3. The Rudolphs note that this idea was resisted by the prominent Madras administrator, historian and legal scholar, J.H. Nelson.

this approach was rejected in favor of one based on local history and experience. The Privy Council in London declared that the standard to determine what should and should not be done in a temple is "usage," or "custom and usage":

> Under the Hindoo system of law, clear proof of usage will outweigh the written text of the law.[4]

Subsequent case law refined how a judge might discover "usage." The most important criterion was that usage be "immemorial or ancient" which, in practice, has not necessarily meant very far back.[5]

For the courts, then, rights are governed by the relevant "custom and usage," or *mamool*, as it is sometimes called. This provides the standards for temple rituals, offices and relationships. Rituals must be conducted according to custom and usage. When custom is not followed, rights are violated, and the trustee has not fulfilled his responsibilities as trustee, particularly if the change is binding on worshippers.[6]

"Custom and usage" is highly specific to each temple; few customs would characterize all temples. One important implication is that the court cannot know in advance how a dispute should be settled. It must conduct a local inquiry and gather evidence regarding the history and rituals of the temple whose affairs are subject to litigation. "Evidence," in turn, usually means "testimony" which is almost always based on hearsay of events far in the past. Witnesses must be heard, after which the court must evaluate what usually is very conflicting evidence.

The court's analysis of temples in terms of property-like rights has enormous consequences. When a given practice is certified as "custom and usage," relationships which in the past may well have been fluid and changing are "settled" and made permanent. Put differently, the court's analysis in no way discourages ambitious individuals and groups from pursuing wealth, status and power in the temple; if anything, it heightens the tendency, since once a position is certified it is secured for the indefinite future.[7] When a particular practice is found to be "custom and

[4] Quoted in S.S. Halker, ed., *Digest of privy council rulings, on appeal from the high courts of Calcutta, Bombay, Madras and Allahabad, the chief courts of the Punjab and Lower Burma, the courts of the judicial commissioner of the Central Provinces, Oudh, etc. 1811–1913* (Rangoon: Hanthawady, Myles Standish and Samuel Presses, 1913), ch. 4, col. 231. See also G.S. Sharma, ed., *Secularism: its implications for law and life in India* (Bombay: N.M. Tripathi, 1966), p. 2.

[5] P.V. Kane, *Hindu customs and modern law* (University of Bombay, 1950), pp. 44–5.

[6] Trevelyan, *Hindu law*, pp. 528–30.

[7] This process was already clear to nineteenth-century observers, as evidenced in the following quotation: "Hindu law is a body of rules intimately mixed up with religion, and it was originally administered for the most part by private tribunals. The system was highly elastic, and had been gradually growing up by the assimilation of new usages and the

usage," it is then a matter of "right," in the western sense, and is guaranteed by the state.

The court here is implicitly connecting the south Indian concept of *urimai* or "shares" with the English concept of "right." The translation is imprecise, however, since "right" adds a dimension of permanence which *urimai* lacks. But the translation is accepted by those who gain from it. A priest or trustee, for example, finds little reason to argue with a court's judgment that his "share" is a property-like right, inheritable by his children. The same is true for any other individual or group with an already well-established place in the temple.

Obviously, the stakes are very high in temple litigation. Not surprisingly, false witness is also widespread. The courts are asking for something which rarely exists. Seldom, that is, is a given practice "customary" in the sense meant by the court, i.e., ancient, immemorial and unchanged. Even a demonstrably old practice is rarely regarded as a permanent "right" in the temple. Temple relationships, like those in most other institutions, are fluid and responsive to changes in both the internal and external environment.

It should by now be clear that the HRCE's and court's theories of the temple and of their responsibilities differ markedly. The court's orientation is basically conservative: to preserve the past and to administer as much as possible by reference to the specific customs of each temple. Precedent, judicial procedure, and long-established legal distinctions are basic and fundamental, including the distinctions between "public" and "private," "denominational" and "non-denominational," "hereditary" and "non-hereditary." The HRCE, for its part, does not believe that long and complicated hearings on the specific nature of each temple are necessary; the important things are already known. Temples are "public" and "religious" and their problems stem primarily from "politics" and mismanagement. To address these problems in the most efficient way possible does not necessarily or even usually mean following local practices or "custom and usage." It means the hard-headed and consistent application of general rules and regulations, for which, if anything, detailed and intimate knowledge of a temple's local circumstance is often a hindrance. In any case, as a branch of the elected government, the HRCE is guided not by precedent but by the current government policy, which is that temple offices, such as those of priest

modifications of ancient text law under the guise of interpretation, when its spontaneous growth was suddenly arrested by the administration of this country passing into the hands of the English, and a degree of rigidity was given to it which it had never possessed." Quoted in Trevelyan, *Hindu law*, p. 1.

and trustee, are not to be regarded as rights and property. Offices should be filled by individuals selected on the basis of merit as measured by criteria relating to objective qualifications, efficiency and honesty.

Incorporating the court

Given these clear contradictions, it might seem striking that the HRCE, an "executive" agency, has never explicitly rejected the court's interpretation. However, the judiciary's analysis is very powerful the HRCE officials are men whose schooling and professional lives are dominated by the British–Indian system of law. The court has exercised major jurisdiction for over a century, and everyone at all close to temple affairs – legislators, litigants, lawyers, trustees – has been touched by its definitions, precedents, categories and analysis. Few would deny that temples involve property and property-like rights and that disputes involving property must sooner or later fall under the court's jurisdiction. On the other hand, litigation exhausts temple finances and proves ineffective against corrupt trustees; an "executive" agency unhampered by precedents and tedious procedures should be able to do a better job. Basically, nearly everyone associated professionally with the temples has wanted simultaneously the best of both "worlds," the world of the temple as defined by the courts and the world of the temple as defined by the presumably more efficient approach of an executive agency.

The judiciary's influence is felt throughout temple administration. It complicates HRCE procedures and organization, reduces efficiency and provides a focal point for resistance to HRCE policies. In crucial areas, indeed, HRCE policies cannot be implemented without tacit judicial approval. All the department's most important orders are subject to judicial appeal. Examples include: decisions to suspend, remove or dismiss a corrupt or incompetent hereditary trustee; decisions on temple budgets; decisions that a given institution or practice falls under HRCE jurisdiction; departmental schemes of administration. Even when its orders are upheld by the courts, the department lacks the instruments to give them effect, so that it must rely on court orders and the civil police. Finally, all disputes over "custom and usage" which have a "property aspect" are ultimately under the court's jurisdiction. Since the judicial concept of property is so elastic, this means that almost any HRCE order can be appealed to the courts.

Provisions for judicial appeal against executive orders are, of course, a feature in other branches of government in India and elsewhere. What makes the HRCE case special is the important difference between the HRCE and the courts as to what is at issue, coupled with the fact that appeals to the court are almost routine. The only way that the HRCE has been able to defend itself is to dilute its own "executive" approach.

Here is the most important legacy of the court's nineteenth-century jurisdiction. The HRCE effectively has incorporated the court – its categories and procedures – into its own administration. This is the inevitable result of the court's intellectual dominance. The HRCE can stem the tide of judicial appeals if it can show that its orders are preceded by careful and measured consideration of the case. The paradoxical result, of course, is to undercut even further the original goal of efficient, summary and effective administration.[8]

The result is the curious amalgam: a "judicial" approach to "executive" administration. The pattern began right with the HRE Board in 1926. The new Board was especially sensitive to the criticism that it would replace the judiciary's considered even-handedness with arbitrary or politically motivated decisions. The first president of the Board, Sadasiva Aiyer, bent over backwards to deny that the term "executive" in fact described the Board's approach. As he reported in 1927:

> Even at the present time, the Board was doing judicial work. Nothing was done in a haphazard manner. [The Board] took evidence . . . and received affidavits . . . About two-thirds of the time of the present Board was taken up by work of a judicial nature.[9]

For Sadasiva Aiyer, in fact, the problem did not lie with the court's definitions and procedures. The problem rather was that the court was too distant and disinterested. "Disinterested law" enabled self-interested parties, especially trustees, to exploit temples for private gain. What distinguished the new Board, according to Aiyer, was its close involvement with and understanding of the issues; the court's approach would be retained within the context of commitment to the welfare of the temple.

The result is that temple administration today is shaped fundamentally by judicial procedures, precedents and definitions. The HRCE is pervaded by an atmosphere of legalism and the culture of the courtroom. Every major order is subject to review in a "quasi-judicial" hearing, governed by formal rules of evidence and adversary proceed-

[8] The parallels between the HRE Board and the Interstate Commerce Commission in the United States, which also replaced a judicial jurisdiction, are interesting. Of the ICC, Huntington writes that if it was to be viable "it must adapt itself to the pressures . . . so as to maintain a net preponderance of political support over political opposition." The end effect, however, was "marasmus," an undercutting of the original organizational goals. See Samuel P. Huntington, "The marasmus of the ICC," *Yale Law Journal* 61 (1952): 470–509.

[9] G.O. 3276 L&M 26 August 1927.

ings. Top officials – commissioners, deputy commissioners and assistant commissioners – have had their viewpoints shaped by legal training. A prominent feature of HRCE buildings, even those in the districts, is the formal "courtroom." Hearings are held several times a week with the HRCE officer presiding over arguments presented by lawyers. The HRCE officer and the lawyers wear the black robes and paraphernalia of the regular civil courts. Evidence can be introduced only in accordance with the procedures of regular civil suits.

> The provisions of the Code of Civil Procedure and the Civil Rules of Practice and Circular Orders shall apply, as far as practicable, to appearance of the pleader and to affidavits, production of documents, examinations of witnesses, taking of oral evidence, proof by affidavits, filing of exhibits, issue of commissions, return of documents not admitted in evidence, and other connected matters; *and the inquiry shall be made, as far as practicable, in the manner laid down in the said Code for the trial of suits.*[10]

It is clear that anyone involved in an HRCE hearing would do well to engage expert legal assistance. On "court days" HRCE offices have the appearance of being regular courts. Clusters of advocates hover in the hallways and verandahs waiting for their cases to be called. Temple litigation within the HRCE is now a sub-field of its own, with many lawyers specializing almost exclusively in it.

The ironic result is that HRCE administration has ended up subject to nearly as much delay as the "judicial" administration it was designed to replace. A deputy commissioner in a district south of Madras invited me to his court to hear a particularly interesting dispute over a temple ritual. With anticipation I travelled down from Madras on the appointed day. But only one of the advocates attended the court that day, and he requested (for the second time) an adjournment for forty-five days. The request was granted as a matter of routine. In fact, of the twelve cases scheduled for that day, only one was actually heard. In each of the other eleven cases a lawyer requested, and was granted, an adjournment. So much for "speedy disposal of cases."

The problem of the dangling trustee

We can now return to the specific problem of temple trustees, where the effect of legalism and the judicial approach is clearly seen. A particular problem is trustee succession. One of the HRCE's greatest frustrations is

[10] See "The holding of inquiries rules," in V. Rajasikhamani, *The Tamil Nadu Hindu Religious and Charitable Endowments Act (XXII) of 1959* (Madras: B. Sundaralingam, 1971?), pp. 90–4, emphasis added.

the problem of the dangling trustee, i.e., the trustee who cannot take office because the incumbent fails to "hand over charge." An incumbent uses a variety of strategies to hang on to office. He may claim that some or all of the temple's property is his own, or that he has a property-like right to trusteeship. Alternatively, he might simply delay handing over charge, waiting for his successor to take legal recourse, all the while continuing to enjoy the benefits of office.

The irony is that the dangling trustee problem is now well over a century old and its solution was a central purpose of the original HRE Act. The "Statement of Objects and Reasons" to the HRE bill notes:

> It is notorious that trustees dismissed by committees under Act XX of 1863 have in several instances refused to hand over possession to the persons newly appointed and have defied the committees by remaining in possession pending the end of protracted litigation started by them.[11]

But the HRCE has always been denied the power of "summary process" and, consistent with its general tendency, has even subjected the little authority it has to a quasi-judicial review.

It is the pattern rather than the exception for incumbent trustees to delay "handing over charge" to their successors. Many new appointees cannot be sure that they will ever take office. Once appointed, a newly appointed trustee is legally more or less on his own, a logical necessity given the doctrine that the HRCE's role is only supervisory. This does not preclude the department from taking an informal interest, which it often does, but formally the conflict is between the two competing trustees.

"Handing over charge" technically means that the old trustee turns over the temple keys, accounts, property registers and other documents. If he does not, the new trustee must go through several steps: he must obtain a certificate from the local HRCE inspector testifying that the incumbent has indeed refused to permit the new appointee to take office; he must request the HRCE commissioner to provide him with a certificate itemizing the moveable and immoveable properties which the HRCE believes to belong to the temple; he must approach a civil court with these certificates and request that the court order the incumbent to hand over charge; finally, he must approach the police with a formal request that they execute the court order.

Each of these steps involves expense, which must be paid by the new appointee, and delay. For example, before the HRCE commissioner (or deputy commissioner, to whom this function is ordinarily delegated) can

[11] Quoted in G.O. 5634 PH 12 May 1943, p. 20.

issue the certificate on the temple's properties, a formal hearing must be held at which the incumbent trustee has an opportunity to challenge what is being itemized. Almost inevitably he will challenge the temple's title to specific parcels of land which must, in turn, be investigated formally. Because of the general uncertainty surrounding temple land titles, getting this certificate alone generally takes at least one year.

If the new trustee has persisted this long, the struggle then shifts to the civil court's jurisdiction. A date in the court's crowded schedule must be obtained to conduct a hearing for the needed court order. It is still not possible to claim victory, however. Because "property" and "property-like rights" may be involved, the incumbent trustee himself can now file a suit in a higher court to appeal either the HRCE commissioner's certificate or the lower court's order. Long before these steps are completed, the new trustee's three-year term of office is likely to have expired.

How widespread is the refusal to "hand over charge"? Annual HRCE reports do not give specific statistics; the issue is not formally under the department's control. A Madras Legislative Assembly's Estimates Committee stated some years ago that deputy commissioners held 200 formal hearings between 1962 and 1965 related to the preparation of property certificates.[12] But these figures scarcely convey the full dimensions of the problem. They indicate only those cases in which new trustees decided to take formal action, not the complete number of trustees who experienced problems when they tried to take over office.

In 1973–74 an inspector in Madras city estimated that fifty percent of the new trustees in his temples experience some sort of delay in taking office. Incumbents, he said, want to hang on as long as possible. They may simply want to give their friends and relatives another year to pay low rents for temple land and properties or, more seriously, they may need more time successfully to alter temple property deeds. An assistant commissioner in Madurai district estimated that difficulties occurred in thirty to forty percent of the cases in his area. The problem is apparently less severe in wealthy "listed" temples. There are fewer of them, deputy commissioners are able to supervise them more closely, and departmental regulations tend to be applied to them more uniformly.

Politics: trusteeships as patronage

Already deadlocked by the courts, the HRCE's ability to control trustees is limited further by the political system. On the surface, trustee

[12] Madras Legislative Assembly, Committee on Estimates, 1965–66, *Hindu Religious and Charitable Endowments (Administration) Department.*

appointments appear to be a routine administrative matter. Applicants are solicited by public announcement. Applicants are screened by inspectors to make certain that none are technically disqualified, e.g., that an applicant is not himself a lessee of the respective temple's land. Final selection is made by the commissioner, in the case of "listed" temples, and by the relevant assistant commissioner for "non-listed" temples. Appointments are for three years.

To appreciate the political nature of most trustee appointments it is necessary to probe beneath these formal procedures. That trustee appointments are politically important is of course nothing new. What has changed is that there now exists an integrated statewide political system, dominated by the competition among centralized political parties, with insatiable needs for sources of political patronage. Trusteeships in this context have taken on an enormous importance. Indeed, the HRCE's very success in two areas – including most major temples under its jurisdiction and reducing the number of hereditary trustees – works against the equally central goal of isolating temples from politics. As an "executive" branch of the government, headed by a cabinet minister, the HRCE is relatively helpless to resist the inevitable.

It must be remembered that the HRCE pervades the Tamil countryside. It administers thousands of public temples, many of them well endowed and major institutions in their respective villages. Given their material and symbolic resources, and the fortuitous presence of the HRCE, it should occasion little surprise that Tamil Nadu politicians watch temple policies and HRCE administration closely. This is true especially of trustee appointments.

The period from 1967 to 1981 affords an unusual opportunity to assess the links between temples and state-level politics. During these fifteen years, four different governments were in power in Tamil Nadu. In 1967 the long period of Congress Party rule ended with an electoral victory for the Dravida Munnetra Kazhagam (DMK); in 1976 power passed to the Governor and his advisers when Presidential rule was declared under the Emergency; and in 1977, after new elections, the All India Anna-DMK (AIADMK) formed the government.

The unstable political climate enhanced the importance of temple resources, and, not accidentally, temples figured prominently in public discussion and debate. Opposition groups, the press, columnists, and the legislature all discussed temple affairs. It soon became clear that temples, especially temple trusteeships, were playing a central role in the strategies of political parties to build, stabilize and extend networks of power and influence.

The HRCE's standard procedure for handling new trustee appointments is clearly laid out in its rule book, and is designed to ensure honesty and competence. The department issues a notice calling on interested persons to present formal applications to fill a vacancy by a certain deadline. Each application is then screened.

This screening is an important aspect and performed by the local "inspector." Inspectors are field officers, who have been called the "backbone of the department." Less intimately involved with particular temples than the EO, the inspector travels throughout the area of his assignment, looking after some of the more mundane tasks that must be performed if temple wealth is not to be misused. He scrutinizes temple accounts; he attends public auctions for temple property leases; he is present whenever the seal on a temple's *hundial*, the padlocked receptacle for devotee offerings, is broken and the offerings, in cash and jewelry, itemized.

With regard to trustee applications, the inspector is responsible for checking that applicants do not have a vested interest in the temple. Is the applicant a temple land lessee? If so, he will probably have disguised the fact, which takes time to find out. What is the applicant's political and social status in the locality? Will his appointment create political difficulties for temple management? Only when an applicant is certified by the inspector as free of all disabilities is he eligible to be considered for appointment.

The final appointment rests finally with the Tamil Nadu government, which means that today most trustees are in some way politically indebted for their appointments. Politicians and local notables take considerable interest when trustee vacancies occur. The scope of the problem is suggested by the following. By 1981 HRCE temples had an annual income of Rs. 16 crores and owned over 400,000 acres. Much of this was owned by 16,500 temples, most of whose trustees were government appointees. Trustee boards usually have from three to five members. Taking as an average four appointed trustees per temple, theoretically 66,300 positions were thus available for patronage.[13]

The actions of the three successive Tamil Nadu governments since 1967 demonstrate a clear awareness of how critical this local resource can be. Their policies differ in detail, but these differences simply reflect the circumstances of each government in pursuit of the same goal of stabilizing its support and minimizing the influence of preceding governments.

Under Congress governments before the 1967 elections, trustees were

[13] HRCE sources, February 1981.

appointed by area committees for terms of five years. Members of the area committees were, in turn, appointed by the government and reflected Congress Party interests. Of the fifty-five area committeemen in 1958–59, for example, fifteen were also Congress MPs (members of the Indian Parliament) or MLAs (members of the state Legislative Assembly), and most others were prominent Congress members.[14] Trustee appointments were naturally shaped by Congress Party interests. Area committee members had permanent tenure and so this bias was not likely to change in the near future.

The threat this situation posed after the 1967 elections for the new DMK government was real and immediate. Still somewhat surprised at its victory and unsure of its strength, the DMK knew that the area committee system ensured that most local temples would continue to be Congress-controlled. The DMK "solution," in an HRCE amendment act of 1968, was to abolish the area committees altogether and reduce the term of trustees from five to three years. The trusteeships of many Congress appointees were immediately terminated. The policy undercut a major base of Congress strength, and lessened the likelihood that temples would be controlled in the future by Congress members.

The suddenness of these changes seems to have politicized temple administration to a new extent. HRCE bureaucrats began to complain that interference by DMK politicians was far more blatant and persistent than it had been under the Congress and that efficient and honest administration was being made even more difficult. By the mid 1970s, according to one estimate, at least 100 DMK MLAs had "opted" for trusteeships, as had many more well-connected businessmen, landlords, *panchayat* board members, and other politicians. Many felt that the new trustees were less conscientious than in the past, and that it was in any case inappropriate for the DMK, which for years had attacked temples as citadels of Brahminism, social reaction, and inequality, to be so closely involved in temple matters.

In early 1976 the DMK government left office when Presidential rule was declared during the Emergency. On 20 April the new government, now under a centrally appointed Governor and non-elected civil servant advisers, set up a special Enquiry Cell to investigate allegations of temple corruption. Most of the complaints touched in one way or another on trustees: unscrupulous appointments, misuse of temple funds, irregularities in land leases. On 1 June, citing these allegations, the government took radical action. All non-hereditary trustees in all temples were dismissed. Pending new appointments, temples were to be

[14] HRCE (Administration) Department, *Administration report, 1959*, Appendix I.

under direct HRCE authority, ordinarily through EOs.[15] There was some suggestion in the press that perhaps this might be a time to abolish the post of trustee once and for all, thereby underscoring the Emergency's emphasis on efficiency. Apparently, however, this possibility was not seriously considered on the grounds that a change of such significance should be left to an elected government, not undertaken during temporary Presidential rule.

The move against temple trustees appears to have been part of a systematic strategy by the central Indian government under Mrs Gandhi to destroy DMK organizational strength in the localities. Similar moves were made against DMK incumbents in rural cooperatives and *panchayats*.[16] It is hard to say how much these measures contributed to the AIADMK victory in the 1977 elections. Without question, however, the DMK was weakened by the measures taken during the Emergency, and by the government's repeated allegations that the DMK ministry had been grossly corrupt.

In any case, the AIADMK enjoyed an enormous opportunity when it formed a new government for the first time in 1977. Thousands of trusteeships were vacant as a result of the Emergency dismissals. In a bid to return to normal, the government announced that it would fill these posts as soon as possible. Ministers' and HRCE commissioners' offices were soon clogged with aspiring applicants, many with endorsements from local AIADMK party units. Soon, temples began to announce new renovation (*tiruppani*) projects. This was surely not a coincidence. After months of Emergency restrictions, construction contracts had emerged once again as a way for trustees to enhance their personal prestige and to reward their friends and allies.

Not everything was as before, however. Anxious to avoid comparisons with the DMK, the AIADMK moved with some caution and circumspection. Regional committees, similar to the old area committees of pre-1967 Congress rule, were established and given authority to screen trustee applicants; the new committees, though, were reportedly stacked in favor of the AIADMK. The government made several highly publicized "non-political" appointments and, repeating promises which earlier had been made by the DMK government, declared that, so far as possible, at least one Harijan would be appointed to each trustee board. Regulations regarding trustee vacancy notices and applications were carefully adhered to. One consequence was that a

[15] *Hindu* (Madras), 2 June 1976.

[16] For a description of similar strategies elsewhere during the same period, see James Manor, "Where Congress survived: five states in the Indian general election of 1977," *Asian Survey* 18 (August 1978): 785–803.

large number of trusteeships in smaller temples, where the pressures for appointment were somewhat less, remained unfilled for several years.

Conclusion

The HRCE's failure successfully to get a handle on the trustee problem means that its capacity to direct temple administration is inherently limited. Trustee appointments are the area where there is the greatest and most persistent political interference in the internal machinery of the HRCE department. Local landlords, panchayat board presidents and members, and state-level politicians are all able to wrangle appointments without much difficulty. Seasoned HRCE inspectors, responsible for evaluating each applicant's qualifications, have become very cynical. Rather than going through the laborious process of investigating each applicant, many inspectors simply check on the politically preferred candidate to ensure that he is not formally disqualified. High HRCE officials report that they must often fight to get satisfactory trustees, that many good candidates do not apply precisely because the general public will consider them to be in some way corrupt or indebted to a political party. A former commissioner was particularly distressed that "dedicated" men were often not approved by higher levels of government:

> In the case of temple X [one of the most prominent temples in Tamil Nadu] a trustee donated a golden cart to the temple. He was obviously dedicated. But minister Y did not want to reappoint him, but to replace him with a political choice. Finally, the minister agreed [with my recommendation], but there were still three other vacancies. The only reason only two of these were ultimately political was that there was some struggle within the government as to who the third trustee should be, so that it was finally left up to the HRCE department.[17]

"But," the commissioner added sardonically, "our choice was also a poor one, as it turned out." Once in office he behaved in as politically motivated a manner as did the government choices.

The politically appointed trustee creates a structural tension at the heart of the temple. The HRCE's agent, the Executive Officer, epitomizes the ideal of de-politicized and efficient management. The politically appointed trustee has loyalties and identities independent of both temple and HRCE. Conflict between trustee and EO is not infrequent, and can quickly embroil the whole temple, with different factions allying themselves with one or the other side. The EO's position is especially

[17] Personal interview, 16 March 1974.

difficult. He is caught between two competing centers of authority. On the one hand, he must manage temple finances, lands and contracts within HRCE guidelines. On the other hand, the Board of Trustees is the formal head of the temple, and thus the EO is nominally responsible to individuals whose political actions, according to HRCE assumptions, are likely to be highly irregular or worse. Whether or not the EO is able to resist his trustees depends on the extent to which his superiors in the HRCE are willing to back him up. And that, in turn, depends on how much clout the particular trustee concerned has with his political party or the government. It is scarcely surprising that one deputy commissioner, observing that politics in trustee appointments exists "throughout the system," commented that trustees are really an "unwanted limb" of the department.

It would seem, then, that though the style of temple administration has changed since the nineteenth century, its functions have not. Trustees continue to use and appropriate the temple's political, economic and social resources. Today, under the HRCE, these resources are filtered through a public bureaucracy, and this undoubtedly has had some effect in controlling abuses. Temple administration is more formal, public and professional. But material wealth, social status and political power remain as much the substance of temple life as they ever were. The difference is only that with the HRCE the locus and language of control have shifted to the center, bringing new kinds of politicians to the fore, and putting the older elites and structures of the localities on the defensive.

5

Economy: the problem of controlling land

The purpose of this and the next chapter is to explore the state's impact on temple economy, especially on temple landholdings. In no other area is the potential for conflict so great. Temple notables jealously guard their rights, while the state sees temple wealth, especially land, as a resource of such magnitude and importance that it simply must assert a jurisdictional interest.

The HRCE finds itself in the middle of this tension. On one side is the impulse to maximize state control, based on the premise that economy is by and large a "secular" matter. For example, it seems reasonable that temple funds should be handled in accordance with standardized accounting practices; the HRCE therefore is quite willing to control the budgeting process, standardize ritual fees and audit temple accounts. The department also has little difficulty with policies which effectively assimilate temple finances to the state's overall economic policy; it is therefore quite willing to regulate where and how temple funds should be invested.

However, when it comes to temple land the HRCE is not so sure. The HRCE agrees in a general way that the way in which temple land is used should not be contrary to broad public policy, especially land reforms. But it is reluctant to go to the full extent of having temple land handled as though it were simply a public resource. Land, after all, is the historical foundation of temples as institutions. It poses a distinct set of problems, and merits special treatment by state authorities.

The disposition of temple land is crucial. How it is handled will determine the future of Hindu temples in south India. Nowhere is the task of the HRCE, and tension between state control and temple autonomy, so important or so difficult. One aspect is the narrow question of jurisdiction: to what extent has the HRCE been able to assert a jurisdiction over the lands belonging to temples? Another aspect is the more general question of effectiveness: how effective has the HRCE been in protecting the land and in ensuring that incomes from land are actually used for the benefit of temples? What sorts of pressures have burdened its work?

This and the next chapter address these questions. The issue of jurisdiction, covered primarily in this chapter, is theoretically and historically prior; I shall deal with it by examining the struggle from 1925 to 1950 between the HRCE and the powerful Board of Revenue. The broader question of effectiveness in land administration will be explored in Chapter 6; the focus will be on major land reforms since Indian Independence and the great challenge they have posed to the traditional economic bases of temples. Before turning to any of these specific questions, however, we need first to discuss land in general terms.

The significance of land

At the outset we should note that the HRCE's general authority over the economy of temples is far more clear and firmly established than it is over either governance or religion. From Regulation VII of 1817 on, the state has consistently been authorized to regulate temple economies. The analogy often made is with the English state in relation to public trusts. Just as the Charity Commissioners have the duty to protect charitable trusts, the HRCE has the responsibility to protect temple endowments.[1] The HRCE's very name, Hindu Religious and Charitable Endowments Department, captures this aspect.

Land is not, of course, the only source of temple finances. Temple economies are complex, and income comes from many sources: fees for particular rituals, interest from bank deposits, sale of jewelry, *tasdik* payments from the government, devotee offerings, pilgrimage and devotee *hundial* offerings, urban properties. The particular mix varies widely. Some institutions have immense land-holdings with little else; others have little land but nonetheless support a lively worship schedule from the offerings of pilgrims and other devotees. Most institutions fall somewhere in between, with modest endowments in land, supplemented by offerings and payments from the local community. But, whatever the mix, the most prestigious source is land. Land provides a dependable and relatively constant income with which to support priests and other temple servants, physical upkeep, rituals, special ceremonies and charities.

Land poses some of the thorniest problems the HRCE has to confront and preoccupies most HRCE officers. It is often hard, indeed, to know exactly how much land the temple has, and what "having it" actually means. A temple's holdings may consist of many different parcels, each from different donors. Each endowment may be attached to particular rituals or services (rather than to the temple itself), be controlled by a

[1] See Appadurai, *Worship and conflict*, p. 173, on problems with this analogy.

particular family or trustee, reflect very particular historical, social and political circumstances, and in general have special conditions attached to its use and administration.

There is also the predictable tendency for unscrupulous trustees to divert the temple's holdings for private use, exploiting the ambiguities in law and administration for maximal personal benefit. The HRCE's task of discovering and protecting the temple's interest is seldom easy, especially because of the intricacies of land use and ownership rights. As one Commissioner put it:

> We are dealing with faults coming from time immemorial ... The problems are manifold, and they go to the very root of the administration of the temples, because without lands, or without trustees, nothing can happen to the temples ... The main problems are only these: the properties of the temples, and the persons in charge of the properties.[2]

Finally, the state has an independent stake in land, one often in tension with temple interests. This constitutes the HRCE's major challenge. Land administration is one of the hallmarks of modern India; it was pivotal in building the colonial state, and has been a major aspect of state policy since Independence. Land administration serves many functions, including provision of a steady revenue to the government, stimulation of agricultural productivity, regulation of social relations, especially among tenants, landlords, moneylenders and laborers, and monitoring of the rural political climate.

The state's land policies have historically been implemented by revenue authorities, especially by the Board of Revenue and local revenue officers, the Collectors. The revenue branch has developed a strong intellectual tradition, of which the central features are an elaborate classification of very diverse tenure systems, and identification of the particular rights associated with the land and the parties to whom those rights belong. The overarching concern, however, is to protect the state's legitimate interests. The *Standing Orders* of the Board of Revenue (hereafter BSO) embodies this tradition, and outlines the procedures to be used for handling the thousands of small decisions and complicated disputes that must be settled each year.

The conflict between the HRE Board and the BOR

Throughout the nineteenth and well into the twentieth century, the Board of Revenue was one of the most powerful branches of the

[2] Interview with Thiru A. Uthandaraman, IAS, former Commissioner, Hindu Religious and Charitable Endowments (Administration) Department.

government. The importance of land to the *raj* would have guaranteed this in any case, but its power was further bolstered by the long and distinguished history of revenue administration and by the extraordinary knowledge and expertise that the Board was able to bring to any policy discussion. Any effort by the new HRE Board to influence temple land use was bound to come up against the BOR's well-established authority.

The HRE Board was established in the context of deepening concern that temples were slowly but surely losing land. The problem was especially severe with land held on *inam* tenure. *Inam* tenure is complicated and controversial, as we shall see in a moment. Basically, *inams* originated as tax-free grants by kings and other rulers of a parcel of land or a portion of the land's produce. *Inam* grants were given for many reasons, e.g., to reward loyal service, to solidify political support, to endow charities, to show piety. Many *inams* were granted for the support of temples or of those performing rituals and other services in temples.[3]

When it began its work, the HRE Board gave immediate priority to the land problem and quickly developed a distinct approach to *inams*. The essential elements of its perspective can be stated briefly as follows: Any *land*, or *income from land*, associated either with a *temple*, or with a *temple servant*, is *owned* by the temple, and is owned *permanently*. Temple land, like the temple itself, is *public*, without private rights attached to it, and because of this is *different from ordinary* inam *land*,

[3] For an overview of the role of *inams* in the structure of colonial rule, see Robert E. Frykenberg, "The silent settlement in south India, 1793–1853: an analysis of the role of inams in the rise of the Indian imperial system," in Frykenberg, ed., *Land tenure and peasant in south Asia* (New Delhi: Orient Longman, 1977). *Inams* bear a clear resemblance to what Max Weber called "prebendal feudalism":

> Prebendal feudalism exists when (1) benefices which are valued and *granted according to the income they yield* are appropriated and where (2) appropriation is, in principle, though not always effectively, *carried out on a personal basis in accordance with services*, thus involving the possibility of promotion ... Finally and above all, (3) it does not involve primarily a free relation of personal fealty arising from a contract of personal loyalty with the lord ... It is rather a matter primarily of fiscal considerations in the context of a system of financing which is otherwise patrimonial ... *This is for the most part made evident by the fact that the prebends are assessed according to their tax value* [emphasis added].

One of the problems Weber noted with prebends is the tendency of the grantee to lay claim to a permanent right to the prebend, i.e., to "appropriate" it. As we shall see in chapter 8, this problem is characteristic of religious *inams* also. See, Max Weber, *Economy and Society*, eds. Guenther Roth and Claus Wittich, 3 vols. (New York: Bedminster Press, 1968), vol. 1, p. 260.

and should be administered through a *distinct set of rules and regulations*, and by a *distinct agency*, the HRE Board.

This perspective may seem unexceptional, a straightforward, common sense view of the term "temple land." Just the opposite is true, however; the definition of *inam* was and still is hotly disputed. Throughout the nineteenth century, *inams* were under the jurisdiction of the Board of Revenue, and were administered on the basis of a quite different tradition and understanding.

The BOR's understanding was as follows: first, like all *inams*, temple *inams* originated as *grants* from local rulers, in this case grants for the support of a temple. *Inams* were not, however, permanent grants. They were made *subject to certain conditions*, at a minimum that the temple and its services be maintained. Second, religious *inam* grants were of two types: those granted *in the name of the temple* itself, and those *in the name of individuals* (such as a priest), and the conditions associated with these two types could be very different.[4]

When a local ruler granted an *inam*, what in fact was he granting? A piece of land, to be cultivated by the temple or its agents? No, was the usual reply of the BOR, and this is the third part of its definition. A typical *inam* did not consist of a piece of land, or even of the right to occupy and farm a piece of land. An *inam* consisted only of the *government's tax on the land*, which the government alienated and gave over to the grantee.

The BOR's definition was based on a reconstruction of what is still widely regarded as the traditional south Indian view of land. According to this reconstruction, land has two "aspects" or "interests," each of which is really a *share* (*varam*) of the *produce* of the land. The *melvaram* (*mel*: upper) is the state's share which the British regarded as land tax. The *kudivaram* (*kudi*: lower) is that portion of the produce due to the cultivator.

Temple or religious *inams*, according to the BOR, could only be *melvaram* grants. They could not be grants of land since the state's share did not include the land itself, or did so only rarely. The proprietary right to the actual land was ordinarily attached to the *kudivaram*, the lower share, and was held by the actual cultivators, or by their landlords. Thus, when the state granted something, the only aspect it *could* grant was the

[4] Of these two types, the Inam Commission Selections states: "The first are held in trust on account of the temples or mosques and are transferred from one manager to another. The second are held by individuals on condition of services rendered or payments to the temples or mosques. These last are transferable by sale or otherwise subject only to the continued performance of the conditions of the grant" (quoted in G.O. 2133 Revenue 16 July 1913).

melvaram, or the land tax. This was a fact often misunderstood, as the BOR constantly reiterated:

> Persons in England, without opportunity of judging from direct observation, and many in India with better means of information, consider an *inam* as a grant of so much land by the State, in which is vested the sole proprietary right to all lands. Such a belief has led to many fatal mistakes.
>
> There is not an acre of land in south India which does not belong, however much the title may have been impaired, to a recognized proprietor or municipality subject only to the payment of a land tax . . . What the ruling power did bestow by the issue of a *sanad* of *inam*, was the alienation of a portion of the land tax to some specific object.[5]

The contrary view, the view that the state could grant the *kudivaram* or the land itself to temples, was a "monstrous fiction," and was based on foreign or English conceptions of land and the state's relation to it.[6]

Although it expressed this view adamantly, the BOR's case was not watertight. *Inams* historically had been given under very diverse circumstances, so that any all-embracing definition was necessarily artificial. There were dozens of *inam* subtypes, each of which was subject to conflicting interpretations. Moreover, the Inam Commission, which worked for nearly a decade in the mid nineteenth century, had unintentionally further complicated matters. The purpose of the Commission was to clarify and stabilize *inam* holdings; in fact, however, the Commission's inquiries, and the title deeds it conferred on *inamdars*, had the opposite effect. The title deeds, for example, seemed to imply that *inams* actually consisted of land. When the deeds were subsequently modified, the situation was made even more ambiguous.

The BOR thus had strong reasons, rooted in the general assumptions on which land administration was based and on recent history, to resist the HRE Board's claim that temples owned *inam lands*. The BOR had been struggling consistently against this interpretation since the mid nineteenth century at least. The BOR's *Standing Orders* in fact declared that, in the absence of evidence to the contrary, a religious *inam* would

[5] Minute of Mr W. Elliot, 16 June 1859 in *Inam Commission Selections*, quoted in ibid.

[6] Actually, the state could conceivably have granted *kudivaram* rights to waste land, unoccupied by anybody. But kings were hardly likely to give waste land to temples, the BOR argued. It wrote:

> It may also be urged that when the old Rajas or chiefs of Governments made over lands in favor of temples, they did not give them waste lands which the temples brought under cultivation. They probably gave them lands and villages already under occupation and under cultivation and what they gave was the Rajabhogam or the Government share of the produce. (G.O. 4026 PH 1 November 1939)

be presumed to consist *only* of the *melvaram*, not the *kudivaram* or the land.[7]

The BOR and the HRE Board had yet another disagreement. According to the BOR, an *inam* was not, properly speaking, "owned" at all. *Inams* were conditional, and could be cancelled at any time. *Inams* were the (more or less) temporary alienation by the state of a portion of its revenue, subject to the condition that certain religious services be performed. An *inamdar* (grantee) could not have any final right or claim to possession. At most, *inam* tenure established a temporary right to use and fruits. Final rights over the *inam* were kept by the ruler, his successors and, by this time, the British government.

The BOR reïterated what it called the state's "paramount right" over *inams* many times. Indian political theory and practice, in the words of one administrator, were "entirely opposed to permanent or hereditary alienations of any portion" of the land revenue. Just as the state had a right to grant a portion of its land revenue, it also had a right to *resume* it when the conditions of the grant were not fulfilled. Resumption was a "crown prerogative based on immemorial custom and prescriptions."[8]

[7] But Mr Moir, in his analysis of *inam* administration up to 1913, remarked that the government's policy varied significantly in matters of detail. This was particularly true, he said, in those cases, very significant for temple endowments, in which both the *melvaram* and *kudivaram* rights coalesced in the same person. His analysis led him to conclude that the variation in governmental policy was based on political considerations: "It is clear, I think, that the extent to which the Government, from time to time, have been prepared to claim that their grants included the land has depended on considerations of a political nature rather than upon an examination of the origins of the grants or of the doctrine held by the department [i.e., Inam Commission] which was responsible for their confirmation." It is not difficult to identify these shifts in political priorities. In 1869, for example, the government was particularly concerned to protect cultivators who might be dispossessed of their land, and so declared that confirmed *inam* grants consisted only of the *melvaram*. By 1910, however, it had become clear that the *melvaram*-only doctrine was resulting in *inamdars* abandoning their service so as to secure a full and unrestricted right to their lands. Growing pressure led to a change in the doctrine in order to make it more difficult for the *inamdar* to establish his occupancy right. Acceding to this change, the Revenue member of the Governor's Council remarked: "... I would not have departed from the previous practice of treating the assessment alone and invariably as the *inam*, had I not been anxious to impede and discourage misapplication of religious and charitable *inam* endowments." The change in 1910 was only a brief interlude, however. Partly because of the influence of Mr Moir's analysis, the government soon returned to the original policy which we have already mentioned, according to which, in the absence of contrary evidence, an *inam* was presumed to consist of the *melvaram* or government assessment only (G.O. 2133 Revenue 16 July 1913).

[8] This position was, to be sure, contested by those arguing that, whatever may have been the position in precolonial times, the British government had by several of its laws (notably Act XX of 1863 and Regulation VII of 1817) introduced self-imposed restrictions on the power of resumption. But respectable authorities could be found who would disagree with practically *any* assertion about *inams*, and the weight of official opinion gradually coalesced around the position that these laws did not add or detract anything from the original grants. In particular, the official policy was that the Inam Commission

The BOR's interpretation of *inams* as conditional grants of the *melvaram* alone was of profound importance for temples. It set in motion a train of events which seriously and adversely affected temple landholdings. The key lay in resumption. "Resumption" is a technical term which means that the *inam* is cancelled and reverts to the state. Resumption ordinarily occurred when an *inamdar* violated the conditions on which the *inam* had originally been granted. Common instances were a priest *inamdar* who did not regularly perform temple rituals, a temple *inam* which was not used to support the temple, or an *inam* which was sold, mortgaged or otherwise alienated to someone else.[9] In such circumstances, according to the BOR, the state was entitled to "resume" the *inam*.

But when the *inam* was resumed, what actually happened? The BOR's answer was narrow and technical. Resumption meant simply that the usual tax was imposed on the land, and credited to the state's general revenues, after which the state's formal interests in the matter ceased. In particular, the state had no specific obligations one way or another to the temple affected. A resumed *inam* was the state's to do with as it chose. The state could, to be sure, reassign the *melvaram* to the temple when conditions were satisfactorily met, or assign it to some other temple. But this was not obligatory. As an assistant secretary in Revenue wrote in 1937:

> When an *inam* is *resumed* on the ground of alienation, there is no obligation on the part of the Government to reassign the assessment to anyone. The *inam* ceases to exist and the Government are at liberty to do what they like with the assessment.[10]

When the *inam* tenure was cancelled, what happened to the *kudivaram*? Again, the BOR's approach was narrow and technical. No longer an

had "confirmed" existing grants as a minimal step, not in order to give their holders any new rights, but merely to free them from "vexatious inquiries" regarding their validity. See G.O. 2133 Revenue 16 July 1913, paras. 68–71. For an analysis of the background and larger political significance of the resumption controversy, see Nicholas Dirks, "Terminology and taxonomy; discourse and domination: from old regime to colonial regime in south India" (Paper at the University of Wisconsin Conference on South Asia, 1983).

[9] See the widely quoted opinion of Sir V. Bashyam Ayyanger: "According to the interpretation placed by the earliest times upon grants made for the maintenance of a charitable or religious institution, the *inam* lapses to the Crown when the particular institution, for the maintenance of which the grant was made, ceased to exist *or* the endowment is not duly appropriated for the maintenance of that institution" (G.O. 262 Revenue 7 May 1898, cited in G.O. 2133 Revenue 16 July 1913).

[10] G.O. 2139 Revenue 20 October 1937. As with most *inam* questions, there was room for disagreement here, and most of the arguments were repeated over and over again from the late nineteenth century. For example, a point of considerable disagreement had to do with *inams* in which the land had been alienated by the *inamdar* to a third party. Could the

inam, the land was "enfranchised," i.e., "placed in the same position as other descriptions of landed properties, in regard to their future succession and transmission."[11] The land became *ryot* land, and the *kudivaram* holder was granted a *ryotwari patta* (certificate) to replace the *inam* title deed. This meant that the *kudivaramdar* emerged as the unconditional holder of the land; the land was subject to no obligation other than the land tax required of all *ryot* holders.

Herein lay the problem so far as temples were concerned. By the late nineteenth century *inamdars* throughout south India realized that the BOR regulations could be manipulated to create private property in favor of those who had or could control those who had the *kudivaram*. The way to do this was very simple: the *inamdar* had only to violate the conditions of the *inam*. As the HRE Board observed in 1926:

> In hundreds of cases, *inamdars* in possession of service *inams* attached to temples have ceased to perform their services and *inam* lands have been alienated or resumed by Government. In many instances, the *inamdars* have deliberately courted resumption of the *inams* by a wanton neglect of the services with a view to get the lands assigned to them on *ryotwari patta*.[12]

The BOR's regulations, in other words, permitted a conditional right to the government's land tax to be transformed into an unconditional, and much more valuable, right to the land itself.

It was, the HRE Board pointed out, of little help if the resumed *inam* (defined now as land tax) was reassigned to the temple (usually in the form of a *tasdik* allowance or *beriz* deduction). Temple wealth depended on the land itself. The Minister for Religious Endowments, Sri T. S. S. Rajan, estimated in 1939 that resumed lands from the famous Srirangam temple yielded the government more than ten times the amount

government exert its "paramount right" to resume these *inams?* One side argued that to do so would violate Act XX of 1863 which was designed to limit governmental interference with religious endowments. Any improper use of an *inam*, such as third party alienations, it was argued, should be dealt with in a civil court. The other side, which ultimately prevailed, argued that resumption was a governmental responsibility both to itself (i.e., to protect its revenues) and to other taxpayers whose tax rates were indirectly affected by all revenue alienations. Mr T.E. Moir wrote: "The Government can do nothing to ensure the *proper application* of religious endowments, but *if they are misapplied* they can withdraw them, not from any obligation to the institutions to see if they are properly applied, but from the right, the immemorial right of the State, and their obligations towards the taxpayers, to render revenues granted but misappropriated once more available to the public service" (ibid. para. 58). A Mr Evans, Under Secretary in the Public Department, expressed a similar view in 1905: "Act XX of 1863 has been quoted as barring all interferences with religious *inams*; but it is, I think, clear that the act does not and cannot affect the Crown's rights as grantor in respect of Crown lands" (ibid. para. 53).

[11] See Act IV of 1862 (The Madras Enfranchised Inams Act), in *The Madras code*, vol. 2, p. 1.

[12] Madras Hindu Religious Endowments Board, *Annual report*, 1925–26, p. 13.

then given back to the temple in the form of *tasdik* allowance, the rates for which had been set in the mid nineteenth century.[13]

It is difficult to know exactly how much the temples were losing. Hard data on temple land-holdings have always been, and to a considerable extent remain, elusive. The Inam Commission reported in 1863 that there were 73,317 *inam* title deeds covering 1,230,227 acres, with an assessment of Rs. 20,43,911 and quit-rent of Rs. 1,29,142.[14] By the 1920s this was already old information, and represented only an aggregate figure. The HRE Board's lack of independent information proved at times embarrassing. In 1932 a member of the Legislative Council asked how much service *inam* land in the city of Madras and its neighboring districts had been "enfranchised, resumed, reassigned or regranted" since the Inam Commission, and how much religious service *inam* land remained. The HRE Board replied that it did not really know, that the question was "not answerable, and getting the information would be hard."[15] Again, in 1939, the Board found itself in the embarrassing position of pleading against resumption in the case of a group of temples which, as the BOR was no doubt pleased to point out, had been "in an abandoned and ruined state for more than a hundred years."[16]

Resumptions were undoubtedly numerous, even so. After 1933, the annual reports on Land Revenue and Settlement began to include information on religious and charitable *inam* resumptions. Table I demonstrates that the annual acreages and assessments involved were substantial. It must also be remembered that these figures include *completed* resumptions only. It can be assumed that significantly more were in the midst of resumption proceedings, or had not even come to the notice of the authorities.

The temple, of course, was the loser in all this. All the other parties involved seemed to gain. The *kudivaramdars* won outright land rights, the state's revenues increased and its jurisdiction over land was safeguarded, and the BOR traditions of land administration were

[13] "There is one other point which is not generally known with regard to the relation of the Revenue Department with these endowments. In the case of big temples, the Government are paying annually *tasdik* allowances and this arrangement originated with the taking over of a number of revenue villages belonging to the *devasthanams* [temples] by the Revenue Department nearly sixty or seventy years ago. The allowance paid to the temple was more or less arbitrary. Today those villages are bringing in large amounts of revenue to the Government although the *tasdik* paid is infinitesimal to the revenue derived" (G.O. 4026 PH 1 November 1939).

[14] G.O. 1155 Revenue 27 July 1925.

[15] G.O. 2195 Revenue 27 October 1932.

[16] G.O. 1612 Board of Revenue 13 April 1939.

Table 1 *Resumed religious and charitable* inams, *Madras Presidency, 1932—43*
(Money amounts in rupees)

Year	Acres	Assessment	Assessment Reassigned	Assessment Credited to General Revenues
1932–33	3,025.97	6,971– 8– 0	5,998– 4–0	712– 9–0
1933–34	2,813.50	6,600– 3– 0	5,707– 4–0	763– 8–0
1934–35	na*	na	na	na
1935–36	1,538.30	2,972– 9– 0	2,199–15–0	772–10–0
1936–37	1,673.41	2,870–14– 4	2,421– 0–0	449–14–4
1937–38	1,728.76	2,761– 7– 8	2,167– 2–2	594– 5–6
1938–39	1,436.15	2,149– 7– 0	1,290–12–7	858–10–5
1939–40	3,626.47	3,687–13–11	3,030– 1–8	657–12–3
1940–41	2,870.53	2,168– 7– 4	2,081– 2–8	87– 4–8
1941–42	na	na	na	na
1942–43	85.43	203– 9– 7	118– 8–7	85– 1–0

Source: Madras Department of Land Revenue and Settlement, *Report on the settlement of the land revenue in the districts in the Madras Presidency*, Faslis 1342–52 (1932–43).

*na: Information not available.

preserved. The whole situation in fact showed dramatically that the temple desperately needed an outside protector.

The mantle of protection fell on the new HRE Board, which faced an uphill task. At first, the HRE Board hoped that the BOR could be influenced to administer more in the interests of temples. It urged that resumption procedures be used sparingly and in a very discriminating way. But the BOR was basically unresponsive. Its job was complicated enough without the new HRE Board pressing its mistaken interpretation of *inams*. With the superiority characteristic of senior agencies, the BOR never had much regard for the HRE Board's competence in land questions.

The only recourse for the HRE Board lay with the legislature, and it began to press for a law which would tie *inams* permanently both to the land and to temples, and which would forbid all alienations. In 1933 Mr Koti Reddy, a member of the Legislative Council, introduced a bill to do just these things. Reddi's proposed amendment to the HRE Act read:

[1] In the absence of evidence to the contrary, it shall be presumed that all *devadayam inams*, and *inams* granted for doing services in temples or *maths* are grants of both *melvaram* and *kudivaram* rights.

[2] Any alienation or encumbrance of an *inam* granted for doing service in temples or *maths* such as *archakam*, piper's service, etc., shall be null and void.

[3] If the holder of a service *inam* alienates or encumbers the *inam* or fails to perform the service for which the *inam* was granted, such *inam* shall be resumed by the Local Government and regranted to the temple or *math* concerned.[17]

The debates over each of these clauses were long and involved, and it is not necessary here to do more than briefly identify the main points. Sensing a clear threat, the BOR protested vehemently that the bill struck "at the root of the administration of [its] branch of revenue." Especially was this true of the *varam* issue:

> At the time of the Inam Settlement, the distinction between *kudivaram* and *melvaram* rights was recognized and the Inam Commissioner confirmed only the Government share of the produce of the land, i.e., the *melvaram* right.[18]

The BOR argued also that the bill was discriminatory, in that it applied only to religious *inams*, and expropriatory, in that an *iruvaram* (i.e., both *kudivaram* and *melvaram*) interpretation would expropriate many peasants of their *kudivaram* rights.

Under dyarchy, the British Governor had to approve all bills, and the BOR's arguments were framed with that fact uppermost in mind. Always sensitive to the issue of "expropriation," the Governor's Council agreed that the bill might well "have the effect of dispossessing the tenants of the *inamdar* who have the *kudivaram* right" and therefore recommended that the *varam* clause be vetoed.[19] The Governor's Council was favorable, however, to having the *varam* issue left open, without any presumption either way, to be decided by local collectors on a case-by-case basis. This represented a partial victory for the HRE Board, although the wording of the revised clause caused much confusion in the next several years.

The legislature's Select Committee reworded the second clause so as to make it more precise. Because the clause was later so important, it would be well to quote it in full:

> Any exchange, gift, sale or mortgage and any lease for a term exceeding five years, of the whole or any portion of any *inam* granted for the performance of a charity or service connected with a *math* or temple, and made, confirmed or recognized by the British Government, shall be null and void.[20]

[17] G.O. 2206 Revenue 5 December 1933; G.O. 1654 Revenue 20 August 1934.
[18] G.O. 2206 Revenue 5 December 1933.
[19] Quoted in G.O. 1654 Revenue 20 August 1934.
[20] G.O. 390–91 Law (Legislative) 22 October 1934.

The Select Committee approved the third clause, which required that the government regrant resumed *inams* to the same institution or to some other purpose designated by the HRE Board. Resumption proceedings could not be used as an excuse for the state to reappropriate old lands or taxes.[21] With these changes, the bill was enacted into law.

The BOR's resistance to change

Although Act XI of 1934 introduced important changes, one thing remained unchanged: the BOR's jurisdiction over religious *inams*. This meant that implementation depended not on the HRE Board, which supported the act, but on the BOR, which did not. Specifically, if Act XI of 1934 was to mean anything at all, the BOR's *Standing Orders* had to be changed.

The Board's *Standing Orders* (BSO) is a prestigious handbook of rules and regulations for revenue and land administration, embodying the accumulated wisdom of generations of dedicated revenue officers. Born initially of problems encountered in the field, the contents of the BSO have been refined over many years through discussion and debate, gradually systematized in the form of definitions, rules and regulations. Once a "standing order" is settled, an immense burden of proof falls on any move to change it. Administrative effectiveness depends in part on consistency, which builds common expectations and understandings among otherwise very diverse parties: collectors, village officers, landowners, *inamdars*, temple trustees and so forth. Changes in the BSO are inherently disruptive and are preceded by long and energetic discussion, in which the Board, the Revenue department and field officers take part.[22]

As far as Act XI of 1934 was concerned, the BOR first made no changes in the BSO. It delayed as long as possible, and when further

[21] An interesting sidelight on government decision-making in Madras is the fact that the draft bill was submitted to the Finance Department to determine whether its provisions would adversely affect government revenues. The Finance Department stated as its opinion that the effect on government revenues would not be "crucial," but once again the extent of bureaucratic ignorance is instructive:

> It does not appear [Finance wrote] that any further examination is likely to enable Government to arrive even at a rough estimate of the probable expenditure from provincial revenues. (Memo from Finance [Accounts] Department, 24 July 1933, in G.O. 2206 Revenue 5 December 1933)

[22] The incremental nature of change in the BSO conforms rather well to Lindblom's description of the "branch method" of administration, in Charles Lindblom, "The science of muddling through," in *Public Administration Review* 19 (Spring 1959): 79–88.

delay was impossible managed to limit severely the Act's overall effectiveness. The next three sections illustrate how.

Ignoring the act

Initially, the BOR simply did nothing. Even after the HRE Board drew attention to the need to change the BSO, the BOR insisted on continuing resumptions under the old BSO: *ryotwari pattas* continued to be granted to the alienee, and the resumed *melvaram* assessments were often absorbed into the state's general revenues. It was only after Koti Reddy intervened that the drawn-out process of revising the BSO started. Even then, however, the BOR argued that the act had no retrospective effect, that it applied only to *future* alienations. There was no urgent need to modify the BSO because five years had to elapse before new alienations could fall within the act's provisions.

Eventually objections were raised in the Legislative Council. The government was forced to acknowledge that, in the nine months following the signing of Act XI of 1934, 111 *inams* were resumed under the old, no longer legal BSO. In forty-seven of these, moreover, the *melvaram* assessment was added to general revenues, rather than regranted to the temple. In an internal memorandum, the Revenue Secretary noted somewhat ruefully:

> It is rather irksome to find that after the publication of Act XI of 1934, there have been as many as 111 cases in which *inams* were resumed and dealt with otherwise than in accordance with the act. Our only excuse is that doubts were felt as to whether the act applied to cases in which alienation of land or cessation of service took place before the publication of the act. These doubts were cleared recently.[23]

New BSO rules were drawn up and published late in 1935.[24]

Applicability of the act: devadayam inams *and service* inams

The BOR had a second line of defense, drawing once again on the problematic legacy of the nineteenth-century Inam Commission. The Commission had distinguished between two kinds of religious *inams*: those held in the name of a temple deity (*devadayam inams*), and those

[23] G.O. 2247 Revenue 24 September 1935. Actually the BOR did send out a preliminary inquiry to the collectors in late 1934. This suggests that it was aware that some BSO changes would have to be made (G.O. 1567 BOR 24 April 1935).

[24] This account summarizes and simplifies a complex series of arguments and negotiations. See G.O. 1929 Revenue 16 August 1935; G.O. 1825 Revenue 7 August 1935; G.O. 1567 BOR 24 April 1935.

held in the name of a person, such as a priest, performing a religious service (service *inams*). The new BSO regulations, the BOR maintained, would apply only to *service inams. Devadayam inams* would fall under the old BSO.

The BOR based this position on a narrow construction of a pivotal phrase in Act XI of 1934: "any *inam* granted for the performance of a charity or service connected with a *math* or temple." Without question, this phrase was ambiguous and would have been clearer had the terms "service and *devadayam inams*" been used. Yet the legislature's intent seems clearly to have been that both types should be included, since the problem of alienation had been identified as especially urgent with *devadayam inams*. The original Koti Reddy bill, before the controversial *varam* clause was rewritten, had mentioned both types explicitly. To many observers, the distinction between service and *devadayam inams* was in any case dubious, since it seemed based less on real functional differences than on admittedly long-standing but questionable conventions in Anglo-Indian law. As one official put in it 1938:

> The object of the act will be frustrated if the act is not made applicable to such *inams* by placing a narrow construction on the wording [of] the act.Maintenance of temples in good repair is also a service connected with the temples.[25]

Throughout the 1930s, however, the BOR persisted in its narrow construction of the legislative language. But its persistence eventually won support, as could have been predicted, from the legal department and from the judiciary. In 1938, the Legal Department agreed that phrasing of the act was imprecise and should be reworded. And in 1942, the Madras High Court came down firmly on the side of the BOR and declared that the phrase "service connected with a *math* or temple" did *not* include *devadayam inams*.[26] Like the BOR, the judiciary had a great investment in established legal distinctions.

The High Court's decision was authoritative. It meant either that Act XI of 1934 would have to be amended, or that the relevant revisions of the BSO, to which the BOR had always been opposed, would have to be

[25] G.O. 977 Revenue 12 April 1938. For the BOR's arguments in 1934, see G.O. 2161 Revenue 25 October 1934; for its arguments in 1937, see G.O. 2610 Revenue 14 December 1937; and in 1938, see G.O. 977 Revenue 12 April 1938. On the issue of the meaning and significance of distinctions such as that discussed here, see J. Duncan, M. Derrett, "Religious endowments, public and private," in *Religion, law and the state in India* (New York: Free Press, 1968), pp. 484–90.

[26] G.O. 977 Revenue 12 April 1938; Appeal No. 198 of 1940, cited and described in G.O. 1706 Revenue 10 May 1943.

cancelled. The country was in the midst of the war effort, and the interim government declared itself unwilling to undertake any "controversial" legislation. The BSO revisions were cancelled – this time with little delay. The BOR had won.

The issue of varams: sanads, muchilikas *and other documents*

The BOR's third strategy dealt with the crucial issue of *varams*. It will be remembered that Koti Reddy's bill initially included the provision that "in the absence of evidence to the contrary, it shall be presumed that religious *inams* are grants of both the *melvaram* and *kudivaram* rights." This provision, objected to by the BOR as well as the Governor, was replaced by a clause which left the determination regarding *varams* up to the local collector without any prior presumption either way.[27]

In accordance with this change, the BOR instructed local collectors to assume nothing, and to decide the *varam* question on the basis of evidence. But what would count as evidence? This question was crucial. The answer the BOR gave was that evidence consisted of available documentation.

> The question, whether an *inam* covered by Act XI of 1934 comprises both the *melvaram* and the *kudivaram* or only the *melvaram*, should be decided with reference to the original *sanad*, *muchilika* and other documents, as may be produced by the parties concerned.

Once again, the BOR had found an approach which, though plausible and reasonable on the surface, had an effect directly contrary to the purpose of the act, which was to end fraudulent *inam* alienations. The problem all along had been that it was rarely in the interests of those who had very old *inam* documents to produce them. If produced, documents might show that the *kudivaram* right belonged to the temple. Without any documents, the *kudivaram* would go to the individual who had customarily been in charge and exercised a proprietary right.

District collectors saw these consequences clearly and began to object. As a Revenue Divisional Officer bluntly reported:

> In the present cases under reference, no such documents were produced. There was also no *prima facie* evidence to show that the *inams* were unoccupied lands at the time of the grant. I consider that the original intention of the Government when granting such *inams* is to see that the institution is not deprived of the

[27] This position of "neutrality" was consistent with a widely quoted, but controversial, ruling of the Privy Council, reported in 1934. The ruling is cited in G.O. 4026 Public Health 1 November 1939.

grant and that the grant constitutes both the rights. I therefore passed orders resuming both the rights.[28]

In late 1937, the Salem collector reported that many subordinate revenue officers were routinely resuming *kudivaram* rights, knowing that, realistically, no one was going to produce *inam* documents.

The fact that local officials were taking matters into their own hands in defense of the temples led the BOR to issue further, more precise, executive instructions in April 1938:

The attention of the collectors is invited to the Madras Act VIII of 1869 (Inams Act) which makes it clear that the word "land or lands" used in the title deeds issued prior to the passing of the Act [i.e., Inam Commission title deeds] does not convey to the inamdars any right to the "land or lands" which they would not otherwise possess. The grants should therefore be considered as grants of *only the net assessment* on the land or lands specified in the T.D.s, unless there is *prima facie* evidence to show that the grants included both the land and the assessment thereon, as for example, when the land was unoccupied waste at the time of the grant. The question whether any grant was of the land also, should be decided with reference to the original *sanads* or other *muchilikas* granted by the ancient rulers, and other documents if available with the parties.[29]

The clear effect of these instructions was to cancel the "no presumption either way" provision of Act XI of 1934. The BOR had made it nearly impossible for a temple to establish a *kudivaram* right.

Lacking jurisdiction, the HRE Board had had no say in the discussions leading to these instructions. All it could do was complain, as it did in its annual report for 1935-36. Revenue authorities were resuming *inams* at an excessive rate, and in most resumptions the temples were losing the *kudivaram* right:

In 455 cases the Revenue Department took action for resumption of *inams* under provisions of Sect. 44-B of the act. **In most cases the institutions have, on resumption, been given only the net assessment and not the lands on the footing that the *inam* consisted only of the *melvaram*. The pecuniary benefit derived by the institutions by such resumptions is very small while they once for all lose all claim to the lands.**[30]

Significantly, the HRE Board's complaint was not included in its entirety in the printed, public version of its report. The sentences between stars in the paragraph quoted above were deleted; someone,

[28] Letter dated 30 September 1937. The BOR instruction, this and other responses are contained in G.O. 3416 4 November 1937.

[29] G.O. 977 Revenue 12 April 1938.

[30] G.O. 875 LSG 4 March 1937.

probably in the BOR, was anxious to limit publicity regarding resumptions and their effects.

A move to wrest jurisdiction: the 1939 Congress bill

Unable to sway BOR policies, the HRE Board staked a claim for independent authority that was based on its own special concern and expertise. It proposed a comprehensive HRE Bill, introduced to the legislature in 1939, which challenged the BOR's historical jurisdiction over *inams*.

Inam issues were covered in section 39. Clause 39 (1), adopted verbatim from the unsuccessful first clause of the 1933 Koti Reddy bill, declared that religious *inams* would be presumed to consist of both *varams*. Clause 39 (2), carried over from Act XI of 1934, voided any sale, mortgage or alienation of temple or service *inams* for periods greater than five years. These two clauses were by now standard HRE Board ideas. The BOR's objections were also standard: clause 39 (1) was a "drastic innovation," and "would be a complete reversal of the policy which has been followed all along in dealing with *inams*."[31]

The more controversial clause was 39 (3), which transferred all jurisdiction over temple *inam* resumptions from revenue authorities to (newly proposed) HRE assistant commissioners:

> The assistant commissioner may, on his own motion or an application of the trustee of the religious institution concerned by order, resume the whole or any part of any such *inam*, on one or more of the following grounds ...[32]

No administrative or judicial appeal could be made from the assistant commissioner's orders.

In a long and forceful memorandum defending clause 39 (3), the Minister for Religious Endowments, Mr T.S.S. Rajan, argued once again that the BSO had "resulted in considerable and widespread loss to Hindu religious institutions in the Presidency," mostly because of "really fraudulent transactions deliberately designed to profit the parties to those transactions." He went on to argue the standard HRE Board interpretation of religious *inams*: that they constituted a special and unique category of land tenure, that they were actually "owned" by temples, and that they should be administered by a separate agency concerned about – and even dedicated to – the temples:

> The Revenue Department has neither the facilities nor the time to embark upon

[31] G.O. 4026 PH 1 November 1939.
[32] Ibid.

an enquiry whether the transaction is genuine or fraudulent ... As between the officers of the Revenue Department and the officers of the new department [the proposed HRCE department], the latter will be far better acquainted with and will be in daily touch with the local conditions relating to the temples which own the *inams* and the considerations, if any, which obtain in respect of any particular institution or group of institutions.[33]

In its objections, the BOR pointed to its well-established expertise in land questions, and doubted whether the new HRCE assistant commissioners were

likely to be the right type of persons competent to handle the intricate subject of *inams*, and whether they will be likely to command sufficient public confidence to warrant the exclusion of the civil courts. It is well known that *inam* questions are complicated and require considerable local knowledge and acquaintance with revenue administration for a proper appreciation of the old *inam* records.

The BOR also objected to having two sets of rules and two sets of administrators for a subject which was, in its opinion, a single area of administration:

Apart from any other question ... uniformity should prevail and it would not do to have one set of decisions for religious *inams* and another set for the secular service *inams* as will happen if the present proposals ... are accepted.[34]

Wider events intervened at this point. World War II opened and the British government declared war on behalf of India. The Congress ministers throughout India resigned in protest. Even though the Madras government had strongly supported the HRE Board and the draft bill, the new interim ministry was unwilling to undertake any far-reaching or controversial legislation, and the matter was dropped.

It is unlikely, however, that the HRE Board's move to wrest jurisdiction from the BOR could have succeeded. The Revenue Department's position within the government was too strong, and the proposal's break with history and tradition too sharp. Even the subordinate officials under the religious Endowments Ministry whose forceful support for the HRE Board was well known wrote in favor of continued BOR jurisdiction:

[33] Ibid.

[34] Ibid. The BOR expressed concern even about the physical security of the old records which were "very valuable and being protected with great care." It wondered about the "risk" involved in dispatching them to HRCE officials. This objection was dealt with sharply by Mr Rajan: "The objection is not entitled to any weight. As a matter of fact, judging from the vast majority of the orders in resumption matters no public documents of the class mentioned by the BOR appear to be in general use. Whatever that may be, the new department is a department of the State and if in the course of its duties it has to handle public documents they must no doubt be made available" (ibid.).

Ever since the inception of the present system of land revenue administration and land tenure the Revenue Department has been dealing with this question of *inams*. *Inams* work forms part of the legitimate duties of the Revenue Department.[35]

On the other hand, a change in the presumption regarding *melvaram* and *kudivaram* rights could be delayed but not ultimately put off. Here, the legal position was ambiguous, the BOR's interpretation of the historical record not entirely persuasive, and the loss to temples from resumptions widely deplored. The matter was opened again soon after Independence. The HRCE Act of 1951 declared finally that religious *inams* would indeed be presumed to consist of both *varams*, the provision for which the HRE Board had been struggling for twenty-five years.

This change was a bit late. In the first decade of Independence far more fundamental questions were raised regarding agrarian relations, and pressure mounted for major land reforms which would alter basic aspects of the south Indian land tenure system. The disputes over *inam* resumptions were soon to be superseded by far more threatening challenges to temple economies based on land.

[35] G.O. 4026 PH 1 November 1939.

6

Economy: the temple's weakness as landlord

No simple statement can capture the complicated and extremely significant effects on temples of the land reforms of the past thirty years. The reforms have focused especially on eliminating as much as possible layered, intermediary ownership of the land, strengthening the rights of actual cultivators and tenants, regulating rents, and scaling down the power and wealth of large landowners. It is important to note at the outset that HRCE officials do not oppose the principles lying behind land reform; they agree that changes are necessary. They go along with the national Hindu Religious Endowments Commission of 1960–62 appointed by Prime Minister Nehru:

> We are aware that consistently with the proclaimed and accepted objective of a socialistic pattern of society it is necessary to benefit the tenants and tillers of the soil and for this purpose the available land has to vest increasingly in the cultivating tenants.[1]

For the HRCE the problems posed by land reform are not theoretical but practical: can a more equitable land tenure system be reconciled with the underlying structure of temple economy and finance? HRCE officials recognize that any reform inevitably means change and short-term dislocation, and they are quite willing to have the temples undergo periods of difficult adjustment. But HRCE officials also believe that it is their responsibility to ensure that temples are provided in the long run with alternative, equally stable sources of financial support. Therefore, while they generally have gone along with land reform, HRCE officials believe that they must oppose measures which do not provide temples with adequate compensation. In their view, opposition was required in 1973. Their action provides a useful entry point for our discussion.

Land reform legislation

In 1973 the Tamil Nadu Legislature passed a statute, the Tamil Nadu Cultivating Tenants (Right to Purchase Landowners' Rights) Act,

[1] Hindu Religious Endowments Commission, 1960–62, *Report* (Government of India: Ministry of Law, 1962), p. 143.

which required landlords to sell land to those tenants who desired to purchase the land they cultivated. Tenants had a choice of purchase arrangements: either pay twelve times the land's "fair rent" in twelve annual installments or pay nine times the "fair rent" in one lump installment.

The act provided for a minor adjustment for temples, exempting the first fifteen acres. Beyond that, temple land was subject to the same provisions as ordinary land. The act therefore would have a major impact. Almost all the 362 listed temples in Tamil Nadu own more than fifteen standard acres (collectively, they own almost 200,000 acres), and nearly one-third of the 9,908 non-listed temples do also (collectively, non-listed temples own 210,000 acres).[2]

The HRCE drafted a strong and closely reasoned memorandum in protest. The memorandum pointed out that most tenants, unable to come up with a large lump sum, would choose to purchase the land in twelve annual installments of "fair rent." Since the "fair rent" was what tenants should be paying anyway,[3] the act, stripped to its essentials, simply meant that temples could go on with their present budgets and services for the next twelve years and then would have nothing. Indeed, the end could come even sooner. According to the worst scenario, a tenant would only make the first annual payment, which would confer equity rights, and nothing thereafter. The temple would have to go to court to get subsequent payments. Sooner or later, in other words, temples would experience drastic reductions in income and services, festivals would have to be curtailed, and, as the memorandum darkly concluded, even "day-to-day performance of *pujas* may come to a standstill."[4]

The simplest solution, the HRCE suggested, would be to exempt temples from the new reform. Barring this (which the HRCE did not really expect), a second alternative was to require that tenants pay the purchase price of (at least) twelve times the "fair rent" *in one lump sum.* This way a temple would at least be able to invest the money and live off the interest, resulting in an assured income for the foreseeable future, if not complete security against inflation.

The HRCE's objections did not move the government, which went ahead and passed the 1973 bill. But the arguments did persuade the Tamil Nadu Governor to withhold his consent from the act and to refer

[2] See summary of the act's provisions in *Hindu* (Madras), 13 August 1974.

[3] Religious institutions were brought under the "fair rent" law by the Public Trusts Act of 1961. The law limited rents to a maximum of forty percent of the produce per standard acre instead of previous rent which had ranged as high as eighty percent.

[4] See "Note on the impact of the new legislation conferring ownership of lands to cultivating tenants on the finances of the religious and charitable institutions" (HRCE, n.d.).

it, as the Indian Constitution provides, to the President of India for advice. In August 1974 the President returned the act to the Tamil Nadu legislature for reconsideration, noting that there had been

> numerous representations received from the religious and charitable institutions in the State, as well as from the members of the public.

The President would not agree to sign until the legislature considered amendments "to enable the institutions to carry on their legitimate functions without any financial difficulty."[5] The 1973 Cultivating Tenants Act has been discussed sporadically in the years since the President's rejection, but has not been seriously considered. So far as the HRCE is concerned, the act was just the culmination of a long series of land reforms in which the very real needs of and consequences for temples had been neglected.

Inam-abolition acts

The earliest reforms were aimed at *inams*, understood here as tenures in which title was vested in a rent-collecting, non-tilling "intermediary." The idea was to do away with the intermediaries, leaving only two parties on the land, the state and the "tiller of the soil." Temple *inams* usually were included since temples generally would rent rather than cultivate their lands themselves, thereby becoming an "intermediary" between the cultivator and the state.

The first measure was the 1948 Estates Abolition Act, which primarily affected larger and wealthier temples owning whole villages on *inam*. Temples able to establish a right to both the *kudivaram* and *melvaram* were not seriously threatened.[6] Where, however, the right was to the *melvaram* only, the *inam* village was abolished and converted into *ryotwari* tenure, with titles (*patta*) given, at least theoretically, to the cultivators.[7] As compensation, the government granted a *tasdik* allowance equal to the "basic annual sum" (rent).

The Minor Inams Abolition Act of 1963 abolished the remaining *inams* in the state, with the same basic provisions. Temples with *iruvaram* rights were granted the *ryotwari patta*, and a temple able to

[5] *Indian Express* (Madras), 13 August 1974.

[6] Conversation with the Special Officer for Temple Lands, HRCE, 27 August 1974.

[7] Here we can mention one of the major difficulties with all land reform measures in south India, not just those affecting religious institutions. The stated intention of these reforms has been to ensure the rights of cultivating farmers. The reforms, however, have been written in terms of the traditional categories of *melvaram* and *kudivaram* rights, and the persons who have been able to establish *kudivaram* rights have not necessarily (or usually) been the actual cultivators.

claim only the *melvaram* was compensated with a *tasdik* allowance equal to the annual "fair rent." If the temple was able to show that the *kudivaram* had been alienated improperly sometime in the previous sixty years, the alienee received the *ryotwari patta* only on payment of twenty times the fair rent.

Compared with the 1973 Cultivating Tenants Act, these *inam* abolition provisions seem quite favorable. But in fact there were substantial losses in temple incomes. The difficulty lay with the way the acts were implemented.

A by now familiar problem is the determination of *kudivaram* and *melvaram* rights. Theoretically the advantage lay with the temple since the presumption, in the absence of evidence to the contrary, was that religious *inams* consisted of both the *melvaram* and *kudivaram*.[8] The problem lay with the fact that most temples, especially big temples, did not cultivate the land with their own staff. For example, a temple owning a whole *inam* village of, say, 300 acres would have perhaps only twenty acres cultivated by its staff. This was called *pannai* or direct cultivation. The rest, amounting to 280 acres, would be non-*pannai* cultivation by tenants. Leases were registered in a separate temple account called the *chitta*, and certificates (*muchilikas*) were issued to the tenants. For the convenience of the temple, *chitta* lessees generally had rights to transfer their leases so long as this was done with other *chitta* account holders.

The non-*pannai* lands proved the temples' undoing. The settlement rules of the 1948 act, for example, regarded a *chitta muchilika* as evidence that the lessee possessed the *kudivaram* right, presumably because *chitta* holders had traditionally been at liberty to transfer their leases to others. In most large *inam* estates, therefore, the temples did not receive *ryotwari pattas* but only the right to a *tasdik* allowance.

To complicate matters further, the government was very slow to give effect to the *tasdik* and other compensation payments. Years elapsed between passage of an act and its implementation. The 1948 *inam* abolition "settlements," as the examination and declaration of each case were called, began only in 1952, and long before then cultivators who anticipated receiving a *ryotwari patta* often stopped paying rent. *Tasdik* payments, however, were not finalized until the early 1960s.[9] Even though the HRCE repeatedly drew the government's attention to the severe financial problems these delays were creating, the government has never stated publicly how much unpaid *tasdik* allowance it still owes the

[8] See pp. 90–2 above.

[9] After three decades, moreover, a considerable amount of the compensation due to temples in Tamil Nadu under the 1948 act had still not been paid. Several temple trustees with whom I spoke were skeptical that the government would ever pay completely.

temples. One officer in the Revenue Department estimated privately that the amount was approximately Rs. 1 crore (Rs. 10,000,000).[10]

Tasdik allowances have been paid fairly regularly since the early 1960s. But HRCE officials argue that the formula by which a temple's allowance was calculated was often unfair. In many cases, only the *melvaram* is being passed on, and the *melvaram* is far smaller than the rent the temples had been actually receiving, and even smaller than a "fair rent" as set by the government's own standards.

Tenancy reform acts

A second category of land reform has focused on tenancy conditions, particularly to stabilize rents and to protect tenants from unjust evictions by landlords. Typical is the Public Trusts Act, 1961. A long-standing HRCE policy was to lease temple lands at public auction, in order to prevent trustees from leasing land at very low rents to personal relations or friends. Auctions had resulted in rents as high as eighty percent of the produce. The Public Trusts Act changed this. It set far lower standards for "fair rent," e.g., forty percent of the produce on surface irrigated wet land or $33\frac{1}{3}$ percent on non-irrigated dry land. It also encouraged cultivators to form tenant cooperatives, and limited "direct cultivation" by the temple (that is, the *pannai*) to twenty standard acres. The Public Trusts Act also narrowed the conditions under which cultivators could be evicted from their lands.[11]

HRCE officials agree that the effect of the 1961 act on temple finances was double-edged. They approve of limiting *pannai* and, indeed, would go even further and abolish it altogether. The income is generally far less than it should be because trustees make private arrangements with

[10] Conversation with official in BOR, September 1974.

[11] Madras Public Trusts (Regulation of Administration of Agricultural Lands) Act, 1961, sects. 4, 16, 18–19, 24, 33–45. The limitation on *pannai* cultivation had not in all cases been implemented in 1974, thirteen years after the act's passage. See, for example, the case of the Navanideswaraswami temple, in Sikkal, Thanjavur district:

> They do continue to have two hundred acres of *pannai* cultivation ... despite the Act's limitation of twenty standard acres, because of a court case.

And the officer went on to indicate some of the complexities involved in effecting land reforms:

> The temple owns some six hundred acres in two to three villages. One village is of three hundred acres. It should have been included in the 1948 act which abolished "estates." Perhaps anticipating this, however, the temple trustees had all the two hundred acres in *pannai* cultivation, so there were no tenants.

(Conversation with former Special Deputy Collector. Thanjavur [HRCE], August 1974.)

friends and relatives. Any hope for increasing the rent of smaller temples with less than twenty acres depends on the elimination of *pannai* lands. For larger temples, however, the "fair rent" standard has definitely reduced income. These were the temples for which the HRCE had made special efforts to lease through auctions; ironically, to the extent that those earlier efforts had been successful the impact of the 1961 act was correspondingly great.

General policy directions

Since in their implementation the land reform acts have not protected temple incomes, several HRCE officials favor a public policy which would dispossess temples of their lands entirely. Given existing trends and ideology, they believe such a policy is inevitable and are simply concerned to ensure that, when it happens, a structure of support be found equivalent to the stability land provides. Here again we see reflected the differences between the assumptions of HRCE administrators, on the one hand, and local priests and temple trustees, on the other. For the priests and trustees, land is intimately wrapped up with the meaning of the temple itself; land means far more than just the rental incomes it brings. For the HRCE administrator, however, land is simply one among several possible methods to finance temples – a method, moreover, which in today's circumstances may no longer be satisfactory. From their perspective, a not unattractive alternative would be to replace land by bank deposits from which a stable and reliable income could be expected each year.

Rents

Once *inam* abolitions were settled, HRCE attention shifted to worrying about the problem of getting the most out of the lands temples *do* still own, in particular, to the problem of rent collection.

In February 1981, the Tamil Nadu government publicly acknowledged a problem which for years had been kept hidden: tenants of temple lands are way behind in rent payments. The full dimensions of the problem, as revealed by the government, are staggering. In mid 1981, Rs. 380 million were owed, and the arrears were rising at a rate of approximately Rs. 50 million per year. It is not possible at this point to give a complete explanation for what has occurred, for the evidence is still fragmentary and, in the absence of reliable historical comparisons, is subject to misinterpretation. But the broad outlines of the problem are known.

Clearly, an indirect effect of land reforms has been to complicate rent collection. The number of persons with which a large temple has to deal has increased sharply. Before land reform, a temple of three hundred acres could deal with a small and manageable number of large tenants, who would undertake to deliver an annual rent, usually in the form of bags of paddy, or sometimes in cash. Although the large tenants would themselves have many subtenants actually cultivating the land, the temple's administrative burden was fairly light. This same temple may now find itself having to handle seventy-five or one hundred tenants; "intermediaries" have been eliminated and another act, the 1961 Public Trusts Act, limits tenants who now may have no more than five standard acres. To ensure that the temple has actually received its forty percent "fair rent," an EO has to know the size of each of these tenant's harvests, and the only sure way to do this is to go to the threshing floor during the harvest and measure out the temple's share on the spot. This is next to impossible when the number of tenants is large.

Second, the provisions of the law place the temple at a severe disadvantage against a tenant who does not pay. The only remedy is eviction. But eviction in the 1961 Public Trusts Act is surrounded by procedural difficulties that rob it of meaning. Eviction authority rests not with temple authorities (trustees, EO) or the HRCE but with an "authorized officer" of the Revenue Department. The authorized officer requires complicated papers, procedures and proofs, and will institute proceedings only after *complete* non-payment on two consecutive crops. Processing an eviction can delay matters further. In 1974, eviction proceedings were backed up generally from two to three years. Finally, the defaulting tenant can easily halt eviction proceedings at any time simply by paying what is owed. Given all this and the near certainty of failure, it is no surprise that most EOs do not attempt evictions.

More important, perhaps, than these specifics is the fact that the general thrust of the state's policies does not encourage tenants to take their rent obligations seriously. The land reform of the 1950s and 1960s, the 1973 Cultivating Tenants (Right to Purchase Landowners' Rights) Act (even though left unsigned by the President), and the rhetoric of political parties: all these work together to convey to tenants the message that tenants have every right to the land they cultivate and that the state is doing its best to secure it for them.

Debt non-payment in fact is becoming an issue throughout rural south Asia. An example is the Tamil Nadu Land Development Bank: it reported in early 1981 that ninety percent of the loans it had advanced were in arrears. The bank, like other government agencies, has found it expedient in the past to ignore these arrears, rather than risk the political consequences of taking action against the delinquent accounts. (The crackdown in 1981 against Tamil Nadu farmers who had not paid their electricity bills was an unusual exception.)

The 1972 Cultivating Tenants Arrears of Rents (Relief) Act was a watershed. It cancelled tenant rent arrears for past years on condition that the rents for that current year (1 July 1971 to 30 June 1972) be paid. It is officially estimated that the loss to religious institutions because of the act was on the order of Rs. 3 crores (Rs. 30,000,000).[12] And the moratorium has more or less been regularly renewed in the years since then. Obviously, legislation of this kind makes life difficult for all landlords. The temple's position is particularly weak. Since trustees have little personal stake in rent collections, they generally do not press the tenants with the same vigor as they do those on their own private lands. Indeed, trustees often have much to gain by not pressing for rents, or even by conveniently forgetting about a lease altogether. While one might expect the temple executive officer – a civil servant – to have more incentive, the EO can jeopardize his career by applying the law rigorously to larger, more powerful and politically connected tenants.

Land ceiling provisions, such as the maximum of five acres specified in the 1961 Public Trusts Act, have also had an indirect but disastrous effect on temple rents because they have encouraged fraudulent *binami* holding. A *binami* holding avoids land ceilings by putting the *patta* title legally in the name of a person who in fact is controlled by another. As a deputy commissioner put the difficulty:

> If we go to the small man, he says, quite rightly, that he isn't in a position to pay anything, having already paid his rent to the *binami* holder. On the other hand, we are not in a position to prove the holdings or liability of the "real" owner.[13]

Tenant Cooperative Societies set up under the 1961 Public Trusts Act constitute a different problem. In Thanjavur district, the center of intensive paddy-growing in the state, nearly fifty percent of temple lands is included within these cooperatives, a deputy commissioner in Thanjavur estimated.[14] By the mid 1970s, it was clear cooperatives were extraordinarily lax in paying rents to the temples.

An important point of contention is whether rents are to be paid in kind or in cash. Temple trustees and the HRCE prefer payment in kind, i.e., bags of harvested grain, which they then sell to the highest bidders

[12] Tamil Nadu Legislative Assembly, Committee on Estimates, 1972–73, *Hindu Religious and Charitable endowments (Administration) Department*, p. 21.

[13] Conversation in Thanjavur district, April 1974.

[14] The complete list is included as Appendix XVI-A in HRCE (Administration) Department *Administrative report*, 1960–61.

on the open market. Many cooperatives, however, pay in cash based on the government's procurement price, generally lower than the market price. This works to the advantage of the cooperative societies, and particularly of their presidents, who often store the paddy until prices rise, then sell and pocket the difference. The temples and the HRCE believe that they are being cheated by this practice, but the Registrar of Cooperative Societies office does not consider this adequate grounds for liquidation of the societies.

Cooperative societies may simply not pay what they owe. For example the EO of a large temple in Thanjavur reported that in 1973-74 the cooperative societies into which his temple's tenants were organized had paid only 2,000 out of 3,720 *kalams*. One of the society's presidents placed the responsibility on non-paying tenants. The EO was skeptical, and noted that he was going to institute eviction proceedings. Non-paying, he believed, was only a temporary expedient, enabling the tenants, or the president, or both to make a profit on the side. "One way or another," he said, "they will certainly pay, because the lands are so valuable."[15]

A legislative committee reported that "huge arrears of rents" were owed to the temples and recommended that the delinquent societies be liquidated:

> The Committee recommends that the concerned temple authorities should apply to the Registrar of Cooperative Societies for the liquidation of such societies in order to realise as much of the arrears of rent as is possible and to recover possession of the lands and lease them to others.[16]

Here is yet another instance in which the HRCE finds itself stymied by another government agency, this time by the Registrar of Cooperative Societies. The rules of the Registrar of Cooperative Societies, however, rarely permit liquidation on the basis of the limited evidence the HRCE or temples are capable of providing.

Paddy grain dealers also participate in the general tendency to bilk the temples. One deputy commissioner described the situation in Thanjavur:

> There are about fifty large grain dealers in Tanjore. By arrangement among themselves, perhaps three only may issue tenders for a given produce.

All three bids will be – "by arrangement" – lower than had a genuine open competitive market existed. Even then it is still uncertain how

[15] Conversation with EO, Palace Devasthanam, Thanjavur, 30 April 1974.
[16] Committee on Estimates, 1972–73, pp. 7–8.

much will be made. Grain dealers often claim that prices fell at precisely the time they sold.[17]

These and other problems connected with rent collection are spoken of repeatedly by HRCE officers and EOs at all levels. Quite apart from non-payment, many leases are at rates below what the temple should receive. The HRCE Special Officer for temple lands reported in 1974 that of 8,797 temples surveyed, rents were low in 44,140 leases covering 76,996.80 acres of agricultural land, and in 9,980 leases covering 1,640.77 acres of urban land.[18]

Some efforts have been taken to rectify the situation. One way is to put pressure on temple EOs, who are directly responsible for rents. A former commissioner reported that his first question on visiting any temple was, "What are the rent arrears?" He would inspect the temple records, try to discover the specific reasons behind each instance of major arrears, and demand to know what action had been taken. After returning to the Madras head office, he would send his "Inspection Notes" to the temple's EO and managing trustee, as well as to the assistant commissioner or deputy commissioner concerned. A "file" on the case would be opened, and he would keep the file pending until "some action" had been reported as having been taken.[19] Occasionally, drastic action is taken against EOs who fail to collect rents adequately. Instances were reported to me of EOs who had been fined or suspended for poor or "lazy" rent collection.

More generally, though, HRCE officials recognize that the political, economic and organizational causes of low rent collection are beyond the control of most EOs. The problem rises with the number and importance of a tenant's connections. In a not untypical example, a tenant with close relatives in the government ministry paid only 700 *kalams* of paddy whereas 3,274 *kalams* were due. The deputy commissioner who reported this added that, had the EO moved legally to recover the full rent, he would soon have found himself transferred.[20]

Effective remedy for this sort of situation requires intervention by higher-level officials. In an innovative effort in Thanjavur district, for example, the deputy commissioner decided simply to ignore the spring *samba* harvest, and to concentrate instead on the fall *kuravai* crop:

The *samba* crop has many demands on it. It is the preferred crop in terms of rice

[17] Conversation with deputy commissioner, Thanjavur, April 1974.

[18] "Report on the investigation of lands by special staff up to 30.6.1974" (mimeo, 1974).

[19] Conversation with Thiru Sarangapani Mudaliar, former commissioner, HRCE (Administration) Department, 31 March 1974.

[20] Ibid.

variety, and so the tenant will want to set aside some of it for himself. Also, the state loaning agencies concentrate on the *samba* crop, and they have legal priority in terms of repayment. For example, the Agricultural Credit Banks, who have made loans to the farmers for implements, fertilizers, seeds, etc., are most active in getting loans repaid during the *samba* harvest in March/April. Now, the temples were not demanding rent repayment from the *kuravai* crop, out of reluctance and fear. The harvest is in December when it is very moist. When the mechanical dryers aren't working (as they usually aren't), there is the danger of the paddy germinating. So, the temples were not trying for this crop.

The deputy commissioner decided to target the December crop, which had few demands on it. Rent collecting rose dramatically, in several cases even covering past arrears.[21]

Encroachments

Any effort to improve rent collection assumes that EOs and trustees can identify the lands from which rent is due. It has been clear for years that this asumption does not hold.

In the early 1970s a "Special Office" branch of the HRCE attempted to itemize *all* temple land and property. This had never before been attempted. Involved was the laborious and time-consuming process of searching through village records and looking up past deeds of ownership and sales to determine whether land transfers had been legal. Special investigators personally inspected the land, submitting reports on such information as the fertility of the soil, the state of irrigation, facilities, the number of fruit-bearing trees, if any, and whether the rent was reasonable.[22]

The inspection reports submitted to the Special Office ordinarily consisted of a few paragraphs, although in some cases reports were much longer. To give an idea of the range of information contained in a routine report, two are quoted below:

Notes of inspection

[1] I inspected Sri Visvanathaswamy temple and overchecked the investigation work of the Special Tahsildar (TL) Thanjavur on 26.5.73.

[2] The temple is situated in an extent of 0.50 acre in R.S.No. 29/5 classed as natham poramboke of Aranthangi village, Aranthangi taluk. The temple

[21] Conversation with deputy commissioner, Thanjavur district, April 1974.

[22] The above two paragraphs are based on conversations with the staff of the Special Office, July–August 1974.

has got compound walls on all sides. The temple building is in good condition and has been maintained well. There are no encroachments in the temple site. Poojas are being performed regularly.

[3] The temple owns 21.91 acres of lands. An extent of 2.97 acres is held under lease. The rate of paddy works out to one half to two kalams per mah. The Executive Officer may be instructed to take steps to increase the rent by negotiation and for fixing the fair rent, if necessary. An extent of 17.64 acres is held under unauthorised occupation while an extent of 0.35 acres is left waste. The waste land in its present state is fit for dry cultivation. The Executive Officer may be instructed to regularize the occupations by entering into lease agreements and lease out the waste lands. An extent of 0.20 acres is covered by the building owns [*sic*] by the temple. The buildings require repairs. The rent collected is fair and reasonable.

[4] The trees belonging to the temple have been duly brought to Special Register No. 15. The usufructs are very negligible and are utilised by the temple.

[5] An amount of Rs. 995.39 is due by way of *tasdik* allowance and *mohini* grant. *Mohini* grant of Rs. 207.37 has been paid up to fasli 1381. The Executive Officer may be instructed to take steps to realise the amount due for fasli 1382 quickly.

Notes of inspection

[1] I inspected Sri Sundarajaperumal temple, Aranthangi town on 26.5.73 and checked the Special Registers prepared by the Special Tahsildar (TL) Thanjavur.

[2] The temple is situated in an extent of 8.00 acres in R.S. No. 28/1 classed as natham in Aranthangi village. The temple is in fairly good condition, but needs repair and renovation. Poojas are being performed regularly.

[3] The temple owns 3.43 acres of urban lands. Except a small extent of natham site the lands are jointly held by the three temples, viz. Sri Sundararaja temple, Sri Veeramakaliamman temple and Sri Rajendra Choleswaraswamy temple. The income derived out of the ground rent collected are apportioned and this temple gets one third share for the sites jointly held. As the rent was fixed some fifteen to twenty years back there is scope for increasing the rent at least by one half times the present rate and if this is done this temple will derive an additional income of Rs. 550 towards its share. The trees owned by the temple are very few in number and have been brought to register no. 15 and the usufructs are used for the temple. There are heavy arrears of rent to be collected. The Executive Officer may be instructed to collect the arrears and to increase the rent as suggested.

[4] This temple is in receipt of Rs. 263.30 by way of tasdik allowance and mohini grant. The mohini grant of Rs. 94.74 has not been paid for fasli

1382. The Executive Officer has been instructed to take necessary steps to collect this amount quickly.[23]

In setting up the Special Office branch, the HRCE's intention was to recover land lost during the *inam* reforms of the 1950s and 1960s as a result of trustees who either intentionally or accidentally had not followed the procedures which would have protected the temple's interests. What surprised the HRCE was a different issue: "unauthorized occupation" or "encroachment," i.e., land which was occupied without the temple authorities knowing that it "belonged" to their temple.

Encroachment is not limited to a few isolated cases. In mid 1974, the Special Office reported that in the 8,797 institutions it had so far investigated, there were 33,040 cases of long standing encroachment, involving 38,801.53 acres of agricultural land and 1,545.32 acres of urban land.[24] This was a striking finding, since all the institutions under HRCE control together owned some 410,000 acres. Some encroachments were relatively unimportant, as when a small thatch *pan* shop was on an otherwise unused corner of a temple's property, but others were more serious:

The mandapam owns 1.27 acres of lands and 1,837 square feet covered by the building. *The entire extent of 1.27 acres is held under unauthorised occupation* by one [individual] of Thirucherai village. Double wet crop is raised. If regularized the institution will derive not less than Rs. 450/per year.[25]

HRCE officers argue that temple land rarely falls into the hands of "third parties" or "encroachers" without the active collaboration of the managing trustee and the village record keeper (*karnam*), and an encroachment is not easily reversed. It is always difficult legally to evict someone, especially when the encroacher has been on the land for years, perhaps for his whole life. A preferable arrangement, recommended by the Special Officer, is for the temple to initiate "tenancy arrangements" with the "encroacher," i.e., formalize tenancy through a lease and then draw fair rent. Commissioners and EOs have been instructed to

take steps to create tenancy relationships in respect of these lands by contracting the parties who are in possession of the land or in the alternative to take steps to evict the occupants through legal means.[26]

[23] Special Office, HRCE, "Notes of Inspection," 1973.
[24] "Report on the investigation of lands . . . up to 30.6.1974."
[25] Special Office, HRCE, "Notes of Inspection," 1973.
[26] "Report on the investigation of lands . . . up to 30.6.1974."

The HRCE knows that it must avoid if at all possible having its administration taken to the arena of the courts.

General policy alternatives

Loss of ownership rights, uncertainty about existing land titles, and non-payment of rents have thrown temple finances into disarray. For years, the government ignored the problem, or attempted to show that it was making every effort to defend the temples.

In 1981, for example, AIADMK government ministers raised the issue of temple finances frequently. They made something of a showcase example of the Nataraja temple in Chidambaram which, though wealthy and famous, is widely believed to be technically landless, on the grounds that the nominal temple land was in fact held personally by members of the *dikshitar* community, who function hereditarily as its trustees and priests. The government, however, claimed to have found that traditionally the land actually belonged to the temple, not to the *dikshitar* community. It registered claims to over 600 acres and as a result of new tenancy agreements negotiated by the HRCE with the *dikshitars*, Rs. 30,000 have been added to the temple's budget.[27] Isolated instances of success, however, do not address the underlying issue: the government is unwilling to strengthen the proprietary rights of any landlord, and, so long as this remains true, temple income from land will continue to decline at an accelerating rate.

Several solutions more general and permanent have been suggested. Under one plan, advocated by former Congress Chief Minister M. Bhaktavatsalam, the government would "take over" all temple lands and distribute them to tenants under whatever arrangement it chose. Fixed bank deposits would be established for each temple, the interest to be applied to budgeted expenditures. Many supporters of temples – in the HRCE, among trustees, and in the general public – support this suggestion as perhaps the best deal the temples can get. Trustees, especially, are weary of the burden and liabilities which landholdings entail, and are tired of pushing for what seems to be a losing cause. However, implementing the policy would cost an estimated Rs. 300 crores, a quite impossible burden on a state budget with total revenues (in 1981) of Rs. 1,200 crores. Another objection is that inflation would eat away at the value of the bank deposits.

A second proposal is to allow temples to sell their land on the open market; present HRCE regulations allow this only in exceptional

[27] *Hindu* (Madras), 31 October 1980, 14 November 1980.

circumstances. The difficulty here is political. There is no certainty – indeed, it is unlikely – that tenant cultivators would be the high bidders in open-market sales, and it would be directly contrary to general policy to dispossess the tenants in favor of the highest bidders. Other alternatives are also unsatisfactory for one reason or another. An arbitrator or settlement officer could fix the price for tenant purchases, but the price would probably be too low to protect the temple's interests and, given the prevalence of debt non-payment, the purchaser might default in future years anyway. A government corporation could be set up to manage the lands on behalf of the temples, thereby relieving them of the burden of rent collection. However, the record of public corporations does not inspire confidence in this alternative either. The simplest solution, perhaps, would be to meet temple expenses directly from the annual state budget. But this would raise major constitutional questions relating to secularism and "establishment," and would involve a major expenditure by the state. It is a commitment which might not be met in the future. Also, this plan would probably just displace the politics of temple finances to a new arena; in the scramble for state allocations, the smaller temples, which most need the money, might end up on the losing side.

Conclusion

Land reform policies were based on state-level political strategies that had little to do with temples as such. The government was not unaware of the potential dangers to temple holdings and income, and at times even attempted to minimize them. But the central concern was to improve tenant and cultivator conditions, and to have excluded temples would have diluted significantly the effectiveness of the reforms. This was particularly true in Thanjavur district, where as much as thirty percent of the paddy land was owned by or associated with religious institutions.

Until very recently the HRCE did not have a systematic picture of temple landholding, and so a systematic comparison with the situation before the reforms began is not possible. It seems clear, however, that the land reforms of the 1950s and 1960s threw temple finances into disarray, and introduced new elements of uncertainty regarding the future. Government compensation has frequently not been paid and, even when paid, is a poor substitute for the flexibility of income derived from land directly. The rent relief acts have reinforced the tendency of many tenants to delay or default altogether on rent payments. And temple trustees, sometimes from ignorance and sometimes from willful negligence, have not done all that they could when land reform acts came to be implemented by revenue settlement officers.

The HRCE's capacity to protect land and income is limited also by local politics. Because those with influence in the temples tend to be powerful in their villages, land leases, titles and rents are frequently manipulated for short-term gain at the expense of the temples. These manipulations, obviously, are disguised and difficult to detect. To find out the "real" facts, one HRCE officer remarked, takes a great deal of work and "in some cases courage." Village factions may be involved, so that an EO who pursues suspected encroachments or fraudulent alienations may be doing so at personal risk as well as hurting administration in other areas. In fact, the EO may very reasonably decide that he has much to lose and little to gain in pressing the matter. After all "the EOs are there for only a short time and want to preserve their careers or further them."

Organizational weaknesses also hinder HRCE land administration. Agricultural productivity in south India varies from year to year. Since rents are calculated as "shares of the annual produce," the task of rent collection is very difficult. The task facing an EO whose temple has extensive landholdings is practically insurmountable. HRCE officials often accuse EOs of "negligence," but this does not seem altogether reasonable. With all his other duties to attend to, with little or no supporting staff, the EO is unable to keep close tabs on each tenant's produce, or go to the threshing floor for the temple's share. Yet it is undoubtedly true that the threshing floor is where the EO can be sure that the temple is getting its fair share. As one commissioner put it, if the EO does not go, he really cannot expect the tenants to pay him later.

> After all, the tenants are poor people, and may not have the rent later and, given the other creditors, are scarcely in a position to save for when the collector from the temple happens to come around.[28]

To put the matter in the most general terms, the temple is an inherently weak landlord, whether "landlord" is defined as trustee, EO or HRCE. Trustees are unlikely to press for rents with the same vigor as they do from private lands; indeed, trustees often have much to gain from *not* pressing for rents, and even from conveniently forgetting that a given parcel of land belongs to the temple. EOs have their own careers to pursue. They occasionally put pressure on small tenants, but they are less likely to with large, more powerful and politically connected tenants. Eviction proceedings are theoretically possible, but are pro-

[28] Interview with Thiru Sarangapani Mudaliar, former commissioner, HRCE, 31 March 1974.

tracted and expensive; the temple budget can stand only so much in lawyer's fees. There remains the HRCE, of course. But legally the HRCE is only a "supervisory body"; it cannot take action on its own initiative but only through EOs and trustees. In any case, as one former commissioner put it, the HRCE does not want to push the matter of rents and encroachments too hard. The temple, he noted, is a "public institution and a religious one." It would be "rather undignified" to use coercive measures for rent collection and tenant eviction.

7
Religion: purifying and organizing Hinduism

Religion has never been very far from the eye of the modern Indian state. For over a century, statutes have attacked such varied practices as caste disabilities, untouchability, the age of consent, and restricted temple entry. Though usually described as social rather than religious reforms, their impact on religion, especially on Hindu practices, has nonetheless been profound.

It is therefore no surprise to find that temple religion is affected by HRCE administration. There is something of a contradiction involved, to be sure, since the principles of Indian secularism would seem to imply that government agencies should not tamper with, or "interfere with," religion. The HRCE Act, indeed, specifically restricts administration to financial and nonreligious matters. But even the most scrupulous secularist would find that supervising temple governance and economy inevitably affects temple religion. "Noninterference," a concept with a long and distinguished history, is a good slogan to legitimate the HRCE, but it is an inaccurate description of actual practice.

What is unexpected and striking is the detail, depth and extent of the HRCE's impact. The department's efforts to transform religion are explicit, elaborate and systematic. It operates on a wide range of religious fronts, some of which have major consequences.

The constant focus which governments give temple religion suggests that religious policy can serve very definite political ends. Certainly publicity about temple religious practices can be diversionary, drawing public attention away from other, often more pressing and controversial areas. Governments have also found that religious policy can be useful in building political alliances and, especially, that it can make a broad ideological appeal. From one point of view, temple religion constitutes a standing challenge to modernity, and symbolizes much that is "backward" in contemporary India. Many features of temple religion seem contradictory to the principles of an egalitarian, just and rational society. Thus, for many politicians and intellectuals, the government's religious policy is an index of public commitment to progressive social change.

One general feature stands out: a distinct absence of political opposition to the state's overtures in these areas. The policy context is shaped fundamentally by "high stateness."[1] As the protector of temples, the state enjoys enormous latitude and is able tightly to control the policy-making environment. Interest groups, particularly those with a material stake in temple policy, approach the government and bureaucracy almost as supplicants, because high stateness enables state agencies effectively to grant or withhold legitimacy from groups desiring a voice in policy making.

The purpose of this and the next chapter is to look more specifically at four areas where the HRCE has explicit religious policies: "religious atmosphere," ritual language, ecclesiastical organization and priestly qualifications. We shall also look at three organizations which have taken an active interest in these areas: the South India Archaka Sangham, an association of temple priests; the Tamil Nadu Deviga Peravai, the state's designated religious organization for over a decade; and the Hindu Temple Protection Committee, an association which continually scrutinizes HRCE administration.

"Religious atmosphere"

The most diffuse area of religious policy is that touching on "religious atmosphere." Annual HRCE reports always include a section on "Religious Atmosphere" describing the effort to make temples serve as "living centers" of religious culture.[2] Both Congress and non-Congress governments have supported these efforts. In 1965–66, for example, when the Congress was in power, the Tamil Nadu Assembly's Estimates Committee reported:

> The Committee is pleased to note [that] the drive that has been launched under the aegis of the HRCE (Administration) Department to maintain the moral, spiritual and cultural atmosphere of the religious institutions has been very successful and hopes that it will be continued with more vigor and enthusiasm.[3]

And the drive was reinforced again in 1972–73, when the DMK was in power:

> A monthly journal by name *Tirukoil* is being published by this Department, since October 1958 ... The Committee therefore recommends that important

[1] On the concept of "stateness," see Introduction above.

[2] HRCE (Administration) Department, *Administration report*, 1958–59, p. 22.

[3] Madras Legislative Assembly, Committee on Estimates, 1965–66, *Hindu Religious and Charitable Endowments (Administration) Department*, para. 85.

articles may be reproduced and printed as separate books or pamphlets for intensive religious propaganda.[4]

Enhancing religious atmosphere can take several forms: arranging for "religious propagandists" and religious discourses on ordinary and special occasions; holding conferences for propagating the Tiruppavai and Tiruvembavai scriptures; appointing of *othuvars* to sing and teach sacred songs; arranging "weekly worship" in several temples; distributing *vibuthi prasadam* to hospital patients; holding special prayers for Independence Day and Republic Day; setting up loudspeaker systems to play devotional music and arranging "convenient worship" for distinguished visitors.

It is also interesting that HRCE officers frequently instruct trustees and priests as to how worship should be conducted. There is no specific department policy here; an officer may simply witness a ritual or practice of which he disapproves and attempt to correct the situation.

Once in a temple I saw some pictures (lithographs) of gods in the sanctum sanctorum. Now, in Hinduism, we have idol worship. Pictures are all right in the homes, but not in the temple. So I called the priest and asked him, "Why did you put that picture there?" He said that he liked it, and thought it was nice. I asked him to take it down immediately. He could have it in his home if he wanted, but not there. In one temple, during the cart festival, the *archaka* was sitting down doing the *puja*. I asked for an explanation. The priest defended himself saying that when the god is carried on shoulder palanquins, the *puja* is said sitting down, so why not here? I replied that given the difficulty of balancing on the shoulders, *puja* could be said sitting down on a palanquin, but not here on the cart where there is no such difficulty. In the Trichendur temple, they were saying the *archanais* of the six faces of Shanmuga in the following way: six persons sitting in a semicircle together said the *archanai*. This is not correct ... I consulted with the Sivacharya of Palani, the most learned man on Shanmuga *archanai*, and he agreed. So it was changed.[5]

HRCE officials worry that temple religion will decay if left to the priests. As one commissioner put it, agreeing with a popular prejudice:

The priests *are* generally ignorant, poor and in their personal habits reprehensible ... They do not know the rituals properly ... This matter of not saying the rituals properly is very important, for we believe that if they are not said properly the state is damaged. The temple, in fact, is intended for prayers for the general welfare of the community and the world at large.[6]

[4] Tamil Nadu Legislative Assembly, Committee on Estimates, 1972–73, *Hindu Religious and Charitable Endowments (Administration) Department*, para. 80.

[5] Interview with former commissioner, HRCE, 18 February 1974.

[6] Ibid. This concern has been a recurrent theme during the history of the department. In 1941, for example, the HRE Board noted: "The question of framing rules under the act or

To rectify the situation, the HRCE has promoted "summer refresher courses" in several of the larger temples to educate *archakas* better. But the priests have not been very enthusiastic, and only a few dozen attend.

Promoting "religious atmosphere" can go even further. For example, in December 1970 the HRCE commissioner, along with other local government officials and religious leaders, joined together at the Arunachaleswara temple in Tiruvannamalai to honor the author of a series of religious discourses and a book containing the temple's religious *purana*.[7] And in October it was reported that the DMK government's Minister for Religious Endowments was expected to lay the foundation stone for a new temple in a village near Tirunelveli city. The newspaper *Hindu* explained that:

> Some eight hundred people came back to the Hindu fold some three years ago. On the occasion of their first anniversary of reconversion they had installed a Vinayaka idol. The minister, on a visit a few months ago, was so touched by their devotion that he undertook to build a small temple for them.[8]

Actually, at the last moment the government minister withdrew from the ceremony, apparently on the grounds that the "majority community" in the area objected to a new temple for the converts. The foundation stone was laid instead by Kunrakudi Adigalar, whose Deviga Peravai organization we will be examining later in this chapter.

It is clear that HRCE officials operate with a highly specific definition of "correct" Hindu practice, and are using their bureaucratic authority to impose this definition on temple priests and others. When the department sets out to improve the "religious atmosphere" of temples, its definition of "religious" is that especially of educated, upper-class Hindus who view temples as "spiritual centers" of high culture: quiet, peaceful and apart from everyday life. This is in tension with actual temples, which are noisy, bustling centers of worship, social intercourse and commerce. Usually a temple is large enough to accommodate both these images at the same time. A quiet side street or hall may be set aside for a concert of *bhajans* by an eminent musician, such as M. S. Subbalakshmi, while elsewhere the temple's ordinary bustle proceeds as usual. Or, when an HRCE officer objects to the presence of shops within

introducing suitable provisions in the act to empower authorities of temples to preclude persons not properly equipped from officiating as priests may soon have to be tackled; so as to ensure priests to acquire the required knowledge the Board has been desirous of establishing institutions for imparting instruction in rituals and *agamas*" (Board of Commissioners for Hindu Religious Endowments, Madras, *Sixteenth annual report*, 1940–41, p. 10).

[7] Reported in *Mail* (Madras), 19 December 1970.

[8] *Hindu* (Madras), 20 October 1970.

the temple, as officers do periodically, the shops will be removed, but will find their way back when the controversy subsides.

Ritual language

While reflecting the conscientious nature of HRCE supervision, "religious atmosphere" policies do not alter central components of temple worship. The state's *archanai* policy, however, affects ritual language, a crucial dimension not only of worship but also of Brahminic orthodoxy. The *archanai* question is thus a matter of great sensitivity, reflecting as it does deep and historically rooted tensions in south Indian society, contemporary ideological movements and social conflict, and political party competition.

Archanai is a popular form of worship, outside the regular cycle of worship in the temple, in which, for a small fee, a devotee receives *darshan* of the deity and an abbreviated *puja* is performed for his personal welfare.[9] Typically, the devotee purchases the ritual necessities, such as coconut, *pan*, camphor, incense and flowers, from the temple shops, buys an *archanai* ticket from the temple office, and then approaches a priest. The *archaka* asks the devotee for his or her name. He then recites the names of the deity, generally 108 in number, along with that of the devotee, and illumines the image of the deity with the burning camphor. The *archanai puja* is customarily performed in Sanskrit, and the sacred Vedic mantra OM figures prominently in the chanting of the deity's names.

In 1971, the HRCE issued a series of circulars instructing temple authorities to change the *archanai* language to Tamil. Many observers discussed this as a maneuver by the DMK government to stoke up again the language controversy, which had been languishing for several years; Sanskrit in worship could easily be made to pose a challenge to heightened Tamil sensitivities. But the place of Tamil in temple worship has a rather more complex historical background. The question was already a source of vigorous doctrinal dispute and sectarian conflict during the medieval period, often interacting with social, political and geographical tensions. At several points in south Indian history Tamil was expressly given prominence. There is evidence that the *Tevaram*, the Tamil hymns of the Saiva saints, and the *Thiruvaimozhi*, the hymns of the

[9] Much resentment surrounds the manner in which *archanai* fees are levied. The HRCE has "regularized" *archanai* fees in recent years by providing that *archanai* tickets be sold from a central box office in large temples. A portion of the proceeds goes to the temple and a portion to the priests. Priests feel that one of the perquisites of their office has been taken from them. *Archanai* ticket scandals have also been reported in the press.

Vaisnava saints, were instituted as integral parts of worship in Saiva and Vaisnava temples respectively by Rajaraja Chola I (d. 1014) and his successors. There is also evidence that Tamil was an important dimension of anti-orthodox *bhakti* movements in the late medieval period.[10] The extent and use of Tamil varies today from sect to sect and from temple to temple. The complexity of the issue is seen in the fact that Vaisnava temples of the Tengalai sect already emphasize Tamil, whereas Vadagalai Vaisnava temples use it much less and Saivite temples hardly at all.

Worship in Tamil was quietly promoted by the HRCE in the 1950s and early 1960s. The HRCE encouraged temples to employ *othuvars* who are specially qualified to sing the popular Tamil devotional hymns. During this period the effort was simply to strengthen Tamil's place alongside Sanskrit rituals. There was no explicit move to substitute Tamil for Sanskrit.

Impetus for a more radical change came with the much publicized attacks on Hinduism in 1953 by E. V. Ramasamy Naicker, a well-known iconoclast and atheist. Naicker claimed that temple practices represented an alien, north Indian based religion, and that both priests and rituals were inherently foreign.[11]

Responding to this criticism, the *mathadhipathi* of a non-Brahmin *math*, Kunrakudi Adigalar, proposed that *archanai* be conducted in Tamil. Kunrakudi, along with many other Dravidianists, shared a love for Tamil and a concern over the virulence of Naicker and his followers' tactics, which included a campaign to smash the small Hindu shrines found on many town and village streets. Kunrakudi argued that the source of this irreligiosity, atheism and iconoclasm was the "unintelligibility" of Sanskrit:

If the *pujaris* were to cast off their superiority complex and to conduct *archanais*

[10] For a brief review of the evidence, see G.S. Ghurye, *Caste and race in India*, fourth edn (Bombay: Popular Prakashan, 1969), pp. 369–74. On medieval *bhakti* and the significance of the language of devotion, see A.K. Ramanujan, *Speaking of Siva* (Baltimore: Penguin, 1973). For a concrete analysis of the interplay of language, sect and political rule, see Appadurai, *Worship and conflict*, ch. 2.

[11] On E.V. Ramasamy Naicker, who died in December 1973, see Charles A. Ryerson, "'Meaning and modernization' in Tamil India: primordial sentiments and sanskritization" (Unpublished Ph.D. dissertation, Columbia University, 1979) ch. 4. Ryerson's analysis includes numerous citations on available sources for studying Naicker. See also his "E.V. Ramasamy Naicker and the Dravidian movement: identity, change and tradition" (paper read at Conference on Religion in South India, Bucknell University, 1975). For earlier, more general treatments, see Lloyd I. Rudolph, "Urban life and populist radicalism: Dravidian politics in Madras," *Journal of Asian Studies* 20 (May 1961): 283–97; P. Spratt, *DMK in power* (Bombay: Nachiketa Publications Limited, 1970).

in a language understandable to the average devotee, there would be no anti-God demonstration in the street.[12]

Fourteen years later, soon after taking office, DMK ministers began to urge temples to introduce Tamil *archanais*. Several "inaugural functions" in late 1970 officially instituted the reform. At the Nellaiyapparkanthimathi temple in Tirunelveli, for example, Tamil *archanai* was begun on 21 October. The program was "inaugurated" by the DMK Minister for Religious Endowments, Thiru K.V. Subbiah, with the HRCE commissioner presiding. Kunrakudi Adigalar also attended. According to the *Hindu*, which described the new *archanais* as "breaking the centuries-old tradition," the cabinet minister said that:

> No language was unknown to God and it was wrong to say that God could follow only Sanskrit. He decried the attempts being made by some devotees to stall the Government's move to introduce Tamil in temples.[13]

In November, the HRCE commissioner announced that Tamil *archanais* had been initiated in one hundred of the listed temples (most of the wealthy and prominent temples in the state), and that he expected the number soon to rise to 150.[14]

From May 1971 the reform was pressed one step further. A circular from the deputy commissioner in Madras instructed trustees and EOs to "make all arrangements to start [Tamil] *archanais*." A follow-up circular in July directed EOs to "pay special attention to the [May] circular and submit a report." It asserted that the reform was a response to popular demand: "The Tamil Nadu people desire that in all temples *archanais* should be performed in Tamil." A month later, in August, the matter was called "very urgent"; officers were ordered to "take immediate steps" to implement the program.[15]

These circulars were appealed to the Tamil Nadu High Court on the ground that they violated constitutional guarantees of religious freedom. In his affidavit submitted to the court, Dakshinamoorthy Bhattar, a priest, argued that the issue was not simply one of translation. Rather, the efficacy of the ritual depended on particular sounds, especially the

[12] *Times of India*, 18 May 1953, quoted in Ghurye, *Caste and race*, p. 371. Naicker and Kunrakudi Adigalar's relations became much more friendly in subsequent years. Their common antagonism to north Indian "cultural imperialism" and attacks on "casteism" apparently drew them together. In the 1960s, Tamilians became familiar with the sight of Naicker, the atheist and inconoclast, sharing the same speaker platforms with Kunrakudi Adigalar, spiritual head of a monastery.

[13] *Hindu* (Madras), 21 October 1970.

[14] *Mail* (Madras), 27 November 1970.

[15] Copies of these circulars are annexed to Writ Petition No. 401 of 1974, filed with the Supreme Court of India (Civil Original Jurisdiction).

nathan which followed the deity's name. He concluded that "disaster" would follow if he "dared to perform the *archanai* in Tamil." The real reason for the HRCE circulars, he argued, was political. The DMK party, a party "with no faith in God," was attempting to "thrust its own religious feelings into the temple and destroy [the temple's] purity."[16]

The High Court rejected the appeal in January 1974. The Court drew a distinction between a *ritual*, on the one hand, and the *language of ritual*, on the other. "No doubt," the court noted, "*archanai* may be part of the religious practice, but we doubt whether language is so." Moreover, the HRCE orders did not rule out Sanskrit *archanais* completely: "Insistence on *archanais* being done in Tamil does not necessarily mean prevention of *archanais* being done in Sanskrit." Therefore:

> The circulars are not shown to affect freedom of conscience or the right to freely profess, practice and propagate religion. *Language is no part of religion* and it cannot be taken that unless religious matters are expressed in a particular language they cease to be religious or religious practices.[17]

Once again the state, here through the agency of the court, was defining what is essential to "Hinduism" or to "religion."

Apparently encouraged by the High Court's decision, the HRCE commissioner's office issued a new, "very urgent" directive in March 1974. Priests were continuing to resist performing Tamil *archanais*, the directive observed, and therefore "some arrangement must be made to help the general public."

> It is therefore suggested that in temples where the *archakas* (priests) are not anxious to perform Tamil *archanais* the *othuvars* may recite the verses and the *archakas* can offer flowers. In such cases a portion of the *archakas*' share must be paid to the *othuvars*. Wherever possible *othuvars* must be appointed in such temples. If there are no *othuvars* steps may be taken to appoint *othuvars* and a decent portion of the ticket collections may be given to them.[18]

Stripped of circumspection, this new directive was little more than a threat to priests that if they did not conform to the *archanai* orders the job would be given to non-priests, with an accompanying loss of income.

At least one deputy commissioner interpreted this directive to mean that Tamil should *completely* replace Sanskrit, and instructed temples in his jurisdiction accordingly.[19] This soon became known as the "Tamil *archanai* only" order, and led to a lively public debate. The Chief

[16] See Writ Petition No. 2666 of 1972, High Court of Judicature at Madras.
[17] Opinion issued 10 January 1974, High Court of Judicature at Madras.
[18] Circular dated 28 March 1974 included in Writ Petition No. 401 of 1974.
[19] *Hindu* (Madras), 20 April 1974.

Minister declared in May that the "Tamil *archanai* only" order would not be rescinded:

A section of the people claim that Tamil language has no divinity and hence there is nothing sacred about it. It is only to controvert this view, the Tamil Nadu Deviga Peravai and the HRCE Department have introduced Tamil *archanais*. The Tamil *archanai* only move is born more out of our love and attachment to Tamil than ill will or hatred towards any other language.[20]

It is not important here to review in detail the course of this public controversy. What is noteworthy is that most public discussion, at least in the press, centered on the government's political motives and on the "correctness" of *archanais* in Tamil, rather than on whether it was appropriate for a secular government to issue such orders in the first place. The *Mail*, for example, made no mention of the constitutional question in its editorial on the orders. Its primary criticism was that the government was trying "to force the pace" of historical change, a pace the *Mail* editors felt should be left to the worshippers. It had no objection *per se* to the government encouraging Tamil *archanais*:

Even the Sankaracharya of Kanchi Kamakoti Peetam has called upon his followers to give equal importance to Tamil *stotras* and hymns. The Government, therefore, in ordering performance of *archanais* in Tamil can be considered to have moved with the times. And having satisfied itself with the reform, it should have allowed the practice to get settled without the Government giving the impression that it is trying to force the pace. It is here the Government acted hastily.[21]

In June 1974 the Supreme Court of India stayed the operation of all the Tamil *archanai* orders pending a full review. This led the Tamil Nadu government to modify its position somewhat. In its affidavit filed with the Supreme Court, the government retreated from the "Tamil *archanai* only" order, denying that there was any intention to exclude Sanskrit altogether. The purpose of the commissioner's circular was to ensure only that worshippers had a choice. The "Tamil-only" order was an error on the part of an overly zealous lower official, and would be cancelled, it said.[22]

The government clearly hoped that this strategic retreat would save the earlier circulars of 1971. But late in August the Supreme Court placed a stay on all *archanai*-related orders until the whole issue could be reviewed. In the interim, temples were instructed to follow their traditional practices in so far as language was concerned.[23]

[20] *Hindu* (Madras), 3 May 1974.
[21] *Mail* (Madras), 20 April 1974.
[22] *Mail* (Madras) 21 June 1974; *Hindu* (Madras), 7 August 1974.
[23] *Mail, Hindu, Indian Express* (Madras), 27 August 1974.

An ecclesiastical organization

The state's commanding presence in religious affairs is also dramatically illustrated by the Deviga Peravai, an organization which for several years in the 1970s was spoken of as a nascent ecclesiastical structure for all south Indian temples. The HRCE founded, organized and indirectly financed the Deviga Peravai as part of its policy of Hindu reform and revitalization. With a few more years of state support the Peravai would possibly have been able to proceed on its own. But in fact the Peravai's vitality was always dependent on state patronage, and when this was withdrawn in the late 1970s, the Peravai underwent a crisis and nearly collapsed. The rise and decline of the Peravai's fortunes over the past two decades demonstrate how pivotal the state is for temple-related associations, and how governments do not hesitate to put this to political advantage.

The remarkable strength of the Peravai was built on a close, almost corporatist[24] relation to the state, on an ideology which skillfully combined sectarian strands in south Indian traditions with nineteenth- and twentieth-century social reform, and on a distinctive blend of traditional, charismatic and legal–rational authority. Let me elaborate these dimensions.

The close connection to the state existed from the very beginning. In 1966 the HRCE commissioner held a meeting with several *mathadhipathis* to explore how *maths* could do more in "active propagandizing." Particularly important at the meeting were the Kanchi Sankaracharya of Kamakoti Peetam, one of the most revered south Indian Brahmin leaders, and Kunrakudi Adigalar, at that time still a somewhat obscure non-Brahmin *mathadhipathi* in Ramnad. The result of their discussion was the decision to found the Deviga Peravai. According to former Congress Chief Minister M. Bhaktavatsalam, who attended the Peravai's inauguration meeting:

> The idea was that the *mathadhipathis* must closely associate themselves in the holy task of propagating the religion, rather than simply retiring and not coming out of the *maths*.[25]

In its annual report for 1966, the HRCE welcomed the Peravai as one of its "landmark" activities.

> [The Peravai was] constituted for conducting and propagating such religious activities in Madras State, as would help the Hindu masses to appreciate the

[24] On corporation, see Philippe C. Schmitter, "Interest intermediation and modes of societal change in western Europe," *Comparative Political Studies* 10 (April 1977): 7–35.
[25] Interview with Thiru M. Bhaktavatsalam, 5 February 1974.

greatness of the religion and strengthen their faith in the Hindu religion and enable them to lead the Hindu way of life in accordance with Hindu Dharma and Ethics ... This has been acclaimed by the public and the press as a great and successful landmark in the activities of this Department.[26]

The original idea of the Peravai was that all the prominent *mathadhipathis* – about fifty of them – would work closely to propagate and revitalize Hinduism. This proved a vain hope, however, as the organization foundered on the traditional jealousies and sectarian rivalries among these spiritual teachers. As the then HRCE commissioner put it later:

I approached the *maths* individually. They all resisted, except for the Dharmapuram Adheenam [the most prominent among the non-Brahmin *mathadhipathis*] ... The problem was the interrelations among the *maths* themselves. Dharmapuram will not have anything to do with Thiruvavadurai, who will not in turn have anything to do with Kunrakudi, who in turn doesn't get along with the Madurai Adheenam, and so forth.[27]

The Peravai turned inevitably to the HRCE itself to solve the problems. The HRCE commissioner became an ex officio vice-president in charge of "supervising the executive work of the society," an HRCE assistant commissioner was "lent" to run the Peravai's central office as secretary, and regional assistant commissioners became vice-chairmen of the Peravai district councils with council meetings held in the HRCE departmental offices.[28]

These links stopped short of making the Peravai a formal branch of the HRCE, however. The Peravai was registered as an independent society under the Indian Societies' Registration Act, and this has enabled the HRCE ever since to reject the criticism that it has a religious wing. Yet, the Peravai's connection with the HRCE was crucial, especially in financial ways. The Peravai asked temples to "donate" one percent of their annual incomes. Temple trustees were not overjoyed at this prospect, however, and many did so only after direct or indirect HRCE pressure. A deputy commissioner commented:

Actually, the collection is nonofficial; there is no official stamp of approval for that, and it would require an amendment to the HRCE Act, and the government has not done that. Under the original plan, the *mathadhipathis* are supposed to pay and support the Peravai. But in fact they do not; and that shows how much they care for religion ... Some temples are paying the one percent, although because of the nonofficial aspect many do not. Those that do pay, do so because

26 *Madras state administration report, 1966* (Government of Madras, 1967), pp. 340–1.
27 Interview with Thiru Sarangapani Mudaliar, commissioner, HRCE, 31 March 1974.
28 Tamil Nadu Deviga Peravai, *Constitution and rules* (Madras, n.d.). p. 4.

they have EOs who are interested and because of instructions emanating from our office.[29]

The EO of a major temple acknowledged that, calculated at one percent of the annual income, his temple owed the Peravai Rs. 75,000. His trustees, he said, figure that that amount could be put more beneficially in buildings or other income producing investments. When I asked what made some temples pay, and others not, he replied:

If they do not pay, you can assume that the temple trustees have enough power or influence at the government level already. If they do pay, it is because they can hardly refuse where our commissioner is the president.

The Peravai's secretary acknowledged that "collection," as he called it, was one of his major duties. Often, he said, he used his position as an HRCE official to cajole or threaten trustees into making a donation. With few exceptions, he said, temples will not pay unless he goes to them in person and uses his status as an HRCE officer.[30] One assistant commissioner summarized the situation from his perspective:

Two weeks ago a temple gave Rs. 2,000. Whenever the Secretary needs money, he comes out to the districts and tries to get it. The poorer temples rarely give . . . I myself do not collect. After all, I am in government service, and it is not proper for me to handle the finances of a religious organization.[31]

The total extent of temple payments is not public information and likely never will be; this is one of the advantages for the Peravai of being an independently registered society. The Peravai itself reported that over the ten years from 1966 to 1976, it received Rs. 17,77,831 (19,38,921 if *maths* are included). This represents an extraordinary sum, even though it is undoubtedly understated, and includes only those donations for which accounts were kept.

How, then, should the Peravai's connection with the HRCE be characterized? The Peravai was always legally separate, but organizationally and financially dependent. One Peravai member described the connection as one of "parallel organizations." An HRCE assistant commissioner, arguing that there was nothing improper going on, said that the "benefit of the department" was simply "loaned" to the Peravai. A temple EO described the payments made by his temple to the Deviga Peravai as "not statutory but obligatory." The last president, Kunrakudi Adigalar, described the Peravai as "quasi-government."[32]

29 Interview, 8 March 1974.
30 Interview, 21 April 1974.
31 Interview, 27 April 1974.
32 Interviews, 8 March 1974; 21 April 1974; 27 April 1974; 17 March 1974.

Kunrakudi's is a telling description, especially in light of the Peravai's meteoric rise and its equally precipitous fall. In its heyday, the DMK government made the Peravai's President, Kunrakudi Adigalar, a member of the Tamil Nadu Legislative Council. Many in Tamil Nadu questioned the propriety of this, believing that *mathadhipathis* should remain aloof and isolated from the world of active politics. Kunrakudi rejected this criticism on the grounds that he was in an unusually good position to advise the government and direct attention to religious concerns. But the government also made use of Kunrakudi Adigalar. When criticized, the government could defend its policies as supported by no less than a major *mathadhipathi*, and thus in a general way representative.

Kunrakudi Adigalar was President during the Peravai's most dynamic years. As *mathadhipathi* of a non-Brahmin *math* in Kunrakudi, Ramnad district, Kunrakudi's authority was at once traditional and charismatic: traditional because he was the successor to a long line of *mathadhipathis*; charismatic because of his closeness to the deity of the Kunrakudi temple, whose charisma he appropriated, and because of his great personal energy and confidence. He shaped the Peravai's goals, personally selected its officers, and most members were indebted and loyal to him personally.

The Peravai organization, however, was formally structured as a bureaucracy. Indeed, it is striking how thoroughly the Peravai, resembling in so many other ways a religious sect, adopted the elaborate and bureaucratized structure of a government department. There was a supervisory staff, close checking of accounts, organizational targets, fines if targets were not met, and, finally, a mass of paperwork. In 1976 there were 2,000 local branches (*sanghams*), 93,000 dues-paying members, and a paid staff of forty persons. The Peravai was well-funded, tightly organized, and approached its goals with close to evangelistic commitment.

The main unit in the localities was called a *sangham*, a Tamil word evoking the past glories of ancient Tamil literature, politics and culture. A book of *Constitution and Rules* governed *sanghams*, and spelled out their responsibilities. The most important activity was the "common worship scheme," to be held once a week. But there were many other responsibilities, some of them indicative of much more general political and religious purposes. For example, *sanghams* were to report any "Propaganda carried on in [their] area[s] against the Hindu faith or practices or any other criticism of Hindu tenets or beliefs"; see that temples were properly maintained; ensure that the temple cart festival was conducted, and "also see that all Hindu residents of all classes in the area take an active part in dragging the temple cart"; arrange visits to hospitals, jails and reformatory schools to distribute *prasadam* and give moral instruction; and start schools for children which would include moral and religious instruction "in accordance with the Hindu faith."[33]

In addition to these regular duties, the central office sometimes sent out special instructions, especially to advise *sanghams* on how festivals should be celebrated in the Peravai context. For example, the Madras office once issued a circular on the Sivaratri festival, instructing members to attend all four *abhisheka* rituals in their local temples.

Most of these activities went far beyond what can be expected of a voluntary membership. The Peravai therefore hired a set of local Peravai workers, called *samaiya pracharaks*, each of whom was in charge of a district or a portion of a district. Most *pracharaks* had a background in Tamil studies, either with a formal degree or some course work. They were chosen personally by Kunrakudi Adigalar, and were paid Rs. 220 to 250 per month, plus a Rs. 90 traveling allowance.

In the early years, a major task was to open *sanghams* throughout the state. The usual approach was to enlist the support of "leading persons" in the area, such as the *panchayat* union members or temple trustees. After their support was certain, the *pracharak* went on to enroll at least twenty-five persons. At the first meeting of the new *sangham* the *pracharak* would introduce the "common worship scheme," after which the membership would elect a president and a secretary. Dues were Re. 1.00 initially plus twenty-five paise annually. One-fourth of this was sent to the central Peravai office, in return for which the *sangham* received free religious pamphlets for all members. *Samaiya pracharaks* and *sanghams* sent monthly reports to the central Peravai office in Madras. Some indication of the range of detail expected can be gathered from Table II.

At the regional level the Peravai was staffed by *muthalmai pracharaks*, who received and then forwarded *samaiya pracharak* and *sangham* reports to the central office. *Muthalmai pracharaks* also oversaw *sangham* financial accounts and, if necessary, disciplined the *samaiya pracharaks*. *Muthalmai pracharaks* were also appointed by Kunrakudi Adigalar. They were mostly older persons with social standing and experience. Frequently they were retired and able to devote their full attention to the Peravai.

The Peravai's line of organization, then, extended from the president and secretary in Madras, through the divisional *muthalmai pracharak* supervisers and the *samaiya pracharak* workers, to the local *sanghams* or

[33] *Constitution and rules*, pp. 9–12.

Table II *Information filed by Samaiya Pracharaks in monthly reports* (selected)

1. *General.* Number of days spent on tour in cities and in villages; number of days spent for starting new *sanghams*, for speeches, for improving Hindu society.
2. *Membership.* Number and names of new members, renewed members, discontinued members.
3. *Sanghams.* Number of new *sanghams* established in villages and in towns, including information on their registration numbers and membership fees.
4. *Sangham Activities.* Meetings held for common worship, for religious instruction, for special events; resolutions passed and actions taken.
5. *Publications.* Details on publications sold, subscriptions collected and free pamphlets distributed.
6. *Information on People.* (a) People interested in or contacted on behalf of the Peravai (e.g., "big shots," volunteers, government officials or teachers); (b) Names and addresses of government officials: District Collector, District Revenue Officer, Superintendent of Police, Assistant Superintendent of Police, Health Officer, Education Officer, District Cooperative Officer, Social Welfare Officer, HRCE Assistant Commissioner.
7. *Hindu Social Service.* Details on visits to slums and homes of poor people and on activities undertaken (e.g., education, cleaning up slums); on visits to hospitals to distribute *vibuthi* (sacred ash); on visits to jails for moral instruction; on special events; on conflicts in local Hindu society related, e.g., to poverty, education, drinking facilities, and on actions taken; on visits to Peravai Hindu schools; on ladies clubs, youth clubs and children's clubs visited or started; on assistance given to temples (e.g., cleaning, festival supervision).
8. *Growth.* Suggestions for extending and encouraging the services of the Peravai.

cells in the villages and cities. Parallel to each of these levels and integrated at each point was the HRCE's organization.

The marked tendency towards central coordination and direction was to some extent balanced in each *sangham* by individual features and emphases. In Tiruchirapalli, for example, the *sangham* based in the Bharat Heavy Electricals Company met each week for common worship and singing at the BHE plant; they did not, as a group, go to temples other than once a month on cleanup expeditions. The Mangayakarasi Mahalir Manram, a women's *sangham* in a fashionable Madras suburb, emphasized Tamil hymn singing led by the Peravai *othuvar*, cooking classes, interior decorating classes and education for preschoolers. The group also constructed a special building at a cost of Rs. 75,000 as a center for these activities. The President of the Tiruchirapalli District Peravai directed his *sangham's* activities towards visiting jails to teach and distribute *vibuthi* (sacred ash) brought from the temples.

A few words on ideology and programs: the strength of Peravai ideology derived not from its being particularly new, but from having linked themes of medieval *bhakti* and Saiva Siddhanta with more contemporary movements of politics and social reform. In an interview,

Kunrakudi Adigalar stated that the main object was to "promote the associational life of Hindus," to create a "mass movement" in which people from different castes and classes come together in "common worship." He quite explicitly viewed the stress on group worship as a departure from traditional temple worship:

In the traditional system, a single man goes to do *puja* for himself and his family, and pays some money for that, whereas now the ideal is to create an associational life, without prejudice to the old system. Under the old system, the cart festival was the only symbol of the congregation in traditional Hinduism.

The *Vara Vazhipadu*, or "common worship scheme," was thus the main activity and requirement for local Peravai units (*sangham*). The *Constitution and Rules* specified that each *sangham* should "unite all the Hindus in a common worship, without caste or creed,"[34] and that common worship should occur weekly:

The *sangham* shall organize *Vara Vazhipadu* once every week on a day convenient to the people of the area and this worship shall be conducted at a convenient open space. The *Vazhipadu* may be conducted on different dates at different places to suit the convenience of the people living in different localities or hamlets so that the people living in those localities or hamlets may not have to travel long distances for reaching the place fixed for worship.[35]

Each *sangham* had to find someone qualified to lead the group and teach the scriptures. In addition, an *othuvar* visited the new *sanghams* to teach their members Tamil hymns.

The "common worship scheme" assumed a set of underlying principles and practices shared by all "Hindus," despite differences of sect, caste and locality. Kunrakudi Adigalar referred to the "Tamil subsect of Hinduism," but acknowledged that the common worship especially "promoted" non-Brahmin Saiva Siddhanta. This is obviously of some importance since it means that the HRCE, through the Peravai, was indirectly supporting a particular religious sect. More generally, Kunrakudi saw religion as a "positive influence" on the character of the people, as distinct from the civil law, which was "negative" in the sense that its effect was achieved by punishment, or the threat of punishment.[36]

Kunrakudi also wanted to overcome the disorganized structure of Hinduism as a whole. In 1974, he spoke frequently about creating an "ecclesiastical organization" modeled on the Jesuit order. A full-time

[34] Ibid.
[35] *Constitution and rules*, pp. 9–10.
[36] This and subsequent quotations from Kunrakudi Adigalar come from a series of interviews conducted in March and April 1974.

sannyasi (holy man, ascetic) would be attached to each temple to conduct common worship, "look after the ceremonies of Hindu families, and take care of Hindus generally." The Peravai *sannyasis*, unlike ordinary *sannyasis*, Kunrakudi emphasized, would have the ideal of "service to society, of helping the society."[37] Here again, Kunrakudi and other Peravai members mentioned the example of Jesuit fathers. *Sannyasis* would be recruited from among college graduates, who would then take a three year training course at the Peravai's Sri Poompugar Peravai College of Indian Culture in Thanjavur district.

In 1974, Kunrakudi Adigalar was working actively to initiate this program. At an organizational meeting called to discuss problems of untouchability, he remarked that the *sannyasis* would be important forces for change. He announced that the program would start with one-hundred trainees, paid for by the Dhandayuthapani Swami temple, Palani, the wealthiest temple in Tamil Nadu. "The government has approved the plan," he added. Presumably, this meant that the HRCE had approved the added expenditure from the Palani *devasthanam* budget.

The clear implication of these projects was to play down the importance and necessity of the Brahmin priest. Kunrakudi argued that temple priests are needed not for worship but only to dress the idols and take care of them and the temples. "You needn't have them there to perform worship for each person. Each person can do it on his own." And he was also hostile to Sanskrit as the language of worship, for this too requires again an intermediary – the knower of Sanskrit. When the Chief Minister Karunanidhi defended the *archanai* orders, he included the Deviga Peravai as a sponsor.

By now it should be clear that, at the end of its first decade, the Peravai was an organization of considerable purpose and energy. In the mid 1970s, the Peravai's Madras office was a center of activity and meetings. Its concerns included, in addition to those already discussed, social reform, untouchability, intercaste marriage, temple entry, *devaram* instruction, religious instruction in schools, and an extensive publication program.

Kunrakudi's aspiration was to have a central ecclesiastical body for Hindus. One plan was that the government constitute a Hindu Religious Council. State religious policy constantly experiences difficulty, Kunrakudi argued, as a result of bad advice given to the government, primarily by secular lawyers. The Hindu Religious Council would replace lawyers as the state's primary adviser. It would be composed of

[37] Kunrakudi noted that from his early childhood in Ramanathapuram district he had been influenced by the example of "service to society" on the part of Jesuit fathers.

mathadhipathis, religious leaders "elected by the legislature," learned men and scholars. It would have statutory authority to advise on and consent to any new law affecting Hindu religious practices and personal law.[38] Not surprisingly, Kunrakudi envisioned the Deviga Peravai as the nucleus of the new Religious Council, and reported in mid 1974 that the DMK government supported the basic proposal.[39]

The flow of support between the HRCE and the Peravai was never in only one direction, however. At its peak, the Peravai occupied a position at which the HRCE and high government influence, on the one hand, and charismatic authority and local politics, on the other, converged. Perhaps inevitably, the HRCE turned to the Peravai as a way of overcoming the fragmented authority, conflicting theories of the temple, and external political pressures to which its administration was subject. The Peravai had an enviable organization in the villages, and Kunrakudi was the only person associated with the HRCE with independent power and authority, rooted partly in his charisma as a spiritual teacher and partly in his connection with top levels of political power. The Peravai was thus able to handle temple disputes expeditiously, avoiding the HRCE's lengthy procedures.

For example, in a temple near Tiruchirapalli, a dispute arose whether the deity should be taken through Harijan streets during the annual temple festival. The Tiruchirapalli city *sangham* brought the case to Kunrakudi's attention, and he intervened successfully on the Harijans' behalf. Kunrakudi observed that in cases such as this the Harijans prefer not to go to the HRCE. Bureaucracy moves slowly and according to its own procedures, he said. There would have to be an inquiry, at which the local caste Hindus would deny that what the Harijans claimed was customary was in fact customary, nothing would be proved, and nothing would come of it. Personal intervention is more fruitful.

Projects could take on major proportions when Kunrakudi became interested. In April 1974 he mobilized a *sangham* to clean a neglected

[38] The Hindu Council's decisions would be based on the original *sastras* and Vedas, Kunrakudi noted. He had no doubt, he said, that when these ancient scriptures are reexamined it will be found that "a casteless society is the main and fundamental tenet of the Hindu religion." Up to now, he argued, these texts have been interpreted by lawyers, and most lawyers are controlled by "orthodox people" whose views are contrary to those of the most ancient scriptures.

[39] The parallel between Kunrakudi's relationship to the DMK government and that of the more classical relationship between Hindu kings and Brahmin spiritual advisers was striking, and occurred to me over and over again during my research. I brought this parallel to Kunrakudi's attention and asked whether he would view his position in this light. Without hesitation, he replied, "Not at all. The rajahs were devout and spiritual men, whereas these men are agnostics. The DK and DMK believe that religion itself is an obstacle to [achieving] Tamilaham."

village temple. Kunrakudi had visited the neighborhood in a different connection, but while there discovered that the local temple, a fairly large structure, was unswept and uncared for. Weeds and shrubbery were growing in the cracks of the stones on the roof which, if unchecked, would soon weaken the whole structure. As I was told the story later, Kunrakudi was so distressed by the sight that offered a glass of milk he refused, saying that he would come back in a week with the Deviga Peravai and clean the temple up, after which he would be willing to take the milk.

A week later, he returned. The local Peravai units, with three dozen or so members, from Tiruchirapalli turned out in force. Many were engineers and technicians from the Bharat Heavy Electricals plant near Tiruchirapalli.[40] Also in the entourage were various government officials and local politicians. Happening to be in the area, I went along for the day-long excursion.

Throughout the morning and into early afternoon the group worked with picks, knives, brooms and ladders. They cleared away the foliage, washed the temple floors, cleaned out the cistern and removed years of accumulated oil and grease from temple sculptures. The project nearly concluded, Kunrakudi met with local leaders in an attempt to resolve the problems and rivalries which had led to the temple's current condition.

Mats were spread out in a shaded corridor and Kunrakudi held an informal inquiry. His presence was an important local event. The temple was beset by disputes among the trustees and between the temple and tenants. The managing trustee had come, along with other prominent officials, including the panchayat board president, the Revenue Divisional Officer, a DMK party man, several large landowners and other interested persons.

After some discussion, Kunrakudi appointed a temple renovation committee. Included were the managing trustee (president), a large landowner (secretary), and five vice-presidents, carefully chosen to represent the major castes of the area. With an eye on the need to raise money for the renovation project, Kunrakudi tentatively added the names of two businessmen from Tiruchirapalli city.

He then explored immediate problems. He heard, without making any particular comment, allegations that a previous trustee had criminally mismanaged the temple; such allegations are frequent. He was more concerned to learn that although the temple owned some fifty

[40] Members of the Arul Neri Thiru Kuttam were also present on this occasion. The ANTK was founded by Kunrakudi in the 1950s to oppose E.V. Ramasamy's "Black Shirt" followers, who were then engaged in a campaign of breaking street idols.

acres, it was receiving rent from only two or three acres because of tenants' claims (presumably under one of the *inam* abolition acts) that the land titles were theirs. The temple was severely underfinanced, and priests were being paid the equivalent of five months' wages for twelve months' work. The Revenue Divisional Officer was able to provide precise information on the status of the tenants' claims then pending in the courts. Unable to do more at the moment, Kunrakudi promised to come back and try to resolve the problem with the tenants.

Finally, Kunrakudi inquired carefully whether political party differences among the newly appointed renovation committee members would hinder the committee's ability to operate. Assured that they would not, he said he would inform HRCE officials regarding the meeting, and seek their approval for the renovation plan. Finished for the time being, the whole group sat down for a late lunch.

I am not able to say how long the agreements reached at that meeting lasted, or whether the temple's immediate financial difficulties were overcome. The point here is that an inquiry was held, various parties were heard, and a working coalition was formed. Kunrakudi's arrival in the village occasioned a kind of small summit meeting among "leading persons," to use his phrase. Present at one time or another during the day were the Block Development Officer, the personal assistant to the Collector, the Revenue Divisional Officer, the panchayat board president, the president of the local agricultural credit society, the managing trustee of the temple, and several other local politicians and wealthy agriculturalists. Had there been no Peravai cleanup, it is unlikely that local politicians, landowners, government officials and temple authorities would have come together under a single roof to discuss an otherwise obscure and unknown temple in Tiruchirapalli district.

Analysis of the Deviga Peravai during its heyday is incomplete without reference to the social, cultural and political movement known to scholars as the Dravidian or non-Brahmin movement. I have left this dimension to the end, however, in order that the Peravai not be seen only within this context, or reduced to it. The matter is more complicated.[41]

Certainly, the Peravai's emphases have much in common with the public image of the DMK. Common to both is a devotion to Tamil and

[41] Of the several works relating to the non-Brahmin movement and the rise of the DMK party, see Marguerite Ross Barnett, *The politics of cultural nationalism in south India.* (Princeton University Press, 1976); Eugene I. Irschick, *Politics and social conflict in south India: the non-Brahman movement and Tamil separatism 1916–1929* (Berkeley: University of California Press, 1969); Rudolph, "Urban Life;" Spratt, *DMK*; Ryerson, "Ramasamy Naicker"; Robert L. Hardgrave, *The Dravidian movement* (Bombay: Popular Prakashan, 1976).

an emphasis on Saiva Siddhanta, a religious system identified by many Tamils as the original system of the Tamil culture, unadulterated by northern, Sanskritic influences.[42] Kunrakudi's conviction that caste distinctions are absolutely contrary to Hindu principles (properly understood) is echoed in the DMK's oft-repeated quotation from Tamil, *onrai kulam, onrai devan* (one community, one god).

It is also important to note, however, that these emphases are not in themselves particularly new. The concern over the religious integrity of temples has been regularly voiced since the nineteenth century, often by orthodox Brahmins. The same is true of temple entry, Harijan uplift and the language of worship. The HRCE encouraged the use of *othuvars* during Congress rule in the 1950s and, if anything, this policy was pursued more vigorously at that time than it has been in more recent years.

Yet it remains true that the Deviga Peravai and the religious policies of the 1970s had overtones of the non-Brahmin and anti-Hindu movements. DMK rhetoric stimulated opposition to reforms which might otherwise have found wider acceptance. In the Tamil *archanai* issue, for example, divisive social and cultural hostilities could not but be brought to the surface when the DMK Chief Minister announced:

> If the right to perform the *archanai* in Tamil is denied, Sanskrit considered as Devabhasha [language of God], and along with that God and religion also, will be driven out from Tamil Nadu to north India.[43]

Or when he stated more bluntly:

> If the gods in the south India cannot tolerate Tamil *archanais* let the gods move to the north India.[44]

The clear alliance between the Peravai and the DMK government (and the Congress government before it) made cynical interpretations inevitable. Many saw the Peravai as simply one more vehicle for ambitious individuals to make good connections and enhance their influence and status. The Peravai was analyzed sociopolitically as a Peravai for non-Brahmins or, more precisely, for the upper non-Brahmin castes who historically have controlled the DMK. There were few, if any, Brahmins in the Peravai, just as there are few Harijans in it.

The union of religious reform, personal advancement, party politics and ideology was epitomized in the person of Kunrakudi Adigalar

[42] On the importance of Saiva Siddhanta in the early construction of non-Brahmin ideology and consciousness, see Irschick, *Social conflict*, pp. 292–3.

[43] *Dinamani* (Madras) 28 September 1971, translated and cited in Supreme Court of India, Civil Original Jurisdiction, Writ Petition No. 401 of 1974, p. 18.

[44] Reported in the files of the South India Archaka Sangham.

himself, *mathadhipathi* of a non-Brahmin *math*. Historically, Tamil Nadu governments have always been sensitive to the views on public policy held by the orthodox Brahmin *mathadhipathis*, especially the views of the Kanchi Sankaracharya of Kamakoti Peetam. This is unlikely to change. But Kunrakudi Adigalar may have extended the boundaries of legitimate advising. The government's patronage went formally and publicly to Kunrakudi, the Peravai was referred to as an authority in religious policy, and both were elevated to unprecedented prestige in modern Tamil politics.

In the final analysis, however, the state's patronage was crucial. This became clear in 1976 when the state withdrew its recognition and support. The Emergency brought President's rule in Tamil Nadu, the DMK government went out of power, as did the particular complexion the DMK had given to religious policy. The new government, the President's Advisers, was immediately swamped with long dormant competing proposals and policies. A variety of ordinances related to temple affairs was passed, designed to wrest control of temple matters from those associated with the DMK. One of these ordinances attacked the Deviga Peravai, after which the Peravai's collapse was quick and nearly complete.[45]

In late April 1976, the Parliamentary Consultation Committee visited the state and heard scathing attacks concerning what was alleged to be the ten percent contribution temples were making to the Peravai. On 1 May the President's Advisers announced that these contributions would stop immediately and that a full scale inquiry would be instituted. This was followed in rapid succession by the resignation of Kunrakudi Adigalar from the Presidency, and the resignation of the HRCE commissioner from the governing body of the Peravai. Reshuffling occurred for a time, until finally in late 1977 the HRCE took charge of the Peravai's press and buildings, and stated that if the Peravai was to continue in the future, it must receive regular contributions from the *mathadhipathis*, as had been the original plan. The HRCE absorbed into its staff a number of the approximately forty *pracharak* workers who were thrown out of work by all this.

When I visited the Madras Peravai offices in 1981, I found that the buildings were closed, looked after by a lone watchman, who is the only regular Peravai employee left. When I met Kunrakudi Adigalar and asked him what had happened to the organization, he made the simple but revealing explanation that the "present regime is not interested in the Peravai." However, he added on a brighter note, he had met recently

[45] *Hindu* (Madras), 2 May 1976.

with the HRCE minister, who had been encouraging about starting the organization up again. Kunrakudi added emphatically that this time the connection with the government would not be as close. He nonetheless waits for a green signal from the state before attempting a revival.

Conclusion

In religious policy the state's primacy and authority stand out in bold relief, uncomplicated by the sharp interdepartmental rivalries and outside pressures characteristic of governance or economic policies. The political context is shaped fundamentally by "high stateness." Indeed, the state is able, in corporatist-like fashion, more or less to structure political participation to suit its own convenience. All agencies and individuals associated with the state – the HRCE, the courts, the cabinet, the legislature – are in positions to articulate compelling, inherently legitimate definitions of the public interest. The state's dominance affects all other groups: their vitality, support, strategies and even survival. All struggle for the state's patronage, despite the fact that many in practice dislike, ignore and even resist state policies. In temple religious policy the constitutive authority of the Tamil Nadu state stands out in bold relief.

In principle, of course, temple religious policy is legally constrained by the HRCE Act and by the Indian Constitution. But actual HRCE policy, despite the lip service paid to "noninterference" and "secularism," shows that these constraints are not treated with any great respect. We have noted several instances in which legal restrictions have been ignored. The major example is the Deviga Peravai, which was intimately bound up with the HRCE but legally registered as an independent society. Indeed, the evidence of this chapter suggests that the HRCE recognizes few, if any, restrictions on its intervention in temple religion. Commissioners tell priests how to conduct worship; circulars are sent altering ritual language; the Peravai, with HRCE backing, sets out to found an ecclesiastical organization for all temples. In each case, the HRCE or its representatives are imposing *their* definition of "real Hindu beliefs" and "correct" ritual.

It is clear also that the administration of temple religion, like HRCE administration generally, has a political dimension. It is one more vehicle by which the temple becomes an arena where the complicated forces which make up the multiple levels of Tamil Nadu politics are played out: individual ambition, village factions, state political parties and ideological and social movements. The Deviga Peravai is particularly revealing here, illustrating the interactions of temple, state and society. In previous chapters the triangular pattern of these interactions was obscured by attention to interagency rivalries and the complicated history of temple governance and economy. The Deviga Peravai, however, was almost autonomous from legal control and other branches of the government, and was unburdened with history. Its political dimension thereby became more prominent, and the structure of state–temple–society interactions emerged clearly.

8

Religion: controlling the priesthood

From the beginning of its administration, the HRCE has made temple priests a target of its administrative efforts. Not that priests have ever posed a threat to overall HRCE control, as have trustees, the courts and the BOR, or even that priests play a particularly large role in temple economy and governance. The HRCE's focus on priests derives from its definition of the temple as fundamentally religious and public. It believes that the priest is the temple's central functionary and that his activities, more than those of anyone else, define the core of the institution. The care or lack of care with which priests conduct daily *pujas*, periodic festivals and other rituals, such as marriages and *archanais*, is seen as a critical index of the temple's overall health.

What have been the effects of HRCE administration on the position and status of priests? Is there any general pattern in the way their interests have been affected over a half century of HRCE administration? How have the priests represented and defended their interests? Have they been able effectively to oppose threatening policies? These questions inevitably raise the issue of India as a secular state. The last chapter suggested that high stateness gives the HRCE considerable latitude. Are there any limits, self-imposed or constitutional, to the control the HRCE exerts over the temple priest, the functionary whom the department itself acknowledges to be preeminently religious?

These questions are explored in this chapter. The answers are complicated, and will require attention both to constitutional questions and to the temple priest's status in Hindu society. A useful way to begin the discussion is with a fairly dramatic government policy: a law to abolish heredity as a qualification for the priesthood.

Abolishing the hereditary priesthood

In 1970 the Tamil Nadu legislature passed a law opening the temple priesthood to "qualified" persons irrespective of caste and birth. The law was framed as simply a social reform measure. Its attempt to remedy disabilities based on caste and traditional restrictions could be construed as just one more in a long line of such measures over the past century. The law was clearly intended to change the general practice and understandings of south Indian society and culture. The assumption, presumably shared by generations of Tamils, that caste and birth were part and parcel of the priesthood was no longer to be true. Concretely, however, the law was widely believed to have been designed specifically to attack the Brahmin priests in large, orthodox temples, and to encourage lower caste members, particularly Harijans (formerly untouchables), to enter the priesthood. Certainly the law's most immediate impact was on the Brahmin priests (*archakas*), who traditionally came to their positions by virtue of their *jati* (birth, sub-caste) and inheritance. The law attacked the security of their livelihood, and their sons' assumed right to be priests if they chose. The demoralizing effect on the *archaka* community was accentuated because it came on the heels of the Tamil *archanai* orders.

It should be noted at the outset that the *archaka* act was not prompted by an explicit demand from the worshipping public. The measure was introduced by the DMK government as a government bill, and was not accompanied by the public debate one would expect over a reform of such magnitude. Yet there was no significant political reaction or protest either, whether from the general public or from those groups and political parties usually most vociferous in their opposition to the DMK. The law could probably have been implemented without serious political disruption had the Supreme Court of India not intervened.

Social reform, efficiency and religious integrity

From the state's point of view, the 1970 *archaka* law could easily be defended on three grounds: social reform, administrative efficiency and religious integrity. In the "Statement of Objects and Reasons" attached to the bill, the DMK government urged that the law be seen as a social, not a religious reform.[1] Like so many other reforms of the twentieth century, this reform would bring Indian society closer to the democratic, egalitarian ideal, since the priesthood would be "open to candidates irrespective of caste, creed or race."[2] In an indirect reference to the Deviga Peravai, the "Statement of Objects and Reasons" also envisioned a day when an "ecclesiastical organization," hitherto absent in Hindu-

[1] Tamil Nadu Hindu Religious and Charitable Endowments (Amendment) Act, 1970. The bill was introduced in Tamil Nadu Legislative Assembly on 30 November 1970, and was passed on 1 December 1970. For an account of the debate, see *Hindu* (Madras), 2 December 1970.

[2] This view was expressed in numerous conversations with DMK leaders in 1973–74. For an early defense of the measure, see the speech by the Minister for Religious and Charitable Endowments, reported in *Hindu* (Madras), January 1971.

ism, would be set up to provide formalized educational training in religious scriptures and rituals for all candidates for the priesthood.[3]

Technically, the *archaka* act abolished the hereditary priesthood simply by reclassifying temple officeholders. The existing classification, under the HRCE Act of 1959, grouped all hereditary personnel, including *archakas*, in a separate category because they enjoyed special rights to their offices and special privileges. One concrete implication of the existing category was that *archakas* had special appeal rights to the HRCE commissioner against disciplinary action or dismissal by temple trustees.[4]

The 1970 *archaka* act simply created a more inclusive classification. All "officeholders and servants," without further distinction, were made subject to the temple trustees in matters of appointment and discipline with limited, but common, rights of appeal. The word "hereditary" was simply deleted from the lexicon of temple administration. This effectively abolished the hereditary priesthood. The priest, who heretofore had been a special sort of person in the temple, became at the stroke of a pen an ordinary "officeholder and servant." To ensure that there be no doubt about this, the bill's framers added a special explanatory clause: "The expression 'officeholders or servants' shall include *archakas* and *poojaris*."[5]

For the HRCE, reclassification is an aspect of efficiency and therefore of its protective function. Administration is improved when diversity is reduced and captured in a few basic, universal categories. But the effects are seldom neutral in human terms. For *archakas*, indeed, classification was the issue of overriding importance. Priests, who regarded themselves as distinct from other temple functionaries and from priests elsewhere, found themselves suddenly placed under a common rubric which threatened not only well-established legal rights and immunities, but their economic security and long term social status as well.

The 1970 law was not the first time under the HRCE that an effort was made to group priests with other temple functionaries. A previous instance occurred in the 1930s when the HRE Board was coping with what it called the "vexing problem" of the north Andhra *archakas*. The HRE Board had discovered soon after its establishment in 1925 that *archakas* in some districts of present-day Andhra Pradesh performed two roles. Apparently, this region of the Presidency, unlike others, did

[3] Quoted in the judgment of the Supreme Court of India, Seshammal and Ors. etc., etc., v. State of Tamil Nadu, (1972) 3 S.C.R. 820.

[4] HRCE Act, sects. 55, 56.

[5] These sections, in their original and amended versions, are contrasted in (1972) 3 S.C.R. 821–2.

not have a separate office of trustee; *archakas* combined in themselves the functions of priest and trustee. The *archakas* conducted the rituals as elsewhere, but also looked after temple lands and finances, accountable within the temple to no one but themselves. Obviously they had unusual power, wealth and prestige.

In the HRE Board's view, this situation was unacceptable, an "anomalous and unjustifiable" combination of two offices. Temple organization in Andhra should look like temple organization everywhere else in south India. Combining both threats and incentives over a period of nearly a decade, the HRE Board gradually forced the Andhra *archakas* to renounce their claims to the trustee function. New trustees were put in charge of the temples, and the *archakas* were demoted to "their legitimate place as servants of the institutions," as the HRE report put it, in order to "improve the general management" of the Andhra temples.[6]

In all its policies affecting priests the HRCE rejects the criticism that it is instituting changes from above. The effect, it argues, is simply to reestablish Hindu practices in their uncorrupted purity. In the case of the *archaka* law, for example, it argued that caste restrictions in the priesthood were not characteristic of earlier south India; each individual could approach the deity on his own behalf. It defended the Tamil *archanai* and Andhra *archaka* policies on much the same grounds: The HRCE was simply encouraging earlier Hindu practices to reemerge.

The HRCE's policies towards *archakas* are shaped also by the concern to protect the temple's spiritual integrity, which they see as threatened directly by the priests. HRCE officials believe that the *archakas* are rather poor protectors of Hindu ritual. This feeling seems to be shared widely by the public. Priests are repeatedly described as dishonest, self-serving and basically ignorant about the rituals they routinely perform; they mutter impressive-sounding but unintelligible phrases, often leaving out crucial parts of the ritual. Priests are constantly making "mistakes," unbeknownst to the devotees and often even to themselves. HRCE officials rarely hesitate, then, to "correct" the priests.

In summary, the 1970 *archaka* law received impetus from at least three directions, each suggesting a concrete dimension of protection. Reclassifying the *archakas* as "temple office-holders and servants" would increase bureaucratic control of recruitment and discipline. Opening the priesthood to all castes, particularly to Harijans, would promote

[6] G.O. 1455 L & M 25 March 1929 10. The Board's *Annual reports* for the years 1926–36 include detailed accounts of the Board's dealings with the *archakas*.

egalitarianism and equal opportunity, recapturing at the same time complementary strands in medieval religious history. Abolishing hereditary recruitment would permit more systematic religious training, thereby enhancing the temple's religious purity. It was anticipated that this reform would lead to a full-fledged ecclesiastical organization regulated by the state.

Associational weakness and dependence on the state

I turn now to the political reaction to the 1970 law and to the handicaps *archakas* face in representing their interests, beginning with a rephrasing of the question asked at the beginning of this chapter: Although the *archakas* were the group most intimately affected by the 1970 law abolishing hereditary priesthood, they were unable to mobilize an effective political opposition to the law. Why was this so?

Archakas have been nominally organized for nearly four decades. The South India Archaka Sangham (SIAS) was founded in 1948 when the bill later enacted as the HRCE Act of 1951 was under consideration. The SIAS submitted memorials to the government on those parts of the bill of particular concern to priests. It was, thus, an interest group which emerged in response to potential changes in public policy.

The SIAS's records of its early years through the 1950s give a picture of fairly vigorous activities.[7] Many petitions were sent to the government; attempts were made to get more representation on governmental bodies dealing with temples; and a long-term project was underway to have sacred *agama* texts printed so that they could be distributed to *archakas* fairly inexpensively. The focal point of the SIAS's activities was the annual conference, usually held during the winter months in Madras. Meetings were held for two or three days and were addressed by government ministers, members of the Legislative Council, newspaper editors and trustees of prominent temples.

However, this picture of organizational vigor, drawn from the files of the SIAS, is probably more appearance than reality. Much of the initial excitement in the SIAS's early years was due to the patronage of prominent government officials who attended its annual conferences. The stature of an organization in south India is measured in part by the stature of the guests who honor it at its conferences and

[7] I should like to express my appreciation to the officers and members of the South India Archaka Sangham, particularly to its Secretary, Sri Swaminatha Gurukkal, and its President, Sri Ganesa Gurukkal. This section relies heavily on the files and historical records of the SIAS.

"functions," but in this case the patronage, and the excitement it caused, obscured a lack of energy and cohesion in the SIAS from the beginning. Indeed, the fact that government recognition was so important illustrates one of several ways that the SIAS is dependent on the state for meaningful action.

Attendance at the annual conferences tends to correlate with the stature of the government officials who are willing to attend. After the DMK government came into power in 1967, for example, attendance dropped significantly. Undoubtedly this poor attendance was a result of the fact that the meetings were being ignored by the DMK government and its ministers. Only about 75 priests came to the 1974 conference, mainly from Madras city and nearby districts, despite the fact that this was during the period in which the *archanai* orders and *archaka* law were posing the most direct and serious challenges priests had faced in years. By way of contrast, when the AIADMK government came to power it adopted a far more conciliatory posture towards the temples generally and towards the SIAS in particular. It is surely no accident that attendance at SIAS conferences and at its regional meetings rose at the same time. In 1981, for example, upwards of 200 *archakas* attended the January conference in Thanjavur, with many having come in from other districts. Yet there were no pressing agenda items.

One obvious manifestation of SIAS weakness is the fact that few of its original projects, though reemphasized again and again over the years, have been successful. Representation on government bodies has not been achieved and, although a few *agamas* were printed, they have remained for the most part undistributed. Most significantly, the SIAS has not been able to create among *archakas* the sense that they belong to a united, cohesive interest association. It has not been a center for communication among geographically and socially isolated Brahmin priests and, with a few exceptions, it has not provided major services to its members. The SIAS has been dominated by a few officeholders, usually enjoying reelection each year. Like so many other *sanghams* and *sabhas* in south India, the SIAS basically surfaces at its annual conference where resolutions are passed calling for some *government* action to solve problems the conference has highlighted.

Strong, vital organizations are crucial for representation in pluralist political systems, particularly for groups, such as the *archakas*, which lack other economic or political bases of influence. But for an interest group to be strong, several conditions must be met. The membership needs to have a sense of identity as a social community. The organization needs a sense of integrity and independence, particularly in relation to state authority. There should be a confidence that the organization's goals and perspective on public policy are worthy and defensible, however much they may be in tension with those of others, including those of the state. And, when the membership is small and marginal, it requires allies in other sections of society.

These conditions are not met in the SIAS. *Archakas* are insecure, individually and collectively, regarding their social and political status; they lack a sense of common identity, integrity and independence from the state; and they lack powerful allies in society. A central reason for these facts is that, throughout at least the modern period of south Indian history, *archakas* have been dependent on the state. Though based in the first instance on economic and material factors, dependence has had important intellectual and psychological ramifications. Especially, dependence has resulted in subjective identification with the state, rather than alienation from it, even though *archaka* interests are clearly at variance with state policies. Let me elaborate these points, starting with the issue of material dependence.

Historically, the temple priests have depended for income on two major sources: offerings and *puja* fees, and land. Data are not available on the relative importance of these two at any given time, and the position undoubtedly varied from temple to temple and region to region. *Archakas* believe, however, that priests in the past enjoyed a secure income from land. The belief is as important as the facts, which remain unclear.

When *archakas* talk, as they do, about the extensive land holdings their forebears enjoyed they are talking primarily about *inams*. The fact of central importance is the state's discretionary power to take away, as well as to give, *inams*. Throughout the nineteenth and early twentieth centuries, the Revenue Department's view was that the *inam* system was a cumbersome and often unjustifiable drain on state revenues, and the department tried to guard what it perceived to be the state's paramount interests. This meant that regional and local revenue officers acted as watchdogs to see that the *inamdars* kept up the services.

The point here is that, under the *inam* system, priests did not control a crucial aspect of their material livelihood: how much land they had, and how much income the land brought. Nor, for that matter, did temple trustees or the worshipping public. The control lay with the state. *Inams* originated from the state and the state maintained its prerogative over them.

Moreover, government bureaucrats defined *inam* rights and adequate "service" on the basis of rules and procedures so complicated that they were seldom comprehended in their entirety even by administrators with years of experience, much less by priests uninitiated into the mysteries of the BSO.[8] And ever changing judicial decisions and administrative reassessments of old regulations periodically gave twists to *inam* regulations which were even less accessible to priests.

The long-term effect is that *archakas* feel uncertain, insecure, dependent and weak. The actual implications of a new law or bureaucratic regulation are seldom clear. This was true in recent years, for example, with land reforms, some of which adversely affected priests and some of which merely threatened to do so. *Archakas* are convinced that their collective material welfare is inexorably declining. Historical comparisons are difficult, of course, and we know that it is by no means the case that all priests in the past were supported directly from land. It is nonetheless true that those today who do have land probably have less ability than had priests in the past to keep it, and less knowledge about what they must avoid doing in order not to violate one or another of the regulations on which their tenure is based. Whether or not priests in the long run will be able to possess land will be determined at least in part by the future of land reforms, about which the priests are already, with reason, pessimistic. Several government departments have recommended that temple lands be given to the peasants who cultivate them, and that the temples be given cash subsidies from the state instead. This recommendation was supported in 1974 by the prominent politician Jaya Prakash Narayan, as he began his national campaign against the government of Prime Minister Indira Gandhi.[9]

Despite all these threats to their material livelihood, *archakas* have been unable to formulate a collective strategy to address the problem. The fact is that the bases for joint action are few, whereas the economic, social and institutional forces which separate and divide are many. This can be illustrated briefly in several ways, starting again with land.

Most land which priests regard as "theirs" was once *inam* land. But *inam* is only a loose category which includes a wide range of arrange-

[8] For the period up to 1913, these rules and the difficulties surrounding them are described in Mr. Moir's report. Later revisions, through 1948, may be traced in Chapter IV of the *Standing Orders* of the Board of Revenue. This volume was kept up to date, subsequent to 1930, by means of "correction slips" pasted in the binding of the relevant page. The multiplicity of "correction slips" on any given page is evidence of the frequency with which *inam* regulations changed – sometimes almost monthly.

[9] *Indian Express* (Madras) 28 December 1973. Commenting on Narayan's well-publicized statements on this matter, the *Mail* (Madras) wrote an editorial entitled "Rapacious". "Why is it that everybody who sets up business as a 'Reformer' of one kind or another suggests that the temples should be deprived of their lands? Perhaps the last man one would expect to find in this rapacious company . . . has now joined in making this demand . . . The tyranny of the impersonal State and its machinery is as grievous to the common man as the tyranny of the big landlord or the big industrialist" (29 December 1973).

ments.[10] Each *inam* was surrounded by distinct conditions; in this sense each former *inamdar* has a relationship with the state distinct from those of his "fellow" *inamdars*. A single change in *inam* regulations would seldom affect more than a small minority at any given time, although the effect on that minority might be severe. Moreover, the revenue bureaucracy has never had the resources to implement systematically every change in the regulations. Implementation tends to occur on a case-by-case basis, often when a particular *inam* comes to official attention for some other reason. It is thus to the advantage of each *inamdar* priest to keep a "low profile," avoiding actions which might draw the notice of government officials.

Social divisions also inhibit collective action. *Archakas* do not form a social community in a subjective sense. Broad sectarian lines divide them, such as those between Vaisnavites and Saivites. These divisions are expressed politically and socially in terms of competing claims of status, prestige and power. That *archakas* come together in the South India Archaka Sangham (to the extent that they do) is more the result of external pressure and circumstance than it is of an enduring sense of fellow feeling. Individual identities are shaped by factors such as sectarian affiliation, sub-caste, the prestige of particular temples, family standing and so forth.

The work situations of *archakas* also divide them. Each temple is unique, possessing a distinct sacred history, tradition and customs, economy and sacred calendar. An *archaka's* life and consciousness are circumscribed by the physical and mental isolation imposed by the life cycle of his temple. Each *archaka* is subject to the directives of his trustees and EO. The relationships he develops with these officials are crucial to his security and welfare and, though governed in broad terms by HRCE regulations, are nonetheless highly specific in character. Here too we can say that each *archaka* has an individualized dependency relationship with the state, since both the EO (directly) and the trustee (indirectly) represent state authority.[11]

It is therefore not surprising that the SIAS has remained a loose association of mostly inactive members. The major activity as we have seen is the annual conference at which resolutions are passed, usually in the form of demands on the state. But these resolutions are nonetheless

[10] See ch. 4 above.

[11] This is somewhat less true, to be sure, in the larger temples with large priest populations, although here my information is only impressionistic. Smooth administration in the larger temples requires that the EO establish more formalized and regulated relations with *archakas* as a group. *Archakas*, in turn, often have leaders to represent them collectively or, at least, to represent their particular faction. But this kind of organization seldom extends beyond the boundaries of a single institution.

very illuminating. Though few have led to concrete results, the annual resolutions reveal much about *archaka* fears and preoccupations. Especially, they indicate how *archakas* handle their dependence on the state intellectually, and how they view themselves.

The first thing which strikes the reader is that *archakas* share with the HRCE the central concept of protection. The term "protection" occurs repeatedly in SIAS conference resolutions, speeches and conversations.[12] On more than one occasion, in fact, the Hindu Religious and Charitable Endowments Act is mistakenly referred to as the Hindu Religion Protection Act. Not surprisingly, however, the meaning which protection has for the priests is not quite the same as that which it has for the HRCE. For the *archakas* protection primarily means preservation: preserving the rights and customs *archakas* associate with their own status:

> The government should protect the *archakas*' rights in receiving *prasadam* as instructed by the *agamas* and *sastras* of our ancestors.

> Vaisnava and Saiva religious opinions should be made known to the ... HRCE department in order to protect their rights.[13]

Archakas of course realize that preserving ancient custom alone does not guarantee protection in modern circumstances, and so many of its other resolutions deal with more mundane matters. For example, the SIAS has appealed for working conditions which are "on par with government servants," including provisions for leave and holidays. It has also asked for formal representation on the Legislative Council and on the Advisory Committee to the HRCE to "advise in the matter of legislation on religious institutions." Most striking, though here they have much in common with other groups in contemporary India, the *archakas* have asked to be included in the "backward classes" list:

> The *archaka* community should be included in the backward classes list and they should be provided free education in the high schools and colleges, reservation of seats in the public institutions, financial help, employment facility, etc.

More than those above, however, the following SIAS resolution encapsulates the issue about which *archakas* feel most threatened and regarding which they believe government policy to be crucial. The government is petitioned to support the *archaka* claim to a higher status than that of their colleagues within the temple:

[12] In Tamil: *padukappu, kapparru.*

[13] These and subsequent resolutions in the following pages are selected from the several dozen SIAS resolutions passed over the years from 1948 to 1973.

> Lastly, it is submitted that the position and status of the *archakas* deserve to be improved. Most of the *archakas* are thought and in some cases treated just as ordinary temple servants. Their position in the conduct of daily worship and other matters are [sic] almost forgotten. This matter requires earnest and serious consideration at the hands of the government.

With only minor changes in wording, this resolution has been passed almost every year since the SIAS was founded. Moreover, the issue it deals with is, in the final analysis, identical to that raised by the 1970 *archaka* legislation.

Priests are profoundly insecure regarding their rank and social status. Mention has already been made of reasons why the public holds *archakas* in low regard: their relative poverty, their alleged ignorance of the *agamas* and their inconsistent performance of rituals. To these must be added the fact that the caste position of the Brahmin temple priest in south India is itself ambiguous.

Although *archakas* are usually classified in the Brahmin *varna*, other Brahmins consider them inferior, question the genuineness of their Brahmin status, and tend to view them with a mixture of bemusement and contempt. Many are quick to observe that *archakas* "get paid" for worshipping, the implication being, on the one hand, that the monetary aspect vitiates the integrity of the worship and, on the other, that *archakas* cannot rank highly since they are willing to receive money ritually from all castes, even the most lowly. One Brahmin lawyer expressed this view notwithstanding the fact that he was representing *archakas* in several legal suits. He repeated what he described as a "commonplace" that *archakas* are *mattyana panchamma*, which he translated as meaning "until he takes his daily bath, the *archaka* is of the fifth and lowest class of the Hindu hierarchy." The uncertain status of the temple priest was also observed in Thurston's classic ethnography of south India. Of the *gurukkals*, or Saiva Brahmin temple priests, he wrote:

> They are temple priests, and other Brahmins regard them as inferior, and will not eat with them. Even in temples, the *gurukkals* sprinkle water over the food when it is offered to the God, but do not touch the food. They may not live in the same quarters with other Brahmins. No *agraharam* will ever contain a *gurukkal*'s house. There should, strictly speaking, be at least a lane separating the houses of the *gurukkals* from those of the other Brahmins.[14]

[14] Edgar Thurston, *Castes and tribes of southern India*, 7 vols. (Madras Government Press, 1909) vol. 1, p. 347. For two more recent analyses of the complex issues involved in the status of Brahmin temple priests, see C.J. Fuller, "Gods, priests and purity: on the relation between Hinduism and the caste system," *Man* (NS) 14:459–76; and Arjun Appadurai, "The puzzling status of Brahman temple priests in Hindu India," *South Asian Anthropologist* 4 (1983):43–52.

The problem is that *archakas* internalize society's negative view of themselves. Their sense of dignity is fragile and their self-esteem is low. Like their critics, *archakas* condemn themselves for being poorly trained and educated, for their ignorance of the scriptures and for their "mistakes" in ritual. They know that their *varna* status is problematic, and that society generally (not only other Brahmins) views them skeptically, is critical of their habits and behavior, and shuns close association with them.

Characteristically, the *archakas* look to government to bolster their position. A major concern is professional training:

This conference requests the government, administrative officers, the *dharmakartas* of large temples, and the Religion Protection Commission [*sic*] to establish *agama* colleges in every district and *taluk* in order that the *archaka* youth may have *agama* education.

The government should distribute *agamic* scriptures and pamphlets to the *archakas*.

There is obviously a tremendous paradox in these resolutions. The *archakas* are demanding not a traditional but a modern form of education, with all the associated trappings of formal classes, syllabi, examinations and diplomas. These are features apparently felt as essential for respectability. It is thus not surprising but nonetheless ironic that in 1953 the SIAS passed a resolution that comes close, in detail if not in spirit and ultimate purpose, to the DMK's 1970 *archaka* law itself:

Some five years or so after the establishment of such schools (for the instruction in *agama sastras* and Sanskrit), no *archaka* should be permitted newly to commence doing *archaka* service *even though he may have a hereditary right* without producing a diploma or certificate that he has undergone the prescribed course of instruction in one of such institutions [emphasis added].

But education cannot change the fact that the *archakas*' status is problematic and ambiguous in caste terms. And this brings us to the second area in which the SIAS looks to the state for support: their classification within the temple, an area which we have already seen was crucial in the 1970 *archaka* legislation.

To support their claim to high status within the Hindu hierarchy, temple priests rely on their highly visible and pivotal role in temple worship. A special dignity and honor is attached to them, they believe, because of their unique privilege in touching the temple idol. They also function as intermediaries between the devotee and the god. The frequency and emotional feeling with which this argument is reiterated makes it worth quoting at length:

The principal functionaries in these institutions (i.e., temples), who have more than any others contributed to the preservation of their sanctity, their glory and their importance, are the *archakas*, – the *battars*, the *gurukkals*, the *pujaris* and the like. Their position in these institutions is unique and at the same time onerous. They alone have the right to enter the Sanctum Sanctorum of the temples. They alone have the right to touch the idol, bathe the idol and bedeck the idol with clothes, ornaments and flowers. They alone have the right to offer worship, offer *naivedynam*, and perform the *archanai*. At the same time, it is they that have to keep care of the priceless ornaments of gold and precious stones worn by the deities and the rich silver ware used in the sannadhies. The *archakas* serve as the medium through whom the public make their offerings, or their *archanais* to the deity. This important office is held by selected families whose members acquire the qualifications required by the *sastras* by tradition from their ancestors and it is only within these families, from generation to generation, for hundreds of years the office has descended. In the distribution of temple honors, they enjoy certain preferential rights. The *archakatvam* office is a spiritual rather than a secular one. Under these circumstances, the holder of the office cannot be treated in the same manner as the holder of other minor or secular offices.[15]

The first part of the above passage draws a picture from which it is difficult not to conclude that the *archakas*' function is indeed a special and elevated one. The point of crucial importance to the priests, which is made in the final three sentences, is that this *elevated status should have concrete social and political consequences*. In other words, the dignity associated with caring for the idol is in the final analysis empty unless it shapes other, human, relations. It should lead to special treatment and special respect, to higher rank in the temple hierarchy. *Archakas* should have "preferential rights" in honors and other perquisites and should not be treated in the same manner as other temple functionaries.

Temple society, as we have seen in earlier chapters, is inherently competitive. Though the state cannot shape status completely it probably has a greater potential here than any other single social institution. EO decisions, HRCE regulations and government laws matter. The EO especially plays a crucial role in the daily making and unmaking of status as he arbitrates disputes among temple factions over various honors and privileges and, in a thousand other ways, shows deference to some and not to others.

It is thus only natural for the *archakas* to be preoccupied with the otherwise mundane question of their classification in HRCE regulations. The 1970 *archaka* law classifying priests as just "officeholders

[15] "Memorandum submitted by the archakas of Madras and south India to the Select Committee, Madras Hindu Religious and Charitable Endowments Bill, 1949" (dated 29 March 1949).

and servants" was unusually blunt and extreme. But it embodied a set of attitudes which *archakas* are very familiar with and which they do not really expect to reverse.

Up to this point, I have tried to show that the *archakas*' weakness is rooted in economic, social and administrative structures largely independent of and predating the specific political context of recent times, during which the DMK and AIADMK parties have been in power. But we must also recognize that the particular emphases in both the 1970 *archaka* law and the *archanai* policies of the same period bore the distinctive stamp of the DMK: extreme enthusiasm for the Tamil language, sympathy for egalitarian forms of worship, and lingering anti-Brahminism. It is unlikely that any other major party would have initiated these policies in quite the same form. Many in Tamil Nadu believe, in fact, that the real force behind the 1970 *archaka* law was E.V. Ramasamy Naicker, the "grand old man" of the Tamil non-Brahmin movement, whose unrelieved hostility to established religion, to Brahmin dominance and to casteism was well known.

As the government in power, the DMK commanded a majority of votes when the *archaka* bill was presented to the legislature. But the bill's smooth passage was further ensured by the fact that the Deviga Peravai's leader, Kunrakudi Adigalar, supported the measure and that, with one exception, no major opposition party actively made an issue of the legislation. The exception was the Swatantra Party, which by this time had only marginal strength.

The lack of party opposition must be put in the context of the overall structure of party politics in Tamil Nadu during this period. The DMK's rise to power was accompanied by a gradual expansion of its support base among the non-Brahmin and ideologically mobilized sections of society. From the mid 1950s, this led to a gradual shift in the Congress party's strategy such that, in ideological terms, both the DMK and Congress were often appealing for the support of the same constituencies.[16]

The *archaka* law was presented to the public as a reforming, egalitarian measure. On public platforms, DMK spokesmen stated their intention of appointing Harijans as priests in the great orthodox temples hitherto dominated by Brahmin priests, a clear appeal for mass support from the lowest sections of the population. The Congress party had split in 1969, and both factions were struggling for supremacy against one another and against the DMK. In these circumstances, little was to be gained by

[16] For more detailed analyses of this period, see V.K. Narasimhan, *Kamaraj: a study* (Bombay: Manaktalas, 1967); Robert L. Hardgrave, *The Dravidian movement* (Bombay: Popular Prakashan, 1965); and P. Spratt, *D.M.K. in power* (Bombay: Nachiketa Publications, 1970).

championing the cause of the *archakas*, who were few in number and insignificant politically. Individual legislators were free to speak out against the measure, and some did, but the parties as organizations did not mount vigorous opposition.

Nor did the *archakas* receive expected support from other organized groups typically concerned with legislation of this kind. Particularly noteworthy was the absence of active support from the Hindu Temple Protection Committee (HTPC). By the early 1970s, the HTPC had emerged as the most vocal and persistent critic of temple administration by the DMK government. The HTPC consists of a loose and sometimes unlikely coalition of smaller groups who express concern for the fate of Hinduism under the "atheist" DMK. Significant ties exist between it and Hindu revivalist groups, such as the Madras branch of the Rashtriya Swayam Sevak Sangh (RSS). It also includes some former members of the DMK's parent bodies, the Justice Party and the Dravida Kazhagam (DK). In the early 1970s, the HTPC demonstrated frequently against government policies it considered harmful or insulting to Hinduism and temples. Sometimes its agitations were mounted independently, other times in conjunction with the "Hindu Mission," an action arm associated with the RSS. One might expect that the HTPC would be a prime candidate for leading an opposition to the 1970 law and, indeed, the HTPC has often expressed a general support for SIAS.

On the other hand, the HTPC's membership and self-definition place considerable distance between it and the *archakas*. The members are drawn almost exclusively from upper non-Brahmin castes, and many were drawn to the HTPC when they found their political fortunes in decline with the rise of the DMK. The Madras branch of the HTPC, in fact, is headed by persons who were members of the Justice Party during the period of E.V. Ramasamy Naicker's leadership, and could not be expected to have any special concern for Brahmin priests. The RSS also is not committed to a hereditary priesthood. In interviews in 1974, RSS members expressed support for the 1970 law, if not for what they perceived to have been its underlying motivation. They pointed out that caste restrictions on physical contact with temple idols (on which *archakas* base much of their case) are the exception rather than the rule in India, and expressed approval of less restrictive north Indian practices.

In late 1970 and early 1971, the *archaka* law was rather low on the HTPC action agenda. Attention was directed at two issues of more transitory importance, but which the HTPC hoped would discredit the DMK in the coming elections. A hue and cry was raised over the "T. Nagar Vinayaka," an idol whose sudden appearance in a field in the T.

Nagar area of Madras was surrounded by mystery and for whose equally sudden disappearance the government was alleged to be responsible.[17] An even more prominent focus of controversy was the "Salem Incident," a procession in Salem town in which the black-shirted followers of E.V. Ramasamy Naicker allegedly testified to their atheism and contempt for religion by beating pictures of Hindu deities with their chappels (sandals).[18] The great energy expended by the HTPC over these issues was in marked contrast to its response to the *archaka* law. The committee made no mention of the legislation in the resolutions of its annual conference in 1970, although the bill had just been passed a few days before.

The Supreme Court ruling

The position we have reached may be summarized as follows. State policy frequently conflicts with the interests of *archakas*. This was certainly the case with the 1970 legislation abolishing the hereditary priesthood. We would expect this conflict to be reflected in the respective interpretations of protection held by *archakas* and by government, and to some extent it is. On the other hand, priests are highly dependent on the state and do not at root reject the government's prerogative over religious policy. To this extent, their interpretation of protection complements rather than conflicts with that of the state.

This analysis substantially explains the routine pattern of temple administration, the terms in which state policy is ordinarily legitimated, and the difficulties encountered in mounting political opposition to government policy. But the analysis is still incomplete so far as the 1970 *archaka* act is concerned. As is true in so many areas, there remains the fact that state authority is fragmented, and especially that the courts are always ready to exercise jurisdiction. Several *archakas*, some in their private capacities and some nominally representing the SIAS, did in fact appeal the new law to the Supreme Court of India.

There are, then, *archakas* who do not accept unequivocally their relation to the state, or at least to the state as it presently exists. These priests argue that the traditional temple–state relationship has little relevance any more. The modern Indian state is based on principles, such as secularism and democracy, which are different from those which

[17] The story of the T. Nagar Vinayaka was covered thoroughly by the Madras newspapers *Mail* and *Hindu*, September–December, 1970. See also, Charles A. Ryerson, "Religious culture and the 1971 elections in Tamil Nadu" (Paper presented at the Society for South Indian Studies, Philadelphia, 1980).

[18] On the controversy, see *Hindu* (Madras), January–March 1971.

historically governed the state's role as protector. Also, temples today are linked up with the larger political party system. The result, these *archakas* argue, is that policy is framed less to benefit religious institutions and more to further the short-range electoral and patronage interests of political parties. This is demonstrated especially by the fact that temple funds are often spent inappropriately and sometimes illegally to enhance the immediate goals of politicians. The state is no longer a protector of temples; it has become an exploiter of temples.

For priests with this point of view, the courts offer distinct strategic advantages. For one thing, effectiveness in the court does not require the kind of political and organizational strengths which the *archakas* so conspicuously lack. To be sure, litigation is expensive, but in the 1970 case the *archakas* found a famous advocate who provided much of his service free of charge. Also, judicial decisions are necessarily informed by different assumptions from those of the government: either by those of the court's well-articulated theory of the temple, or by constitutional understandings of "secular" religion–state relations, or by both. Indeed, in an interesting and somewhat ironic reversal, the *archakas* based their appeal more on modern constitutional arguments, such as the separation of religion and state and the inviolability of religious custom; whereas the government based its public defense more on prerogatives enjoyed by the state in south Indian history and on the traditional duty of protection.

To read the Supreme Court's decision on the 1970 *archaka* law is to enter a world the assumptions of which are quite different from those of the *archaka* memorials or government statements discussed so far.[19] No reference is made to protection, nor is there mention of the economic and political dependence of priests on the state. Instead, the Court's decision was shaped basically by three questions: Do the *agama* scriptures govern the ritual in the temples concerned in the case? Is the hereditary principle of appointment a well-established "usage" and therefore possibly inviolable, or is it a mere "matter of convenience"? Is the appointment of a temple priest a religious or a secular act?

Regarding the first question, the Court found that the *agamas* indeed regulate who may touch the temple idol and officiate at worship, and that the restrictions which these scriptures impose are protected by the Constitution:

> The *archaka* undoubtedly occupies an important place in the matter of temple worship. Any state action which permits the defilement or pollution of the image by the touch of *archakas* not recognized by the *agamas* would violently interfere

[19] Seshammal and Ors. etc., etc., v. State of Tamil Nadu, (1972) 3 S.C.R. 814–34.

with the religious faith and practices of the Hindu worshipper in a vital respect, and would, therefore, be prima facie invalid under Article 25(1) of the Constitution.[20]

Thus, the Court confirmed that only members of particular "denominations," e.g., those born of Vaikhanasa parents in Vaikhanasa Vaisnava temples, are competent to officiate in the large class of temples governed by the *agamas*.

Regarding the second question, the Court found that, legally, the hereditary principle of appointment must be regarded as a usage peculiar to the temple. The government had argued to the contrary that heredity was merely a "matter of convenience," a rule of thumb procedure whereby the next qualified person can be easily selected. But the court found otherwise:

It, however, appears to us that it is now too late in the day to contend that the hereditary principle in appointment was not a usage. For whatever reasons whether of convenience or otherwise, this hereditary principle might have been adopted, there can be no doubt that principle had been accepted from antiquity and had also been fully recognized in the unamended section.[21]

So far, the Supreme Court's decision moves in the direction of supporting the *archakas*. It affirms that the *agama* prescriptions against defilement of the image must be respected, thereby restricting the priesthood to members of a few families. It also affirms that hereditary appointment is an established usage in the temples, a finding which means that heredity cannot be summarily abolished without further investigation.

But the third question remained to be answered: Is the act of appointing a temple priest a religious or a secular act? The 1970 *archaka* law, it must be remembered, did not directly attack the *agamas*; it only changed the appointment procedure for *archakas* to make it common with that of other officeholders and servants. The crucial question in deciding the constitutionality of the act, therefore, was whether the government was competent to make this change. To affirm that hereditary appointment was a usage was not enough:

The real question, therefore, is whether such a usage should be regarded either as a secular usage or a religious usage. If it is a secular usage, it is obvious, legislation would be permissible.[22]

Here, the Court's decision was doubly disappointing to the priests. Not

[20] Ibid., 826.
[21] Ibid., 830.
[22] Ibid., 831.

only did it answer that appointment was essentially secular, it also tied this answer to a series of comments affirming that *archakas* were basically ordinary servants in the temple. Should the *archakas*' status be considered essentially similar to that of a *mathadhipati*, the spiritual head of a monastery? Definitely not, in the view of the Court:

The *archaka* has never been regarded as a spiritual head of any institution. He may be an accomplished person, well versed in the *agamas* and rituals necessary to be performed in a temple, but he does not have the status of a spiritual head.[23]

On the contrary, the *archaka* is essentially a "servant." The Court quoted prior decisions as well as the HRCE Act to demonstrate that the *archaka* is subject to the trustee: a trustee can inquire into an *archaka's* conduct and dismiss him for misconduct, for example. From these observations on the status of the priest the Court drew its conclusion regarding the nature of the act of appointment:

That being the position of an *archaka*, the act of his appointment by the trustee is essentially secular. He owes his appointment to a secular authority.[24]

Thus, although the *agamas* impose restrictions on who can be a priest, and these restrictions are protected on religious grounds by the Constitution, the appointment act itself is nonetheless secular. Apparently recognizing that the resulting position was somewhat paradoxical, the Court reiterated it several times:

It is true that a priest or an *archaka* when appointed has to perform some religious functions, but the question is whether the appointment of a priest is by itself a secular function or a religious practice.[25]

Thus the appointment of an *archaka* is a secular act and the fact that in some temples the hereditary principle was followed in making the appointment would not make the successive appointments anything but secular ... That after his appointment the *archaka* performs worship is no grounds for holding that the appointment is either a religious practice or a matter of religion.[26]

In summary, the Court upheld the constitutionality of the 1970 *archaka* act, but did so in such a way as to render the act ineffective. Its ruling contained a tension which did not suggest a single course for public policy. It affirmed that the government could abolish heredity as a principle of priestly appointment, but it also affirmed that the state was bound not to violate the regulations laid down by the religious *agamas*.

[23] Ibid., 831–2.
[24] Ibid., 832.
[25] Ibid., 831.
[26] Ibid., 832.

The *agamas*, in turn, declare that only persons following certain traditions and born of certain priests are competent to perform worship, and this obviously comes to much the same thing as heredity.

In the final analysis, the Court's decision left neither side satisfied. The government's view that the 1970 act was constitutional was confirmed, but confirmed in such a way that its immediate political and ideological purposes were rendered ineffective. In 1974, the Tamil Nadu legislature passed a resolution that the Constitution must be amended so as to ensure effectiveness of social reform legislation. On the other side, the priests achieved their short-range objectives in that their tenure and the tenure of their sons within the temples were not immediately threatened. But they were discouraged that once again their claim to having a higher status than that of "servants" was denied.

Conclusion

In this and the previous chapter I have argued that interest representation must be understood in the context of a generalized dependence of groups such as the Deviga Peravai and SIAS on the state for recognition, support and organizational resources. The strength of the HRCE is based on its clear legal authority, its administrative power to strengthen or undercut the positions of temple actors, and the continuity between its position at the head of temple administration and that of governments and rulers in the past. Tamil Nadu governments have shown repeatedly that they are willing to interpret the principle of protection liberally in order to legitimate quite specific religious reforms. Groups which might oppose the state's religious policy are automatically on the defensive. The state is able to designate some associations, as was done for the Deviga Peravai for nearly a decade, as *the* legitimate representatives of society's interests in the temple, and to relegate groups such as the SIAS to the status of "special interest" groups.

The weakness of the SIAS as in interest association derives first from the economic, political and ideological control the HRCE has over the *archakas*. The probability of priests forming a strong organization is also lessened by sectarian divisions among *archakas*, their social and political isolation from society generally, and their lack of self-esteem. In the early 1970s the prominence of the Deviga Peravai weakened the position of priests further. The HRCE promoted the Deviga Peravai as a partner in encouraging its version of "correct" Hinduism. Groups such as the SIAS and HTPC were dismissed as disruptive pressure groups, ordinarily ignored or else manipulated in ways that advanced HRCE goals.

This chapter has also suggested, however, that the SIAS, and presumably other associations, have learned skillfully to manipulate fragmented state authority to achieve ends otherwise rejected by the HRCE and the government. The HRCE may rely ideologically on the principle of protection, but protection is a principle of little relevance in the court. The standard for the court is not the current vagaries of public policy, but the court's own theory of the temple, the law and the Indian Constitution. The latter, especially, focuses on the necessity to ensure freedom of religious practice and enunciates "secularism" as the state's basic posture.

Ordinarily, the dependence of priests on the HRCE translates into a ready acceptance of the state's dominance in temple affairs, including temple religion. Yet, the fragility and seemingly inexorable deterioration of their position have led *archakas* more than once to challenge the government in the courts. This dual posture – at once accepting dependence through "protection" and challenging dependence through "secularism" – is surely inconsistent. But it is merely a specific instance of the fragmentation characterizing the political, legal and administrative institutions of modern India, caused by the diverse historical and cultural elements introduced in the last two centuries. As we have seen in previous chapters, this fragmentation has hindered effective HRCE administration, enabled corrupt trustees to exploit temples for personal gain, and perhaps rendered ineffective many social reforms properly on the public agenda, such as land reform. As the example of the *archakas* and the 1970 *archaka* act illustrates, however, this same fragmentation has also ensured that channels exist for otherwise powerless groups to defend themselves from powerful bureaucracies and governing political parties, to safeguard local religious customs, and to articulate interests and values which would otherwise go unheeded.

9
Conclusion

Over the half century of HRCE administration, temples have been transformed from localized, more or less distinct institutions into an organized and constituent part of the Tamil Nadu political system. Social reform, cultural protection and efficiency – ideals closely linked with modernity and the modern state itself – justified and promoted this reconstruction. Yet conflicts over the theory of the temple, and the constitutional limits on interference have repeatedly made difficult any mechanical incorporation of temples into the state's structure and have given a significant twist to temple administration. The HRCE has the advantage of high stateness, but in practice its administration is shaped by the struggle for jurisdiction among state agencies, by the specific issues involved (economy, governance or religion), and by the changing shape of political ideologies and opposition.

At the outset of the nineteenth century, most south Indian temples were embedded in and circumscribed by their respective localities. Each temple drew on local history, geography and memory to create for its village or town a sacred history, sacred geography and sacred story which were distinct and unique. These local traditions were based on regional and great Hindu traditions, but were altered and given special meaning in their local variations. The local temple was also organizationally specific. Authority and management were shaped by local distributions of power and wealth, by the special ways its priests and trustees were selected, and by other factors such as certain conditions attached to whatever *inam* lands the temple enjoyed. The local temple thus had an individual character and identity, and ordinarily its affairs were conducted with a fair degree of autonomy. This was the broad picture, though there were of course some exceptions, particularly among temples which were religiously prominent and regionally important.

Since the late nineteenth century the south Indian temple has been on the defensive, normatively, organizationally and politically. Social reformers have attacked it on the grounds that its practices are corrupt, obscurantist, caste-ridden and contrary to "true" Hinduism and "genuine" religion. Bureaucrats have threatened it by favoring a pattern of management which is standardized, centralized and depoliticized. Central politicians and policy-makers have eroded its autonomy through their attempts to direct the purposes to which its material and symbolic resources are put. At the beginning of the nineteenth century, those groups and individuals involved in the struggle for wealth, status and power tended to come from the temple's locality. More recently, the struggle for place has been linked to the struggle among state-level politicians and political parties. Priests, tenants, landlords, hereditary trustees and others find that their fortunes are increasingly affected by a centralized bureaucracy over whose policies they have little or no control.

These challenges to the local temple are part of a larger transformation in the macro-character of the south Indian state since the mid nineteenth century. Locality has become linked with province and province with nation.[1] Central authority has expanded its scope and penetrated Indian society, overcoming pockets of resistance by political, administrative and even military means. Disparate forms of politics, economy and culture have been brought under central control through expanded bureaucracies working out of Madras city.

The state's effort to control temples did not just "happen" in an impersonal, evolutionary sense. Politicians, bureaucrats, judges and colonial rulers (to mention only a few) had a hand in it, acting at different levels of the political system and for different ideological, institutional and political purposes. Centralization culminated in the HRE Board and in its successor, the HRCE. This extensive bureaucracy was created specifically to make the local temple more responsive to state and national policy. The clear design was to modify local traditions, customs and practices to bring them into line with the political interests and ideological preferences of westernized elites, bureaucrats, political parties and social reformers. The effort to draw the temple to the center was systematic, elaborate and self-conscious.

To a striking extent, however, the local temple has withstood the challenge of centralization. The nineteenth-century temple remains intact today to a degree which is remarkable given the fact that the forces of the modern state have been arrayed against it, in different ways and with varying degrees of intensity, for over a century. Most of the "problems" which Regulation VII of 1817, Act XX of 1863, Section 92 of the Civil Procedure Code, the HRE Act of 1927 and the HRCE Act of 1951 were designed to address and "solve" are still present: corrupt trustees, poorly trained priests, irregular trustee succession, excessive

[1] For a good description of this process, see Christopher J. Baker, *The politics of south India 1920-1937* (Cambridge University Press, 1976), esp. pp. 322 ff.

expenditures, internal conflict and factionalism and, in general, the use of the temple for personal wealth, status and power.

The local temple's resilience in the face of the challenges by the modern state is an instructive example of administrative ineffectiveness in postcolonial states. This study has highlighted several dimensions of the problem.

In part, the causes of the temple's resilience are related to what scholars of political development have called the crises of penetration, integration and centralization.[2] The task which central policy-makers in Madras set for themselves was that of penetrating and integrating under central control over 50,000 separate and locally based institutions, many of them in isolated, relatively inaccessible regions of the state. This was an enormously complex task. In simple organizational terms, it assumed a level of technical and bureaucratic capacity which is only now being approached. On top of this, persistent conflict has characterized the relations between central administrators and those over whom they would exert control. Penetration, integration and centralization are not simply technical, value-neutral processes. By definition, they imply the destruction of the often unique patterns which historically have prevailed in the locality, and are informed by the ideological preferences and material interests of individuals, groups and institutions at the center. It is therefore natural that centralization and integration are resisted by local groups and individuals who see that they have much to lose and little to gain at the hands of central policy-makers.

Thus, the task of centralization would have been difficult in any case. Seriously complicating administration and accentuating the likelihood of ineffectiveness were the conflicts, examined throughout this book, among operative ideals or theories. In the universe of temple administration there is no agreement on such basic issues as what the unit of administration, "the temple," really is, how its relations to society and politics should be analyzed and described, and what the obligations and rights of the state towards it are.

The underlying source of these conflicts over the theory of the temple can be found in British colonial rule. When they first came into contact with south Indian temples, British administrators were faced with new and unexpected phenomena. They quickly had to make "sense" of these phenomena in order to handle the social, political and economic problems that temples posed. Because of their different institutional starting points, British administrators (and later Indian administrators

[2] Leonard Binder et al., *Crises and sequences in political development* (Princeton University Press, 1972).

following in their intellectual footsteps) in the BOR, court and HRCE came up with very different images of what goes on in temples, and how temples should be regulated. These images drew on and combined different aspects of the western past and south Indian reality. Some features of the resulting theories were fairly congruent with local processes and perspectives, while others were radically different.

The HRCE's operative ideal is the most sharply different. Its assumptions – that temples are "public," "religious" and "non-political" – place great distance between it and the localities. The traditional temple is an institution where public and private, the religious and the secular, and power and authority meet and become nearly indistinguishable. The temple is fundamentally a locus, often the central locus, for distributing and redistributing local resources which make for power, wealth and status. The boundaries between temple and society are fluid and permeable, and temple processes are an integral part of social and political processes generally.

The court's approach is more congruent with the traditional temple. The court is more responsive to local customs and traditions, and less committed to separating the temple from society and politics. The court is willing to adjudicate the struggle for power and place in the temple in terms of the historical concept of "shares." Indeed, because it tends to define "shares" in terms of the western concept of "rights" and because it respects "custom and usage," the court is favored by temple actors interested in consolidating positions already achieved.

The BOR's approach falls midway between those of the court and the HRCE. On the one hand, the BOR was basically sensitive to the special cultural and historical character of the south Indian region. It took pride in the *Standing Orders* precisely because the regulations managed to capture and depict the extraordinary complexity of the south Indian land tenure system. On the other hand, the BOR is a bureaucratic agency whose policies are formally responsive to changing government priorities. More than the HRCE or the courts, the BOR defined itself unambiguously as a state agency whose primary responsibility was to the state's material and strategic interests. In the twentieth century, this has come clearly at the overall expense of temples.

The discrepancies between these four theories of the temples – those of the locality, HRCE, court, BOR – go a long way toward explaining the pervasiveness of jurisdictional conflict, the diversity of norms and expectations, and the general ineffectiveness of HRCE administration. State authority over temples is fragmented. The HRCE does not have exclusive jurisdiction over temple affairs and, because of this, crucial aspects of its administration depend on cooperation among several government agencies. This cooperation seldom exists.

Fragmented authority regularly presents temple actors with opportunities to undercut HRCE policies and goals. Temple actors know that they can manipulate jurisdictional disputes in such a way that their chances of achieving their goals, of making a successful claim to a part of the temple's resources, are enhanced. Manipulating jurisdictions means manipulating political cultures, i.e., rules and procedures which channel demands and regulate conflict, and languages and concepts which define "reality," issues and problems.

Quite naturally, temple actors choose to work within the jurisdiction where they have the greatest skills and resources and where greatest recognition is given to their claims. An *inamdar* in the 1930s who wanted to keep personal hold on "his" land would discontinue his service to the temple and bring this to the attention of the BOR, knowing that this would set in motion a set of resumption procedures which the HRE Board was almost powerless to stop. A "hereditary" trustee in the 1960s who wanted to consolidate his position for the indefinite future would appeal an HRCE trustee appointment to the court, relying on the latter's respect for "shares" and "property-like rights" to buttress his claim for a permanent temple position.

Fragmented authority shapes the nature and speed of change and the character of political representation. Multiple government jurisdictions tend to favor the status quo. HRCE policies which would radically depart from the past are balanced by the basically conservative stance of the BOR and the court. Fragmented authority also means that politically weak groups and individuals, such as temple *archakas* and hereditary trustees of smaller temples, have been able to defend and to some extent protect their interests and values. The court has played an especially important role here because of its relatively greater sensitivity to local traditions.

In a sense, then, the positive aspect of policy ineffectiveness is greater political representation. As the *archaka* legislation showed clearly, the persons most directly affected do not necessarily have a formal and direct voice in shaping temple policies. Temple policies are shaped more by ideological currents and the interests of central elites, politicians and bureaucrats. Groups such as the South India Archaka Sangham lack vitality and independence, and the HRCE, rather than being responsive to their pressures, is quite hard-nosed and closed in its priorities. Representation in this context is typically achieved *indirectly* through exploiting jurisdictional conflicts and the conflicting theories those jurisdictions represent.

Given the pervasive character of the tension between the temple and the state, it is only reasonable to raise the general question of legitimacy. "The classical problem of legitimacy," Clifford Geertz has written,

> is peculiarly acute in a country in which long-term colonial domination created a political system that was national in scope but not in complexion. For a state to do more than administer privilege and defend itself against its own population, its acts must seem continuous with the selves of those whose state it pretends to be, its citizens; to be, in some stepped-up, amplified sense, their acts.[3]

A major feature of the HRCE is that its actions are *not*, in Geertz's sense, "continuous with the selves" of those it would administer. The HRCE administers in terms of an image of the temple which conflicts fundamentally with the customs, traditions and processes of temple life as they have traditionally existed. Much of the HRCE's work consists precisely of defending "itself against its own population": protecting departmental rules and goals against those in the localities who would subvert them.

One might therefore expect the HRCE to be beset by a deep-seated "crisis of legitimacy," but nothing in this study has suggested that this is in fact the case. How can this paradox be explained? Three explanations suggest themselves. The first can be stated quite briefly. Fragmented government control over temples results in a series of "cracks" in the system which, as has been shown, enable actors in the localities to further interests within existing institutional arrangements. The tension between the HRCE and the localities is thus less serious than it would otherwise be.

Second, the HRCE has been in continuous existence for over half a century. It is a commonplace that legitimacy problems are most critical in the first few years of a new regime. It is then that the regime's credentials are most seriously challenged and opposition most vehement. Legitimacy problems diminish as the new regime (or bureaucracy) gains confidence, as "new" patterns become "old" and established, and as vested interests build up around the new distribution of power, resources and authority.

The HRE Board in its early years was plagued by challenges to its authority, but these challenges diminished as the years went by.

[3] Clifford Geertz, "Afterword: the politics of meaning," *Culture and politics in Indonesia*, ed. Claire Holt (Ithaca: Cornell University Press; 1972), p. 325.

Legitimacy was an issue of uppermost concern in the first administration report of 1925–26.

One important thing that engaged the attention of the Board of Commissioners at the very outset was to remove misconceptions in regard to the purposes of the act. With this end before them, the commissioners took great pains during their several tours to meet as many of the trustees of temples as possible, to interview members of committees and other leading men and the general public.[4]

A few years later, the commissioners reported optimistically:

During the year under report, the improvement in the general attitude of the public towards the Act and the Board was kept up. Judging from the fact that the worshippers resort to the Board more and more for redress of grievances, its activities are becoming more and more popular and there are clear indications of a growing consciousness in the minds of the public that the machinery introduced by the Madras Hindu Religious Endowments Act is fraught with immense potentialities for good which would fructify more and more as its work progresses in due course of time. Even the general attitude of the trustees may, on the whole, be said to have improved.[5]

Today, fifty years later, the HRCE's right to exist is rarely challenged, its legality has been upheld by the Indian Supreme Court, and several generations of trustees, priests and other temple actors have patterned their activities within the structure of HRCE supervision and control.

The third, more fundamental, reason for the absence of a crisis of legitimacy is related to the principle of protection. It is important that this principle not be misunderstood or oversimplified. The weakness of strictly cultural analyses of legitimacy is the temptation to portray a society's norms, symbols and values in such an abstract way that legitimacy becomes non-problematic. The political values of the society are displayed as an integrated and consistent system, stable over time, and shared equally and in the same sense by all groups in the society. We have already seen that this is not the case in temple policy. In any case, it would not seem to be a very useful vantage point from which to approach legitimacy in the modern Indian state where, it is clear, the values and norms of the polity are embodied in an amalgam of local, regional and national institutions with diverse historical and cultural origins.

Accordingly, in this study we have avoided the temptation to treat the abstract norm of protection in isolation from concrete economic, social and political processes and the conflicts surrounding them. We have examined the principle of protection only as it manifests itself in the

[4] G.O. 1337 L & M 9 April 1927.
[5] G.O. 1455 L & M 25 March 1929.

concrete interactions of groups and institutions. Although we have argued that protection is *the* principle defining temple–state relations, we have shown that its actual meaning varies historically. Protection had one set of implications in the nineteenth century when the BOR was the agent of the government; it has a quite different set of implications today when the HRCE is the agent. Protection means one thing to temple priests and has a different meaning for EOs.

The concrete meaning of protection at any given time is shaped by conflicts among individuals, groups and institutions attempting to enhance their respective interests. The political values in temple society do *not* form an internally consistent and interdependent system. Temple society is complex, involving a plurality of political values with the same problematic relations among them as have the groups which hold them. The abstract principle of protection is indeed taken seriously by almost everyone, but this does not mean that it is understood in the same sense by everyone. The richness of the principle of protection, in fact, derives precisely from its vagueness, generality and multivocality, such that it can be understood in many ways and be put to many different uses.

The great achievement of the HRCE is that it has managed to appropriate the concept of protection and establish its interpretations as "correct" and dominant. Legitimation in any polity or bureaucracy occurs in contexts of inequality: of unequal power, authority and resources. What protection in the final analysis means depends in part on the person defining it, and here the strong have a more important voice than the weak. In the south Indian context, powerful groups, such as westernized elites, and superordinate institutions, such as the HRCE, have had enormous advantages in the struggle over the meaning of protection as compared with less powerful groups, such as the South India Archaka Sangham and isolated temple trustees, who have had fewer choices open to them and diminished capacity to manipulate public power and authority. In this sense, protection's concrete meaning is a political outcome, shaped by changes and continuities in the distribution of power, authority and resources.

What, then, of the overall structural relationship between temple and state? What, on balance, is the extent of change since the nineteenth century? Three major continuities and one major change may be mentioned.

The primary continuity is the very fact of state jurisdiction over temples. The solicitude of the state for temples, which, as we have seen, is a leading characteristic of modern "secular" south India, is definitely not new. It characterized the early British *raj*, for example, when temple endowments were regarded as religious trusts, and was also a feature of the medieval period. What Professor T.V. Mahalingam observes of premodern times illustrates that the underlying purposes of HRCE policies are essentially identical with those which have stimulated state action in temples for hundreds of years:

> Sometimes the kings instructed the authorities of the temples to sell away by public auction the lands and rights of the temple servants who had embezzled money from the temple treasury and thereby committed the crime of *Sivadroha*. Under normal circumstances, the temples were not to part with their lands either by mortgage or sale, and anyone who bought them was liable to be punished with the confiscation of his property. At one period a number of villagers at Chidambaram had taken up on mortgage lands purchased, presented to or otherwise owned by temples and refused to give back such lands to them. So the temple tenants had to abandon the villages which resulted in the stopping of worship in the temples. Hence the king ordered that temple lands were not thereafter to be let out on (long) lease nor were they to be assigned to anyone as tax-free hereditary property.[6]

The pivotal role of the state is undoubtedly related to the absence in Hinduism of an ecclesiastical organization able to impose controls against temple mismanagement and to arbitrate conflicts among trustees, priests and worshippers.[7] Historically, the south Indian state has performed this role and this activity is, in the final analysis, the core meaning of state protection.

The second major continuity in temple–state relations is intimately related to the first: political power can be enhanced through the temple. This is true of political power at both the state and local levels. Today as in the past, for example, temple resources (land, trusteeships) enable those who control them to dispense patronage and solidify political support. *Periyavars* – that is, "big men," VIPs, local notables – have for years enhanced and consolidated their status and authority through *mariyathe* and other rituals. The opponents of the HRE Act in the 1920s were quick to perceive that this underlying pattern would not be changed by the existence of a new bureaucracy. The most likely change would be that the locus of control over patronage would shift from the localities to the center, so that the political benefits of the temple would now accrue to a set of new political entrants whose fortunes were to be found at the state level of the political system.

The third area of continuity is the state's active role in shaping temple religion. In the nineteenth century, British policies shaped temple religion directly and indirectly even after noninterference was adopted

[6] T.V. Mahalingam, *South Indian polity* (University of Madras, 1967), p. 384.
[7] Appadurai, *Worship and conflict*, ch. 2.

as the guiding principle of state action. In the 1970s the state expressed its commitment to a particular kind of "pure" temple religion in the Tamil *archanai* policies, the *archaka* law and the Deviga Peravai.

These three areas of continuity suggest that the pattern of temple–state interdependence has remained relatively untouched in the twentieth century, despite ideologies of secularism and noninterference. There is, however, one area of major discontinuity. A crucial dimension of the traditional pattern of interdependence no longer exists. In premodern times, the interdependence was an organic one, tangibly embodied in a set of exchanges, which placed obligations on and brought benefits to both state and temple. The temple gave the state access to temple resources in return for donations of land, jewelry and other forms of support. The state thereby buttressed its authority and the temple thereby enhanced its wealth, status and prestige.

In the twentieth century, this organic link has been broken. Politicians still use the temple to enhance their power, but the state's authority in the final analysis derives from nonlocal sources, particularly from the principles enshrined in the Indian constitution. Equally important, the state no longer acts as the temple's major donor. On the contrary, rather than donating resources, the state extracts resources in the form of temple "contributions" which are used to finance a far-flung bureaucracy, the HRCE.

The fundamental character of this change has not been lost on temple personnel or on others. Once again, we can look to the debates on the original HRE act in the 1920s to find a succinct statement of the change. The following passage was quoted earlier in this study, but is worth repeating:

> Our kings in the old days, *the Hindu kings, endowed properties* for temples and *maths*. They appointed trustees or constituted themselves as trustees. That is how they exercised the kingly duty of interfering with the temple properties. *But what is the case now? The government which has got an ecclesiastical department for itself has nothing to do with the endowments of the properties of the Hindus*, but yet wants to interfere with the religious institutions.[8]

It is, of course, true that the state today, in the form of the HRCE, has "nothing to do with" temples in the direct, personal sense praised by the speaker in the above passage. But most HRCE officers would regard this as the HRCE's outstanding virtue. The passage of the HRE Act of 1925 symbolized the rejection by the modern state of the traditional, organic link between public authority and temples. The HRCE today is a bureaucratic organization designed specifically to eliminate all signs of

[8] *Proceedings*, 26 August 1926; emphasis mine.

personal, patrimonial-like interests on the part of those with authority in temples, whether they be trustees, EOs or commissioners. Ideally, trustees should have no personal stake in their temples. EOs are transferred frequently to ensure that they do not develop more than a temporary and career-oriented interest in their institutions.

It is impossible to make a final assessment of the historical choice made in favor of "pure" bureaucratic administration at the expense of the more patrimonial forms which preceded it. Most historians, political scientists and public officials would probably argue, for a variety of reasons, that the choice was a good one. At least as measured by the criterion of administrative effectiveness, however, the result has been problematic, as we have seen over and over again. Many HRCE officers have tried over the years to stem temple corruption and mismanagement, to resist external political interference, and genuinely to protect the temples under their charge. It is no reflection on their efforts to note that one of those who was, during my research experience, particularly energetic and successful in this regard was a commissioner who had personally endowed the major temple of his home district. This HRCE officer approached his job with unusual dedication, sustained concern and, most notably, a very personal and direct interest. In his person the traditional connection, now ordinarily nonexistent, between gifts and donations, on the one hand, and authority and trusteeship, on the other, had been reestablished.

Bibliography

Government records

Government of Madras
    Board of Revenue
    Revenue Department
Government of Madras. *Proceedings*
    Board of Revenue
    Revenue Department
Government of Madras. *Government orders*
    Board of Revenue
    Education and Public Health Department
    Home Department
    Legislative Department
    Local and Municipal Department
    Local Self-Government Department
    Public Department
    Public Health Department

Public documents

India. Hindu Religious Endowments Commission, 1960–62. *Report*. Government of India: Ministry of Law, 1962
Madras. Board of Revenue. *Standing orders*
  Hindu Religious Endowments Board. *Annual reports*
  Legislative Assembly. Committee on Estimates, 1965–66. *Hindu Religious and Charitable Endowments (Administration) Department*
  Legislative Council. *Proceedings*
  The Madras code. 4 vols. Government Press, 1940
  Madras state administrative report, 1966
Tamil Nadu. Hindu Religious and Charitable Endowments (Administration) Department. *Administrative reports*
  Legislative Assembly, Committee on Estimates, 1972–73. *Hindu Religious and Charitable Endowments (Administration) Department*

Newspapers

Hindu (Madras)
Indian Express (Madras)
Mail (Madras)

Bibliography

Books and articles

Allison, Graham. "Conceptual models and the Cuban missile crisis." *American Political Science Review* 63 (September 1969): 689–718

Appadurai, Arjun. "Honor and conquest: warrior-kings and vaisnava sectarianism in South India 1350–1700." Paper presented at the Conference on Religion in South India, Bucknell University, 1975

"The puzzling status of Brahman temple priests in Hindu India." *South Asian Anthropologist* 4 (1983): 43–52

Worship and conflict under colonial rule: a south Indian case. Cambridge University Press, 1981

Appadurai, Arjun and Breckenridge, Carol Appadurai. "The south Indian temple: authority, honor and redistribution." *Contributions to Indian Sociology* (NS) 10: 187–211

Baden-Powell, B.H. *The land systems of British India.* 4 vols. Oxford: Clarendon Press, 1892

Baker, Christopher J. *The politics of south India 1920–1937.* Cambridge University Press, 1976

Barnett, Marguerite Ross. *The politics of cultural nationalism in south India.* Princeton University Press, 1976

Beer, Samuel H. *British politics in the collectivist age.* New York: Knopf, 1965

Binder, Leonard; Coleman, James S.; LaPolambara, Joseph; Pye, Lucian W.; Verba, Sidney; and Wiener, Myron. *Crises and sequences in political development.* Princeton University Press, 1972

Breckenridge, Carol Appadurai. "Betel-nut and honor: exchange-relationships and temple-entry in a south Indian temple." Paper presented at the annual meetings of the Association for Asian Studies, San Francisco, March 1975

"'Dry-nurse of Siva': withdrawal and temple endowments, 1833–1863." Mimeo, 1976

"The Sri Minaksi Sundaresvara temple: worship and endowments in south India, 1833, to 1925." Unpublished Ph.D. dissertation, University of Wisconsin, 1976

Chattopadhyay, Rakhahari. "The political role of labor unions in India: an interstate study of labor unions in West Bengal, Karnataka and Rajasthan." Unpublished Ph.D. dissertation, University of Chicago, 1975

Coupland, Reginald. *The Indian problem: report on the constitutional problem in India.* Oxford University Press, 1974

Derrett, J. Duncan M. "The reform of Hindu religious endowments." In *South Asian politics and religion*, pp. 311–36. Edited by Donald Eugene Smith. Princeton University Press, 1966

Religion, law and the state in India. New York: Free Press, 1968

Dirks, Nicholas. "The structure and meaning of political relations in a south Indian little kingdom." California Institute of Technology: Humanities Working Paper No. 14, 1978

"Terminology and taxonomy; discourse and domination: from old regime to colonial regime in south India." Paper presented at the University of Wisconsin Conference on South Asia, 1983

Embree, Ainslie T. "Religion, nationalism and conflict." In J.S. Bains and R.B. Jain, eds. *Contemporary political theory*. New Delhi: Radiant Publisher, 1980

Etzioni, Amitai. *A comparative analysis of complex organizations*. New York: Free Press, 1961

Frykenberg, Robert E. "The silent settlement in south India, 1793–1853: an analysis of the role of inams in the rise of the Indian imperial system." In Robert E. Frykenberg, ed., *Land tenure and peasant in south Asia*. New Delhi: Orient Longman, 1977

Fuller, C.J. "Gods, Priests and purity: on the relation between Hinduism and the caste system." In *Man* (NS) 14: 459–76

Servants of the goddess: the priests of a south Indian temple. Cambridge University Press, 1984

Galanter, Marc. "Secularism, east and west." In V.K. Sinha, ed., *Secularism in India*, pp. 159–91. Bombay: Lalvani Publishing House, 1968

Geertz, Clifford. "Afterword: the politics of meaning." In Claire Holt, ed., *Culture and politics*, pp. 319–35. Ithaca: Cornell University Press, 1972

Ghurye, G.S. *Caste and race in India*. 4th edn. Bombay: Popular Prakashan, 1969

Grew, Raymond, ed. *Crises of political development in Europe and the United States*. Princeton University Press, 1978

Halkar, S.S., ed. *Digest of Privy Council rulings on appeal from the high courts of Calcutta, Bombay, Madras and Allahabad, the chief courts of the Punjab and Lower Burma, the courts of the judicial commissioner of the Central Provinces, Oudh, etc. 1811–1913*. Rangoon: Hanthawady, Myles Standish and Samuel Presses, 1913

Halperin, Morton. *Bureaucratic politics and foreign policy*. Washington: Brookings Institution, 1974

Hardgrave, Robert L., Jr. *The Dravidian movement*. Bombay: Popular Prakashan, 1965

Huntington, Samuel P. "The marasmus of the ICC." *Yale Law Journal* 61 (1952): 470–509

Hutchins, Francis G. *The illusion of permanence: British imperialism in India*. Princeton University Press, 1967

Irschick, Eugene F. *Politics and social conflict in south India: the non-Brahman movement and Tamil separatism 1916–1929*. Berkeley: University of California Press, 1969

Kane, P.V. *Hindu customs and modern law*. University of Bombay, 1950

Kuhn, Thomas S. *The structure of scientific revolutions*. University of Chicago Press, 1962

Lindblom, Charles E. "The science of muddling through." *Public Administration Review* 19 (Spring 1959): 79–88

Mahalingam, T.V. *South Indian polity*. University of Madras, 1967

Manor, James. "Where Congress survived: five states in the Indian general election of 1977." *Asian Survey* 18 (August 1978): 785–803

Marriott, McKim. "Little communities in an indigenous civilization." In

McKim Marriot, ed., *Village India*, pp. 171–222. University of Chicago Press, 1955

Mudaliar, Chandra Y. *The secular state and religious institutions in India: a study of the administration of Hindu public religious trusts in Madras*. Wiesbaden: Franz Steiner, 1974

Mukherjea, B.K. *B.K. Mukherjea on the Hindu law of religious and charitable trusts*. 3rd edn. Calcutta: Eastern Law House, 1970

Narasimhan, V.K. *Kamaraj: a study*. Bombay: Manaktalas, 1967

Potts, E. Daniel. "Missionaries and the beginnings of the secular state in India." In Donovan Williams and E. Daniel Potts, eds., *Essays in Indian history in honour of Cuthbert Collins Davies*, pp. 113–26. New York: Asia Publishing House, 1973

Rajasikhamani, V. *The Tamil Nadu Hindu Religious and Charitable Endowments Act XXII of 1959*. Madras: B. Sundaralingam, 1971?

Ramanujan, A.K. *Speaking of Siva*. Baltimore: Penguin, 1973

Rudolph, Lloyd I. "Urban life and populist radicalism: Dravidian politics in Madras." *Journal of Asian Studies* 20 (May 1961): 283–97

Rudolph, Lloyd I., and Rudolph, Susanne Hoeber. "Authority and power in bureaucratic and patrimonial administration: a revisionist interpretation of Weber on bureaucracy." *World Politics* 31 (January 1979): 195–227

The modernity of tradition: political development in India. University of Chicago Press, 1969

Rudolph, Susanne Hoeber, and Rudolph, Lloyd I., eds. *Education and politics in India: studies in organization, society and policy*. Cambridge: Harvard University Press, 1972

Ryerson, Charles A. "E.V. Ramasamy Naicker and the Dravidian movement: identity, change and tradition." Paper read at the Conference on Religion in South India, Bucknell University, 1975

"Religious culture and the 1971 elections in Tamil Nadu." Paper presented at the Society for South Indian Studies, Philadelphia, 1980

"'Meaning and modernization' in Tamil India: primordial sentiments and Sanskritization." Unpublished Ph.D. dissertation, Columbia University, 1979

Schmitter, Philippe C. "Interest intermediation and modes of societal change in western Europe." *Comparative Political Studies* 10 (April 1977): 7–35

"Still the century of corporatism?" *Review of Politics 36* (January 1974): 85–131

Sharma, G.S. ed. *Secularism: its implications for law and life in India*. Bombay: N.M. Tripathi, 1966

Singer, Milton. *When a great tradition modernizes*. New York: Praeger, 1972

Smith, Donald Eugene. *India as a secular state*. Princeton University Press, 1963

Religion and political development. Boston: Little, Brown and Co., 1970

Smith, Vincent A. *Oxford history of India*. Oxford University Press, 1923

Spratt, P. *D.M.K. in power*. Bombay: Nachiketa Publications, 1970

Stein, Burton. *Peasant, state and society in medieval south India*. New Delhi: Oxford University Press, 1980

Stokes, Eric. *The English Utilitarians and India*. Oxford University Press, 1959

Thurston, Edgar. *Castes and tribes of southern India*. 7 vols. Madras: Government Press, 1909

Tilly, Charles, ed. *The formation of national states in western Europe*. Princeton University Press, 1975

Treveleyan, Ernest John. *Hindu law as administered in British India*. Calcutta: Thacker, Spink and Co., 1912

Venkatarama Aiyer, T.L. *Mulla on the Code of Civil Procedure Act V of 1908*. 13th edn. Bombay: N.M. Tripathi, 1965–67

Washbrook, David. *The emergence of provincial politics: the Madras presidency 1870–1920*. Cambridge University Press, 1976

Weber, Max. *Economy and Society*. 3 vols. Edited by Guenther Roth and Claus Wittich. New York: Bedminister Press, 1968

CAMBRIDGE SOUTH ASIAN STUDIES

These monographs are published by the Syndics of Cambridge University Press in association with the Cambridge University Centre for South Asian Studies. The following books have been published in this series:

1 S. Gopal: *British Policy in India, 1858–1905*
2 J.A.B. Palmer: *The Mutiny Outbreak at Meerut in 1857*
3 A. Das Gupta: *Malabar in Asian Trade, 1740–1800*
4 G. Obeyesekere: *Land Tenure in Village Ceylon*
5 H.L. Erdman: *The Swatantra Party and Indian Conservatism*
6 S.N. Mukherjee: *Sir William Jones: A Study in Eighteenth-Century British Attitudes to India*
7 Abdul Majed Khan: *The Transition in Bengal, 1756–1775: A Study of Saiyid Muhammad Reza Khan*
8 Radhe Shyam Rungta: *The Rise of Business Corporations in India, 1851–1900*
9 Pamela Nightingale: *Trade and Empire in Western India, 1784–1806*
10 Amiya Kumar Bagchi: *Private Investment in India, 1900–1939*
11 Judith M. Brown: *Gandhi's Rise to Power: Indian Politics, 1915–1922*
12 Mary C. Carras: *The Dynamics of Indian Political Factions*
13 P. Hardy: *The Muslims of British India*
14 Gordon Johnson: *Provincial Politics and Indian Nationalism*
15 Marguerite S. Robinson: *Political Structure in a Changing Sinhalese Village*
16 Francis Robinson: *Separation among Indian Muslims: The Politics of the United Provinces' Muslims, 1860–1923*
17 Christopher John Baker: *The Politics of South India, 1920–1936*
18 David Washbrook: *The Emergence of Provincial Politics: The Madras Presidency, 1870–1920*
19 Deepak Nayyar: *India's Exports and Export Policies in the 1960s*
20 Mark Holmström: *South Indian Factory Workers: Their Life and Their World*
21 S. Ambirajan: *Classical Political Economy and British Policy in India*
22 M.M. Islam: *Bengal Agriculture 1920–1946: A Quantitative Study*
23 Eric Stokes: *The Peasant and the Raj: Studies in Agrarian Society and Peasant Rebellion in Colonial India*
24 Michael Roberts: *Caste Conflict and Elite Formation: The Rise of a Karāva Elite in Sri Lanka, 1500–1931*
25 J.F.J. Toye: *Public Expenditure and Indian Development Policy, 1960–70*

26 Rashid Amjad: *Private Industrial Development in Pakistan, 1960–70*
27 Arjun Appadurai: *Worship and Conflict under Colonial Rule: A South Indian Case*
28 C.A. Bayly: *Rulers, Townsmen and Bazaars: North Indian Society in the Age of British Expansion, 1770–1870*
29 Ian Stone: *Canal Irrigation in British India: Perspectives on Technological Change in a Peasant Society*
30 Rosalind O'Hanlon: *Caste, Conflict and Ideology: Mahatma Jotirao Phute and Low Caste Protest in Nineteenth-Century Western India*
31 Ayesha Jalal: *The Sole Spokesman: Jinnah, The Muslim League and the Demand for Pakistan*
32 N.R.F. Charlesworth: *Peasants and Imperial Rule: Agriculture and Agrarian Society in the Bombay Presidency, 1850–1935*
33 Claude Markovits: *Indian Business and Nationalist Politics, 1931–39: The Indigenous Capitalist Class and the Rise of the Congress Party*
34 Mick Moore: *The State and Peasant Politics in Sri Lanka*
35 Gregory C. Kozlowski: *Muslim Endowments and Society in British India*
36 Sugata Bose: *Agrarian Bengal: Economy, Social Structure and Politics, 1919–1947*
37 Atul Kohli: *The State and Poverty in India: The Politics of Reform*

INDEX

For EU product safety concerns, contact us at Calle de José Abascal, 56–1°, 28003 Madrid, Spain or eugpsr@cambridge.org.

www.ingramcontent.com/pod-product-compliance
Ingram Content Group UK Ltd.
Pitfield, Milton Keynes, MK11 3LW, UK
UKHW012344130625
459647UK00009B/505

9780521053679